BLACK FEMINIST EPISTI RESEARCH, AND PRAXIS

While there has been an increase of Black women faculty in higher education institutions, the academy writ large continues to exploit, discriminate, and uphold institutionalized gendered racism through its policies and practices. Black women have navigated, negotiated, and learned how to thrive from their respective standpoints and epistemologies, traversing the academy in ways that counter typical narratives of success and advancement. This edited volume bridges together foundational and contemporary intergenerational, interdisciplinary voices to elucidate Black feminist epistemologies and praxis. Chapter authors highlight relevant research, methodologies, and theoretical or conceptual frameworks; share experiences as doctoral students, current faculty, and academic administrators; and offer lessons learned and strategies to influence systemic and institutional change for and with Black women.

Christa J. Porter is an Associate Professor of Higher Education Administration and Student Affairs at Kent State University, USA.

V. Thandi Sulé is an Associate Professor of Higher Education at Oakland University, USA.

Natasha N. Croom is an Associate Professor of Higher Education and Student Affairs at Clemson University, USA.

Diverse Faculty in the Academy
Series Editor: Fred A. Bonner II

Racial Battle Fatigue in Faculty: Perspectives and Lessons from Higher Education
Edited by Nicholas D. Hartlep and Daisy Ball

Building Mentorship Networks to Support Black Women: A Guide to Succeeding in the Academy
Edited by Bridget Turner Kelly and Sharon L. Fries-Britt

Black Feminist Epistemology, Research, and Praxis: Narratives in and through the Academy
Edited by Christa J. Porter, V. Thandi Sulé, and Natasha N. Croom

BLACK FEMINIST EPISTEMOLOGY, RESEARCH, AND PRAXIS

Narratives in and through the Academy

Edited by Christa J. Porter, V. Thandi Sulé, and Natasha N. Croom

NEW YORK AND LONDON

Cover image: © Getty Images

First published 2023
by Routledge
605 Third Avenue, New York, NY 10158

and by Routledge
4 Park Square, Milton Park, Abingdon, Oxon, OX14 4RN

Routledge is an imprint of the Taylor & Francis Group, an informa business

Library of Congress Cataloging-in-Publication Data
A catalog record for this title has been requested

ISBN: 9781032026381 (hbk)
ISBN: 9781032027258 (pbk)
ISBN: 9781003184867 (ebk)

DOI: 10.4324/9781003184867

Typeset in Bembo
by codeMantra

CONTENTS

FIGURES

TABLES

ACKNOWLEDGMENTS

...To the Black women who paved a way, to those persisting alongside, and to those coming after—we will forever honor, uplift, and center our narratives...

-Christa, Thandi, and Natasha

SERIES EDITOR'S INTRODUCTION

Fred A. Bonner II

As Editor of this Series, *Diverse Faculty in the Academy*, what most inspires me are the opportunities to explore via each proposal submission, new plateaus, vistas, paradigms, and alternative frameworks that allow for a more expansive view of the higher education landscape, especially the terrain traversed by diverse faculty. What Porter, Sulé, and Croom have contributed by way of this cutting-edge tome, *Applying Black Feminist Epistemology, Research, and Praxis Narratives: In and Thorough The Academy* is a place to enter—reminiscent of Paula Giddings' opining in *When and Where I Enter* more than three decades prior, in which she illuminated the key contributions of Black women from Ida B. Wells, Mary McLeod Bethune to Ella Baker during from 1890 to 1945.

In the same vein of Alice Walker, Audre Lorde, Patricia Hill Collins, bell hooks, and Kimberlé Crenshaw, the editors and authors of this tome collectively and individually underscore challenges that Black women experience given their intersecting identities and engagements with multiple and interlocking systems of oppression. *Applying Black Feminist Epistemology, Research, and Praxis Narratives: In and Thorough The Academy* provides a *third base*, an orthogonal perspective to look at how Black women go about the ontological task of divining what it means to "be" as well as the epistemological task of what it means to "know."

Perhaps, what is most exciting about this book is how it draws clear lines of demarcation that encourages Black women to codify, develop, and engage and (re)theorize about the construction of knowledge across myriad topical areas—a rarified place that people of color and individuals representing diverse communities are seldom allowed to occupy.

Inclusive of, and steeped in the tradition of Black Feminism, Black Feminist Thought, Intersectionality, and Womanism (Cleage, Collins, Crenshaw, hooks, and Walker), *Applying Black Feminist Epistemology, Research, and Praxis: Narratives In and Thorough The Academy* is certain to become ensconced in the pantheon of critical works that chronicle who Black women were, who they are, and who they are to become. That is, raising up their voices and giving them a space of belonging. My blessing is that this masterpiece is part of the Diverse Faculty in the Academy Series.

Yours Truly,

Fred Bonner II

Fred A. Bonner II, Ed.D.

FOREWORD

"Speak Your Names"

Despite common knowledge and popular myth, Black people do go on to college and advance on to post-graduate degrees. In fact, Black people have been integrating colleges and universities as well as receiving doctoral degrees since the 1800s in the USA, and Black women specifically began acquiring doctoral degrees in the early 1900s. In 1921, Sadie Tanner Alexander, Eva B. Dykes, and Georgiana R. Simpson were the first Black women to earn doctoral degrees in the USA. To the memorized and forgotten Black women doctorates who came before us—I *speak your names*,[1] and to the scholars' who share their stories in the pages of this book, "Applying Black feminist epistemology, research, and praxis: Narratives in and through the academy"—I *speak your names*.

At different moments in their lives, the Black women scholars' mentioned above (and nameless others who came after them) were systematically excluded from opportunities to teach in their fields of study at universities reserved for the white intelligentsia while at other times they practiced, taught, or wrote in their respective fields of study alongside Black men at Black universities, colleges, training schools, independent Black schools, churches, community organizations, etc. Enduring racial oppression and gender discrimination in academia, many Black women intellectual trailblazers decided to find refuge in civic engagement work such as the practice of law, formation of civic institutions, or advising political officials on federal civil rights policies as the nation reckoned with the moral prospect of building a democracy that was racially and gender-inclusive. Since the early 1900s, degreed Black women—welcomed or unwelcomed—have integrated into all sectors of society with the intent to pursue intellectual curiosity, economic prosperity, and political freedom for themselves and the race.

Today, nearly 100 years later (2021), the Black women scholars presented in the chapters of this book dare to walk in the footsteps of our academic foremothers. As they inscribe their truths from the perspective of a Black feminist standpoint, in a moment of sociopolitical unrest and educational uncertainty, the discussions in this volume continue a long legacy of unveiling the historical and contemporary precarity of Black women's visible and invisible, intellectual and emotional, paid and unpaid labor in the academy. Black men scholars like W.E.B. DuBois, Carter G. Woodson, and John Henry Clarke have a long tradition of wrestling with the condition of Black intellectuals in white educational institutions. These pioneer intellectuals raised important questions about the utility of white educational training and socialization. They openly debated the socio-political worth of white science for Black intellectuals truly concerned with the sociopolitical condition of Black people in the USA and across the African Diaspora.

Similarly, Black women intellectuals such as Inez Beverly Prosser, Jeanne Nobel, Barbara Sizemore concerned themselves with topics such as politicizing the perils and possibilities of white schooling on the psyche of Black children, the relevancy and importance of Black teachers, and the state of Black women in institutions of higher education as students and faculty. In discussions led by Black men intellectuals (and propagated by white male-dominated academe) very rarely were race and sex considered in the plight of the Black academic. Without a conscientious intersectional prism in which to consider the role of Black people in higher education training and socialization, Black men pioneers of Black educational theory failed to garner more nuanced theorizations on the role of scientific thought, intellectual stimulation, and educational attainment as potential vehicles for human freedom.

For instance, historically, Black women were deemed by the very scientific communities in which they were entering into as graduate students to be inherently biologically and physically inferior to men; biologically and physically (even aesthetically) inferior to their white women counterparts. Expectantly, Black women in pursuit of higher education in the 1900s, prior to entering universities or exiting them as degreed people, would have already been determined to be innately intellectually inferior to white people and to those of the male sex. Like today, imperialism, colonization, white supremacy, and patriarchy influenced the types of scientific questions white men scientists asked and influenced many of the theories about human intelligence and biology that white scientists held about both Black people and women. The quest for white domination fueled science and science fueled white domination.

Popular culture (e.g., movies, print media, cartoons, music, etc.) only further cemented Black women to the bottom of the human imagination. In popular culture representations or scientific considerations of who or what group of people are capable of rational thinking, scientific investigation, and contributing to the advancement of society, Black women would have been the least likely to come to mind. They would have been regulated to the domestic sphere as "the help" or domestic workers (i.e., cooks, house cleaners, or childcare providers) or entertainers at best. Like their predecessors, Black women academicians of the 21st century continue to battle against a popular imagination and discourse which views Black women as "less than."

Often from start to finish, our preparation, credentials, and potential contributions to the profession or our respective disciplines are questioned by colleagues and students alike. Unlike our white colleagues, rarely are Black women extended the benefit of the doubt that we have keen insight into methodologies of teaching or the intellectual aptitude to ponder reality and existence for the purpose of solving challenging scientific and/or social problems. For many Black women, as hinted at throughout this book's chapters, from the moment they are invited to the "job talk," extended a tenure track appointment, during the review of their student evaluations, or upon the review of their portfolio for consideration of tenure and promotion, too many Black women report feeling perceived as *less than* and are not given the benefit of the doubt. Rarely are they viewed as exceptional in their gifts and talents in the same vein as their degreed white men and women peers.

Consequently, to navigate and survive academia, Black women scholars of our past, present, and future have drawn upon the individual and collective agency to thrive in research and teaching spaces that do not always view them as fully human, let alone fully capable of engaging in intellectual sparring or the meaningful cultivation of the next generation of scholars. There are many Black intellectual activists, including me, who wonder, "Why now, why this?" More specifically, we ponder the reason why at this moment in history that colleges and universities are actively targeting Black people for recruitment into doctoral studies programs (especially into colleges of education or student support services programs) at a time when university funding is so low, yet tuition and fees are higher than at any other time in the history of higher education. And we openly or secretly wonder why so many Black women are entering into post-graduate programs and choosing to enter academic work at a time when we know university work is not necessarily a ticket into the middle class. We also must acknowledge that for most Black women, it is a ticket to lifelong debt and financial insecurity.

These are complex questions Black women scholars grapple with sometimes publicly and most times privately. We find ourselves contemplating these complex questions in the published chapters presented in this volume, our research investigations, and in our professional presentations and musings. Privately, we wrestle with such convoluted questions about our purpose and existence in higher education at home with our family members, in between the pages of our reflection journals, during laughing or cussing sessions on the phone with other sister scholars, or in our after-conference briefings (i.e., over libations). Publicly and privately, seriously or in jest, we ask, "Have we become the nannies of academia? In our determination to be called 'Dr.' or 'Professor,' are we accepting our fate of suffering and marginalization simply to appear more important than our non-academic Black and Brown siblings?"

Although there is no short answer to these overt and not so obvious ponderings, those of us who embrace Black feminism as political theory and praxis can state unequivocally that we are committed to racial and gender consciousness-raising, cultural literacy, political empowerment, and the decolonization of higher education. We believe Black feminist standpoint theory is a useful political apparatus to alleviate and mitigate the deleterious effects of white supremacy patriarchy capitalism.[2] Without a doubt, in this nation, colleges and universities (and all levels of education) continue to be politically contested sites. Especially in a moment of racial reckoning, these Black women scholars are not only risking job security or economic stability when they stand up against white supremacy as a set of university policies and practices, but many also risk physical and mental safety.

In "Applying Black feminist epistemology, research, and praxis," you will see/feel/hear Black women scholars (as educators, mentors, advocates, sisters, daughters, and mothers) *take up space,* and concomitantly, *refuse* space. Black feminism reminds us that Black women's presence represents in this culture a body politic of resistance, refusals, and compromises. Epistemologically, Black feminism is a theoretical and analytical tool used to comprehend Black women's individual and collective agency as well as our individual and collective struggle. Black feminism, for many of us, is also a spiritual bulwark in the face of inconvincible white supremacy in higher education cloaked as benevolence. A 100 years after the desegregation of higher education, many Black women still face threats to our spiritual, intellectual, mental, and physical well-being.

With this harsh reality in mind, to the Black women academicians presented throughout this book, as I acknowledge the fortitude of our academic Black women ancestors, I must too unabashedly "speak your name." Throughout this text you all boldly engage in narrative inquiry, storytelling, poetry, and prose as cultural productions that serve to speak against dominant narratives that attempt to render Black women intellectual activists invisible and erase us from the historical record. Thoughtfully and with gratitude, we "speak your name" to acknowledge the emotionally charged intellectual labor and cultural work you engage in as you do your part to document our people's humanity, and equally important, keep Black women visible in the archives of human knowledge. Finally, your embodied and inscribed hope paves the way for another generation of Black women to dare to imagine and walk unapologetically in educational, career, political, and spiritual endeavors that protect and encourage our full humanity!

We speak your names—yesterday, today, and tomorrow!

Venus E. Evans-Winters

Notes

1 We "Speak Your Names" was spoken by Pearl Cleage in a poem with the same title to honor Black women trailblazers who inspired and paved the way for other Black women icons. Cleage, P. (2006). *Speak Your Names.* The Random House Publishing Group.

2 bell hooks (1997) first used this phrase during an interview to describe how power overlaps in dynamic ways to complicate individuals lives and that of members of marginalized social groups differently. Retrieve here: https://www.mediaed.org/transcripts/Bell-Hooks-Transcript.pdf

1

APPLYING BLACK FEMINIST EPISTEMOLOGIES, RESEARCH, AND PRAXIS

An Introduction

Christa J. Porter, V. Thandi Sulé, and Natasha N. Croom

For years, Black women have shared their (extra)ordinary lived realities within higher educational institutions (i.e., "the academy"). Recently, however, one of these many narratives illuminated how and the extent to which Black women experience gendered racism (or anti-Black woman oppression) despite credentials or status. With overwhelming support, Nikole Hannah-Jones' tenure materials moved through the typical academic process at various levels at the University of North Carolina (UNC) Chapel Hill. Yet, her process of earning tenure and promotion halted after the Board of Trustees decided not to vote on her materials. Hannah-Jones threatened the Board with legal action, UNC students and faculty protested the decision, and ultimately the Board agreed to grant her tenure. Hannah-Jones declined their offer and instead took her tenured position at Howard University, a historically Black college and university in Washington, DC. She emphasized,

> For too long, Black Americans have been taught that success is defined by gaining entry to and succeeding in historically white institutions. I have done that, and now I am honored and grateful to join the long legacy of Black Americans who have defined success by working to build up their own.
>
> *(Legal Defense Fund, 2021, para. 27)*

Hannah-Jones' experience unfortunately represents all too often, Black women's narratives in and through the academy. Black women across rank or status (i.e., doctoral students, faculty in tenured and non-tenured positions, and academic administrators) traverse along the margins of higher educational institutions – often without appropriate support and remuneration.

DOI: 10.4324/9781003184867-1

> When they confront race and gender stereotypes, Black women are standing in a crooked room, and they have to figure out which way is up…Sometimes Black women can conquer negative myths, sometimes they are defeated, and sometimes they choose not to fight. Whatever the outcome, we can better understand sisters as citizens when we appreciate the crooked room in which they struggle to stand upright.
>
> *(Harris-Perry, 2011, pp. 29, 32)*

Harris-Perry (2011) asserted the politicization of Black women; she analogized their standpoint in the crooked room to depict how they make meaning of their positionalities in society. The academy is no different. While there has been a numerical increase of Black women faculty in higher education institutions (mostly in contingent positions; see Gregory, 2001; NCES, 2019; Porter et al., 2020), the academy writ large continues to exploit, discriminate, and uphold institutionalized anti-Black woman oppression through its policies and practices (Boss et al., 2019; Collins, 1986; Croom, 2017; Croom & Patton, 2012; Harley, 2008; Porter, 2019). Black women have (re)navigated, (re)negotiated, and (re)learned how to thrive from their respective standpoint and epistemologies, no matter how crooked the academy or any other space or context within which they find themselves (Carter Andrews, 2015; Collins, 1990; Fries-Britt & Kelly, 2005; Mabokela & Green, 2001; Porter et al., 2018; Sulé, 2009, 2014). Black women have chosen to traverse the academy in ways that counter typical narratives of success and advancement; they have (re)imagined how to embody their praxis (Collins, 1990; Dillard, 2006; Evans-Winters, 2019).

Black Feminist Epistemologies, Research, and Praxis Defined

Collins (1986) petitioned Black women academics "…to produce facts and theories about the Black female experience that will clarify a Black woman's standpoint for Black women" (p. S16). Black feminisms or Black feminist epistemologies (how one makes sense of, understands, and embodies their ways of knowing) were created not only to center the lived experiences of Black women but also to capture the situatedness of Black women's sociohistorical positioning within the US society (Collins, 1990; hooks, 1994). When developing the outline and proposal for this edited book, we desired to highlight the varying ways folx engage Black feminist epistemologies, research, and praxis.

We acknowledge the evolution of, bridging together, and building upon Black feminist epistemologies – from Anna Julia Cooper's 19th Century *Voice from the South* (1892/1988), double jeopardy (Beale, 1979), womanism (Walker, 1983), Black feminist thought (Collins, 1986, 1990), and intersectionality (Crenshaw, 1989, 1991), to endarkened feminism (Dillard, 2006) and critical race Black feminism (Alexander-Floyd, 2010) – each theoretical framework elucidates intersectional (i.e., raced and gendered) experiences for, with, and alongside Black women. These intersectional experiences speak not only to the convergence of Black women's identities but also about how institutions concenter and conspire to oppress Black women. Black women used their stories to bear testimony to the contours of their oppression, and in articulating those experiences they laid the foundation for their theory, research, and praxis (Combahee River Collective, 1982).

Although this edited book examines how Black women in academe employ Black feminist epistemologies, we want to be clear that Black women's ways of knowing emanate from their everyday Black woman lived experiences (Smith, 1983). Through their home spaces, Black women organically learned about Black feminism. Smith (1983) expressed, "I learned about Black feminism from the women in my family-not just from their strengths, but from their failings, from witnessing daily how they were humiliated and crushed..." (p. xxiv). Black feminist epistemologies are generational and generative as Black women, by simply living, they bestow wisdom. Black feminist research then, embraces the subjective (Dillard, 2006). It is an exploration steeped in the cultural traditions, concrete experiences, and perspectives of the researcher. Research is a spiritual endeavor to engender healing and transformation. Walker (1983), in searching for how Black women express their creativity while simultaneously being disregarded and stifled, asserted Black women's creativity survives as familiar, yet taken for granted, aspects of Black women's culture. From healing practices, horticulture, to haircare, Black women's epistemology expressed through their creativity is abundant. Regarding her mother's artistry, Walker (1983) shared, "guided by my heritage of a love of beauty and a respect for strength – in search of my mother's garden, I found my own" (p. 242).

The everyday enactments of Black feminist epistemologies correspond to the mundaneness of anti-Black women's oppression. Informed by Hughes and Giles (2010), Croom (2017) noted, "*Praxis* requires the bringing together of theory and practice to act toward the empowerment of womyn of color and the elimination of racism, sexism, and classism" (p. 567). Because Black women's ways of knowing and being are grounded in their work for personal and communal development, Black women's epistemology and praxis are entwined. Elsa Barkley Brown (1989) speaking about Maggie Lena Walker emphasized,

> Her theory and her action are not distinct and separable parts of some whole; they are often synonymous, and it is only through her actions that we clearly hear her theory. The same is true for the lives of many other Black women who had limited time and resources and maintained a holistic view of life and struggle.
>
> *(p. 631)*

Within Black women's lives, the boundaries between epistemology, research, and praxis are fluid. In conceptualizing Black women's resistance, Collins

(2000) asserted Black women strategically engaged in everyday acts of opposition by feigning adoption of prescribed roles while developing their own criteria for what has value and beauty. Evans-Winters (2019) also discussed blurring the margins between theory and practice as their research with girls was aligned with their personal need for the validation found in Black feminism. Black feminisms, as an amalgamation of epistemology, research, and praxis, are tools of affirmation and navigation. Black feminism also "offers original suppositions into how Black women are able to confront the social world order, while being simultaneously vulnerable and resilient in the face of systematic inequality, including marginalization in the academy" (Evans-Winter, 2019, p. 18). Such validation is needed within the academy because it perpetuates "dominant Eurocentric/androcentric ideological, epistemological, methodological, and pedagogical traditions that are meant to maintain the hegemonic order" (Perlow et al., 2018, p. 7). Black women navigating academia have few options to examine and affirm their experiences with gendered racism as both feminist and anti-racism schools of thought are limited. Crenshaw (1991) stated,

> The failure of feminism to interrogate race means that the resistance strategies of feminism will often replicate and reinforce the subordination of people of color, and the failure of antiracism to interrogate patriarchy means that antiracism will frequently reproduce the subordination of women.
>
> *(p. 1252)*

Black women have led the call to name and affirm themselves. Their knowledge creation process runs counter to normative practices in the academy (Collins, 2000; hooks, 1994). It derives from how they engage a world that punches down on them. Drawing from their home spaces, Black women, out of necessity, employ approaches that allow them to authentically assess and assert themselves. Their epistemological traditions speak to the necessity of pushing against hegemonic norms that shape Black women's raced and gendered experiences.

Epistemic Violence and Agency

Black feminist epistemologies and praxes are direct responses to the epistemic violence Black women have experienced for centuries. The Nikole Hannah-Jones incident, noted above, can best be described as the most recent, and very public, display of epistemic violence against Black women intellectuals and scholars. Simply put, fear and, thus by extension, violence, are at the root of resistance to Black women's onto-epistemologies. The following section provides a brief treatment of epistemic violence and the epistemic agency Black women scholars have enacted to articulate said violence.

Epistemic violence refers to a type of oppression that manifests through the silencing of minoritized communities (Spivak, 1999, 2010). Dotson's (2011) distinction between *instances* and *practices of* silencing is notable. Dotson remarked, "This is not to say that an instance of silencing is not harmful, but that epistemic violence concerns a practice of silencing that is harmful and reliable" (p. 241). We tap into this distinction as a way of suggesting that while individual Black women in the academy may be experiencing various forms of problematic silencing, the disappearing, erasure, and marginalizing of Black women's ways of knowing and knowledge are systemic. That is to say, the epistemic violence Black women face in the academy manifests ideologically (i.e., hegemonic ideas, beliefs, and attitudes held about Black women), culturally (i.e., social norms enacted in everyday practices meant to immobilize Black women), and structurally (i.e., policies, in/formal rules and customs that disproportionately disadvantage Black women).

Given these systemic realities, Bunch (2015) further summarized three classifications of epistemic violence – discriminatory, testimonial, and distributive. Discriminatory epistemic violence establishes the "other" (i.e., minoritized communities) by dehumanizing them, making them illegible and unintelligible, and by withholding reciprocity from them (Bunch, 2015). Testimonial epistemic violence describes a reduction in credibility and silencing and often manifests as discrediting minoritized communities as experts (Bunch, 2015). "The refusal to acknowledge an actor's contributions to the broader epistemic community, or to bar them from it altogether, impairs their epistemic agency" (Bunch, 2015, p. 12). Distributive epistemic violence refers to the withholding of resources via structural inequities. This could include, for example, keeping folx from (in)formal educational and professional opportunities.

The Hannah-Jones and the Board of Trustees of the UNC debacle serve as an exemplar of these various forms of epistemic violence. According to the UNC faculty who submitted a petition after the Board's decision, the Board's failing to act on Hannah-Jones tenure "unfairly moves the goal posts and violates longstanding norms and established processes" (Robertson, 2021, para. 9). In addition to the procedural inconsistency, that is withholding tenure in this case when all others in the position prior to were granted tenure, the Board also attempted to deemphasize her intellectual contributions by going against the assessments and judgments of those qualified to make such assertions. The slap in the face becomes even more resounding when one realizes that instead of offering the Pulitzer Prize winning, MacArthur Fellowship "Genius Grant" recipient Hannah-Jones a lifelong appointment via tenure, they offered and fully expected her to accept a five-year fixed-term contract with a Professor of Practice rank to accompany the named Knight Chair position. To be clear, named sponsored and/or endowed chairs most often, if not always, are given to tenured faculty (Kamath et al., 2004; Tang, 1993; Tang & Griffith,

1997/1998; Worthington et al., 1989). Moreover, according to the Knight Foundation (n.d., n.p.),

> Knight Chairs in Journalism are top professionals who bridge the newsroom-classroom divide with innovative teaching, major outreach projects and their own journalism. Since the program began in 1990, Knight has endowed 26 chairs and professors at 23 universities. The chairs have helped lead journalism and media education – and journalism itself – toward a better future in the digital age.

Not to belabor the point, but the faculty and administrators who made the decision to provide an affirmative vote on Hannah-Jones's portfolio concluded that this nationally, if not globally, recognized journalist was an appropriate and adequately (and likely overly in comparison to the rest of the School of Journalism) qualified candidate.

Additionally, many media outlets reported the external political tensions exuded from what they called "conservative" groups as a primary rationale for the Board's decision (Killian, 2021). Thus, in response, the Board chose to discredit the expertise of not only its own institution's faculty, but ultimately that of Hannah-Jones for fear of political backlash – a move that only serves to maintain imperialist white supremacist patriarchal capitalism. As Dotson (2011) noted, "An epistemic side of colonialism is the devastating effect of the 'disappearing' of knowledge, where local or provincial knowledge is dismissed due to privileging alternative, often Western, epistemic practices" (p. 236). Withholding tenure and creating doubts about one's expertise ultimately serve to create inaccurate narratives about Black women intellectuals which then get taken up to make their knowledge inaccessible. As a result, these narratives also get enacted as rationales for excluding Black women from formal opportunities/positions. Furthermore, withholding the avenues by which academics might more fully participate (e.g., tenured professorships) also serves to keep Black women from being able to shape and dispute controlling images (Collins, 1990) from the inside – where these caricatures are often maintained. Lastly, the material consequences of such decisions keep Black women from higher earnings, which has long-term consequences for economic stability over a lifetime. These discursive and practical moves serve as exemplars of the types of epistemic violence introduced above. Further, they signal a cross-cutting or intertwining phenomenon – that is to say, the examples simultaneously represent discriminatory, testimonial, and distributive forms of epistemic violence.

Black women intellectuals, however, have never been passive victims of epistemic violence. In fact, many have engaged in the epistemic agency by thinking, speaking, and writing our onto-epistemologies into the world (Evans-Winters, 2019; Sulé, 2014). Notably, Black women intellectuals and academics have described the various ways Black women might experience epistemic violence. In considering the purpose of this book, we want to surface three theories articulated by Black women academics – spirit murder, gendered racism, and misogynoir.

Critical race legal scholar, Patricia Williams, introduced the term spirit murdering in the mid-1980s to describe how racism (and the intersections of sexism and classism) slowly kills the humanity, life force, and will (Williams, 1987). Gendered racism was introduced by Philomena Essed in the early 1990s. Drawing on the work of Patricia Hill Collins and others, Essed coined this term to explicitly describe a system of oppression informed by both sexism and racism (1991). Finally, in the late 2000s to the early 2010s, Moya Bailey introduced the term misogynoir (Bailey & Trudy, 2018). Similar, yet distinct from gendered racism, misogynoir is meant to capture the particularities of discrimination experienced by Black women (like how misogyny can be used to describe discrimination experienced by white women). Too often, the claim is made that "me" search is a less rigorous, self-involved form of scholarship; however, Black women are literally writing themselves, ourselves, into myriad existences because of the epistemic violence that has been enacted upon them, us, over time. Epistemic agency requires surfacing our knowledge and valid realities, as well as our praxes as valuable possibility models for ideological, cultural, and structural shifts in the academy and beyond. A kind of epistemic agency in action!

Hannah-Jones' final decision demonstrates epistemic agency in action. While the Board of Trustees at UNC ultimately decided to grant her tenure, she decided to not accept their offer and move on to a different institution – Howard University. At Howard, she serves as the Knight Chair in Race and Journalism as a tenured (full) Professor. In an interview with National Public Radio, Professor Hannah-Jones shared, "...it's not my job to heal the University of North Carolina. That's the job of the people in power who created this situation in the first place" (NPR, 2021, n.p.). Her decision was a shock for many but serves as a constant reminder of the agency we can enact when faced with on-going and ever-present epistemic violence. It is our goal that the work in this book serves to demonstrate an active participation in and engagement with Black women's ways of knowing and agency in the academy.

Organization of Book

Our book serves as a crucible text, a bridging together of seminal and contemporary intergenerational voices through interdisciplinary narratives, that elucidate Black feminist epistemologies, research, and praxis. Co-editors and chapter authors highlight relevant research, methodologies, and theoretical/conceptual frameworks; share experiences as aspiring faculty, current contingent, tenure-track, and tenured faculty; and offer lessons learned and strategies to influence systemic and institutional change for, with, and alongside Black women. We intentionally decenter whiteness by choosing not to capitalize the "w" in white and whiteness throughout the book.

In addition to the foreword, conclusion, and afterword, this edited book consists of 19 chapters divided into 4 sections. Twelve full-length chapters situate Black women in and through the academy/pipeline in relation to the professoriate. Seven shorter chapters foster dynamic discussion toward applying Black feminist epistemologies in new and emerging ways. We imagine the interplay between the full-length and short chapters will generate broader, more emboldened, and yet unarticulated conceptualizations of Black feminist epistemologies, research, and praxis. The body of chapters, then, is synchronistic, pushing up against conceptual boundaries and welcoming liminality.

In Section 1, the authors historically frame how Black women have traversed the academy. In Chapter 2, Mabokela and Mlambo employ an international pan-African feminist lens to interrogate experiences of Black women academics both in North America and in other parts of the world. Gregory reflects on decades of experience as a Black woman academic researching other Black women in the academy in Chapter 3. In Chapter 4, Harley reexamines her earlier work – Black women faculty as Maids of Academe (2008) – to contemporarily situate our lived realities within the context of the Black Lives Matter movement. Templeton concludes Section 1 with a call to action. She calls for the uplift and elevation of Black women to disrupt white supremacy.

Section 2 highlights the utility of Black feminist epistemologies, research, and praxis through possibilities of practical application. In Chapter 6, Patterson-Stephens and Njoku illuminate Black cyberfeminism as resistance to the media's (mis)representation of Black womanhood. Ngadjui discusses misogynoir within counselor education in Chapter 7. In Chapter 8, Haynes, Stewart, Allen Moore, Joseph, and Patton describe intersectionality methodology as a lens through which Black women can write themselves into existence. In Chapter 9, Collins and Hunter embody education as a practice of freedom by teaching African dance in their courses. Aya, in Chapter 10, analogizes Black women doctoral students' realities in the academy as spirit murder. Davis and Peters conclude Section 2 with a focus on mentorship in graduate education. In Chapter 11, they engage sista circle methodology as praxis to support and socialize Black women doctoral students.

Chapter authors within Section 3 narrate how Black feminisms have grounded/guided their existence as Black women in academic spaces and specifically on their journeys toward reappointment, tenure, and promotion (i.e., through teaching, research, and service). In Chapter 12, Wright Fields and Overby make meaning of Black women's tweets via the hashtag #BlackintheIvory through a found poem. Through visual and textual sources, West shares her experience transitioning from administrator to academic in Chapter 13. In Chapter 14, Brown and Murray center on a womanist caring framework to recount personal and pedagogical narratives of teaching within the social foundations of education programs. In Chapter 15, Steele names Black feminist thought as a guiding frame through which she narrates her experiences as a doctoral student turned faculty/scholar. To conclude Section 3, Hylton centers on positionality to ground the histories of Black women faculty teaching in literacy programs.

Canary in the coal mine, or Section 4, highlights narratives of Black women faculty who have attained tenure and promotion, as well as academic leadership positions. In Chapter 17, Garrett and Croom discuss how and to what extent interlocking oppressions (i.e., racism and sexism) influence Black womyn's trajectories into a full professorship. Hailu and Cox contextualized Dr. Cox's journey as an institutional leader within a department of engineering education in Chapter 18. In Chapter 19, we as co-editors highlight and converse with excerpts from an interview with two full professors turned department chairs. In the concluding chapter, Sulé revisits her concept of enact, discard, and transform to highlight Black women's agentic epistemology.

References

Alexander-Floyd, N. G. (2010). Critical race Black feminism: A "jurisprudence of resistance" and the transformation of the academy. *Signs: Journal of Women in Culture and Society, 35*(4), 810–820.

Bailey, M., & Trudy (2018). On misogynoir: Citation, erasure, and plagiarism. *Feminist Media Studies, 18*(4), 762–768.

Beale, F. (1979). Double jeopardy: To be Black and female. In T. Cade (Ed.), *The Black woman: An anthology* (pp. 90–100). New American Library.

Boss, G. J., Davis, T. J., Porter, C. J., & Moore, C. M. (2019). Second to none: Contingent women of Color faculty in the classroom. In R. Jeffries (Ed.), *Diversity, equity, and inclusivity in contemporary higher* education (pp. 211–225). IGI Global.

Brown, E. B. (1989). Womanist consciousness: Maggie Lena Walker and the independent order of Saint Luke. *Signs, 14*(3), 610–633.

Bunch, A. J. (2015). Epistemic violence in the process of othering: Real-world applications and moving forward. *Scholarly Undergraduate Research Journal at Clark, 1*(2), 11–18.

Carter Andrews, D. J. (2015). Navigating raced-gender microaggressions: The experiences of a tenure-track Black female scholar. In F. A. Bonner II, A. F. Marbley, F. Tuitt, P. A. Robinson, R. M. Banda, & R. L. Hughes (Eds.), *Black faculty in the academy: Narratives for negotiating identity and achieving career success* (pp. 79–88). Routledge.

Collins, P. H. (1986). Learning from the outsider within: The sociological significance of Black feminist thought. *Social Problems, 33*(6), S14–S32.

Collins, P. H. (1990). *Black feminist thought: Knowledge, consciousness, and the politics of empowerment.* Unwin Hyman.

Collins, P. H. (2000). Black feminism, and Black political economy. *The Annals of the American Academy of Political and Social Science, 568*, 41–53.

Combahee River Collective. (1982). A Black feminist statement: The Combahee River Collective. In G.T. Hull, P. Bell-Scott, & B. Smith (Eds.), *All the women are White, All the Blacks are men, but some of us are brave: Black women's studies* (pp. 13–22). The Feminist Press at CUNY.

Cooper, A. J. (1892/1988). *A voice from the south.* Oxford University Press.
Crenshaw, K. (1989). Demarginalizing the intersection of race and sex: A Black feminist critique of antidiscrimination doctrine, feminist theory and antiracist politics. *University of Chicago Legal Forum, 8*, 139–167.
Crenshaw, K. (1991). Mapping the margins: Intersectionality, identity politics, and violence against women of color. *Stanford Law Review, 43*(6), 1241–1299.
Croom, N. N. (2017). Promotion beyond tenure: Unpacking racism and sexism in the experiences of black women professors. *The Review of Higher Education, 40*(4), 557–583.
Croom, N. N., & Patton, L. D. (2012). The miner's canary: A critical race perspective on the representation of Black women full professors. *The Negro Educational Review, 62* & *63*(1–4), 13–39.
Dillard, C. B. (2006). *On spiritual strivings: Transforming an African American woman's academic life.* State University of New York Press.
Dotson, K. (2011). Tracking epistemic violence, tracking practices of silencing. *Hypatia, 26*(2), 236–257.
Essed, P. (1991). *Understanding everyday racism: An interdisciplinary theory.* Sage.
Evans-Winters, V. E. (2019). *Black feminism in qualitative inquiry: A mosaic for writing our daughter's body.* Routledge.
Fries-Britt, S., & Kelly, B. T. (2005). Retaining each other: Narratives of two African American women in the academy. *The Urban Review, 37*(3), 221–242.
Gregory, S. T. (2001). Black faculty women in the academy: History, status, and future. *The Journal of Negro Education, 70*(3), 124–138.
Harley, D. A. (2008). Maids of the academe: African American women faculty at predominantly White institutions. *Journal of African American Studies, 12*(1), 19–36.
Harris-Perry, M. V. (2011). *Sister citizen: Shame, stereotypes, and Black women in America.* Yale University Press.
hooks, b. (1994). *Teaching to transgress: Education as the Practice of freedom.* Routledge.
Hughes, R., & Giles, M. (2010). CRiT walking in higher education: Activating critical race theory in the academy. *Race Ethnicity and Education, 13*(1), 41–57. https://doi.org/10.1080/13613320903549685
Kamath, R., Meier, H. H., & Rao, S. R. (2004). A comprehensive study of named Marketing chairs at colleges and universities in 2002. *Marketing Education Review, 14*(2), 69–78.
Killian, J. (2021, May 13). UNC hire of acclaimed journalist sparks conservative ire. *NC Policy Watch. http://www.ncpolicywatch.com/2021/05/13/unc-hire-of-acclaimed-journalist-sparks- conservative-ire/*
Knight Foundation. (n.d.). *Knight Chairs in Journalism.* https://knightfoundation.org/knight-chairs/
Legal Defense Fund. (2021, July 6). *Nikole Hannah-Jones issues statement on decision to decline tenure offer at University of North Carolina-Chapel Hill and to accept Knight Chair appointment at Howard University.* https://www.naacpldf.org/press-release/nikole-hannah-jones-issues-statement-on-decision-to-decline-tenure-offer-at-university-of-north-carolina-chapel-hill-and-to-accept-knight-chair-appointment-at-howard-university/
Mabokela, R. O., & Green, A. L. (2001). *Sisters of the academy: Emergent Black women scholars in higher education.* Stylus.

National Center for Education Statistics. (2019). *Full-time faculty in degree-granting postsecondary institutions, by race/ethnicity, sex, and academic rank: Fall 2015, fall 2017, and fall 2018.* Table 315.20. https://nces.ed.gov/programs/digest/d19/tables/dt19_315.20.asp
NPR. (2021, July 6). *After tenure controversy, Nikole Hannah-Jones will join Howard faculty instead of UNC.* National. https://www.npr.org/2021/07/06/1013315775/after-tenure-controversy-nikole-hannah-jones-will-join-howard-faculty-instead-of
Perlow, O. N., Wheeler, D. I., Bethea, S. L., & Scott, B. M. (2018). *Black women's liberatory pedagogies: Resistance, transformation, and healing within and beyond the academy.* Palgrave MacMillan.
Porter, C. J. (2019). Metaphorically speaking: Being a Black woman in the academy is like. In D. J. Mitchell, Jr., J. Marie, & T. Steele (Eds.), *Intersectionality & higher education: Theory, research, and praxis* (2nd ed., pp. 99–109). Peter Lang.
Porter, C. J., Davis, T. J., & Boss, G. J. (2018, December 13). *My sister's keeper: Advancing scholarship and sustaining one another through an academic writing (life) group.* National Center for Institutional Diversity. https://medium.com/national-center-for-institutional-diversity/my-sisters-keeper-1c814c96ce5d
Porter, C. J., Moore, C. M., Boss, G. J., Davis, T. J., & Louis, D. A. (2020). To be Black women and contingent faculty: Four scholarly personal narratives. *The Journal of Higher Education, 91*(5), 674–697.
Robertson, K. (2021, May 19). Nikole Hannah-Jones denied tenure at University of North Carolina. *New York Times.* https://www.nytimes.com/2021/05/19/business/media/nikole- hannah-jones-unc.html
Smith, B. (1983). Introduction. In B. Smith (Ed.), *Home girls: A Black feminist anthology* (pp. xxi–lviii). Kitchen Table: Women of Color Press.
Spivak, G. C. (1999). *A critique of postcolonial reason: Toward a history of the vanishing present.* Harvard University Press.
Spivak, G. C. (2010). "Can the subaltern speak?": Revised edition, from the "history" chapter of critique of postcolonial reason. In R. C. Morris (Ed.), *Reflections on the history of an idea: Can the subaltern speak?* (pp. 21–78). Columbia University Press.
Sulé, V. T. (2009). Black female faculty: Role definition, critical enactments, and contributions to predominantly White research institutions. *NASPA Journal about Women in Higher Education, 2*(1), 93–121.
Sulé, V. T. (2014). Enact, discard, and transform: A critical race feminist perspective on professional socialization among tenured Black female faculty. *International Journal of Qualitative Studies in Education, 27*(4), 432–453.
Tang, R. Y. W. (1993). A profile of accounting chair professorships in 1992. *Journal of Education for Business, 68*(3), 133–138.
Tang, R. Y. W., & Griffith, D. (1997/1998). Accounting chair professorships in 1997. *Journal of Applied Business Research, 14*(1), 137–147.
Walker, A. (1983). *In search of our mother's gardens: Womanist prose.* Mariner Books.
Williams, P. (1987). Spirit-murdering the messenger: The discourse of fingerpointing as the law's response to racism. *University of Miami Law Review, 42*(1), 127–157.
Worthington, J. S., Waters, G. L., & Fields, K. T. (1989). A profile of chairholders based on chair efficiency ratios. *Accounting Educator's Journal, 2*, 87–103.

SECTION I

Historical Overview

Situating (Counter)Stories in the Academy

2

TWENTY YEARS LATER... THE NARRATIVE FOR BLACK WOMEN IN THE ACADEMY REMAINS THE SAME, OR DOES IT?

Reitumetse O. Mabokela and Yeukai A. Mlambo

Twenty years ago, a team of 15 women of African descent collaborated on an edited volume entitled, *Sisters of the Academy: Emergent Black Women Scholars in Higher Education* (Mabokela & Green, 2001). At that time, the co-editors, Drs. Reitumetse Obakeng Mabokela and Anna L. Green, and most of the contributors to this scholarly endeavor were early career academics, navigating what at times seemed like an indecipherable maze. The subsequent establishment of the Sisters of the Academy (SOTA) Institute under the leadership of Dr. Green recognized the need to create a safe space dedicated to facilitating the success of Black women in higher education, by providing a community and network of support to women who would often feel the isolation of "being the first" or "the only" in many academic spaces.

Despite these earlier calls for interventions by and for Black women in higher education that emerged from the book, today the plight of Black women and their positioning within institutions of higher learning remains largely unchanged. Furthermore, while the experiences of women who collaborated on SOTA were anchored in, and informed by the U.S. higher education context, they bear remarkable similarities to accounts shared by academic women, and especially Black women in various international milieus today. In this chapter, we demonstrate how gendered and racialized experiences for Black women in the academy transcend national boundaries, with varying degrees of disparities across different socio-political contexts. We employ both a postcolonial feminist lens to interrogate and acknowledge the diverse experiences these women face, as well as a pan-African feminist lens to illuminate the transnational Black woman experience and to demonstrate the necessity of finding the unity in that diversity as we work to improve Black women academic's experiences around the world.

DOI: 10.4324/9781003184867-3

Gleaning from experiences Black women shared 20 years ago in SOTA, many of which are still pervasive, we juxtapose the current realities of what it means to be a Black academic woman in a global academic context. We extend beyond previous works to highlight the growing significance of context and identit(ies) in understanding Black women's experiences in higher education. More importantly, we reflect on the collective global experiences of Black women and amplify the need for more urgent and deliberate actions by institutions of higher education to secure Black women's success in the academy.

Postcolonial and Pan-African Feminism(s)

In advancing our understanding of Black women's experiences beyond the North American experience, we leverage postcolonial feminism and pan-African feminism to highlight both the importance of acknowledging the different contextual experiences of Black women in the diaspora, as well as the necessity of "mobilizing multiple energies that work to demystify, resist and overcome sex- and gender-based oppressions" (Mama, 2017, p. 1) that operate in the institutions Black women inhabit.

Postcolonial Feminism

Postcolonialism is a critical and transformational perspective that not only draws attention to, but works to disrupt Eurocentrism, racism, and ethnocentrism that exists in institutions, societies, and ways of thinking. *Postcolonial feminism* by extension aims to disrupt the superiority of Western knowledge related to women's lives, through amplifying the voices of racialized women who are often silenced in mainstream, hegemonic feminist lenses. In relation to North America and the broader Black woman diaspora whose experiences are rarely visible in mainstream conversations, "postcolonial feminism is a means to grasp cultural differences by decentering knowledge production, where the culturally different Other is heard and understood from standpoints located at the margins" (Racine, 2003, p. 97).

Chakraborty (2017) noted, "unidirectional and linear theories and world views are not always sufficient to understand every society"; furthermore, "to see the oppression of women in the First World and the global South as the same, and to work through the same structures would be to ignore the specificities of their different locations" (p. 53). Therefore, postcolonial feminism challenges the use of gender as a homogenizing boundary marker that delineates belonging between national, ethnic, or religious groups. Instead, it calls for identifying and celebrating diversity, both to challenge homogenous ideas of representation and to disrupt the "Othering" which occurs when discussing gendered experiences of people from otherwise marginalized geolocalities (Marchand, 2009). Through amplifying alternative perspectives, postcolonial feminism pushes to "avoid reframing or re-presenting current injustices and social inequalities in a white Western hegemonic" discourse (Racine, 2003, p. 97).

For postcolonial scholar Mohanty (1988), "sisterhood cannot be assumed on the basis of gender" alone, instead it must be built with an understanding of the nuances of history, politics, and specific practices related to the place. Mohanty asserted the ties that bind women together as a group are the struggles against imperialism, class, race, and gender; and women, and specifically Black women must navigate wherever they are located. Therefore, while interrogating Black women's experiences in the USA provides one perspective, our objective is not to essentialize the US experiences, but to illuminate varied insights of Black women academics around the globe, which transcend particularities of geography, politics, and culture and offer a collective understanding of Black women experiences.

Pan-African Feminism

Building upon SOTA, we also leverage pan-African feminism as part of a conceptual framework with postcolonial feminism. Pan-African feminism advocates for "collective organising with coherent feminist consciousness informed by sound theories of gender oppression and change" (Mama, 2017, p. 1). Rooted in the notion of unity in diversity, where it is important to build and acknowledge diverse feminist perspectives, pan-African feminism encourages us to leverage the common desire for Black women's liberation as a pathway to realizing a collective force for change. Like postcolonial feminism, pan-African feminism demands space(s) for Black women in the broader diaspora including Africa, the Caribbean, Europe, and Australia to be included in driving demands for change for all women of African descent wherever they may be located.

In the next sections, we first reflect on the experiences of Black women in North America, tracing their oppressions and liberations to date, building on the stories shared in SOTA. Additionally, guided by the notion of collective organizing espoused by pan-African feminism, we expand the discussion to highlight Black women's experiences around the world, showing the differences and similarities among Black women academics in the diaspora. We conclude with calls to action for individuals, higher education institutions, and for policymakers and implementers to consider in the pursuit of supporting the liberation and humanization of Black women in the academy.

The U.S. Academic Landscape: 20 Years Ago and Current Realities

Narratives shared by women in SOTA in 2000–2001 are strikingly comparable to accounts of the Black academic women experiences in 2020–2021. A review of the literature indicates that progress has been primarily stagnant, in terms of representation, inclusion, and qualitative experiences of women of African descent in the U.S. academic ranks (Bartman, 2015; Corley, 2020; Jaschik, 2020; Patel, 2021). Notably, 20 years ago there were pervasive disparities across racial and gender lines, with respect to academic rank, mean income, teaching, and research activities, which persist today (Flaherty, 2020; Walkington, 2017). In terms of academic rank, racial and ethnic minorities and women were and continue to disproportionately occupy lower academic ranks as assistant professors, lecturers, or instructors (Bartman, 2015; Corley, 2020; Jaschik, 2020; Jones et al., 2015; Patel, 2021), while at the rank of full professor, men outnumber women at a ratio of almost three to one (Flaherty, 2016). The impact of legislative and institutional policies including affirmative action to redress racial and gender disparities over the past two decades has been uneven. A 20-year study by the TIAA Institute indicated that while the proportion of women and faculty of color has increased slightly, the majority hold non-tenure track positions (Flaherty, 2016).

According to the National Center of Education Statistics (NCES), in 2018, Black women comprised 3% of the 1.5 million academics in U.S. universities and 4% of faculty in tenure track positions (NCES, 2018a, 2018b; Patel, 2021). While women represented just over half (52.9%) of assistant professors, Black women at 4%, were chronically under-represented in the entry-level faculty positions. Similarly, among associate professors whose representation was near parity at 46.4%, only 3% of academics at this rank were Black women. While the pursuit for full professorship remained elusive, with only 34% of these positions held by women, Black women occupied only 2% of these senior academic positions (NCES, 2018a, 2018b; Patel, 2021).

Aside from numerical representation, the intersection of gender and race underscores fractured academic experiences of women of African descent, irrespective of academic rank institutional prestige or geographic location. Various scholars (Britton, 2017; Croom, 2017; Frazier, 2011; Jones et al., 2015) contended higher education institutions created an environment that Turner and Myers (2000) characterized as a "chilly climate" where Black women and women of color feel unwelcome. Bell et al. (2021) used the term anti-Blackness to describe the "disdain, disregard and disgust" for Black people in higher education (p. 43). Black women continue to report denials of their racialized experiences, being subject to persistent discriminatory practices including microaggressions and silencing (Aiston & Fo, 2020; Bell et al., 2021). All these dehumanizing structures and experiences have encumbered the professional progress and contributions of Black women faculty and academic administrators.

A study of U.S. college presidents conducted by the American Council on Education (ACE, 2017), further highlighted continuing disparities in the representation of women in presidential ranks. In 2016, 83% of all university presidents were white, 8% were of African descent, 4% Latinx, and 2% Asian or Asian American. When considering gender and racial-ethnic composition, 30% of all university presidents in the U.S. were women. Of this representation, 36% of women led two-year colleges, 28% Baccalaureate universities, 29% Master's, and 29% Doctoral granting institutions. Minority women presidents comprised only 5% of presidents, the majority of whom led two-year colleges (ACE, 2017). As will be demonstrated in the ensuing discussion, like the U.S., arguably the trends in the global context demonstrate that women are not numerically under-represented in higher education, however, they continue to be relegated to lower academic ranks. However, the intersection of race intensifies marginalization for academics of African descent, relative to gender among their peers.

Global (Under) Representation of Black Women in the Academy

In most high-income and some middle-income countries, women represent most students enrolled in undergraduate programs, with the exception of STEM disciplines where under-representation persists (Mlambo, 2017). However, these robust undergraduate enrollment trends are not reflected in academic and administrative ranks where women faculty continue to be relegated to the margins. Although there are global variations in terms of the degrees of success toward the attainment of gender parity in education broadly, and the higher education sector specifically, what is consistent is that even in countries with extensive legislation and policies to redress gender inequities, disparities persist. Patterns of gender marginalization observed in countries including the United Kingdom (Rollock, 2019), Australia (Winchester & Browning, 2015), Canada (Canada Education Board, 2018), New Zealand (McGregor, 2018), South Africa (Mabokela & Mlambo, 2017), and other sub-Saharan countries (Assie-Lumumba, 2006; Mama, 2006) revealed remarkable similarities to those articulated in SOTA, which endure two decades later.

An analysis of data in the United Kingdom, Canada, Asia-Pacific, and Sub-Saharan Africa reveals similarly disturbing themes of inequity in pay, fewer opportunities for promotion and tenure, imbalanced workloads, and sexual harassment in the academy. While socio-cultural conditions and political particularities in these countries and regions of the world differ significantly from the United States, women's experiences are extra-ordinarily similar. Nicola Rollock's (2019) report, *Staying Power: The Career Experiences and Strategies of UK Black Female Professors* portrayed a disheartening account of the academic landscape in the UK, where there were 85 Black professors across all higher education institutions, of which 25 were Black women. She further conveyed, only 4.6% of all Black faculty occupied this senior academic rank compared with 11.2% of white faculty. Similar to the U.S., studies conducted across 28 countries in the European Union, New Zealand, and Australia revealed a disproportionately high percentage of women were employed as part-time or contract workers, similar to non-tenure positions, and occupied the lowest academic ranks (e.g., lecturers, junior lecturers, or tutors; McGregor, 2018; Winchester & Browning, 2015).

Australia demonstrated similar patterns and further highlighted the institutionalization of inequitable practices. In 2018, women held fewer academic positions than men at the senior lecturer level and above, but more than 50% of all lecturers and below-lecturer positions. Women occupied 46.8% of senior lecturer positions and just one-third of above senior lecturer positions. On the lower end of the academic rank spectrum, women occupied 54.7% of lecturer positions and 53.8% of below-lecturer faculty positions (Catalyst, 2020a, 2020b). In terms of race, although Australian institutions have seen an increase in diversity among students and staff with higher international student numbers and more Aboriginal and Torres Strait Islander staff, academia itself "remains a space that perpetuates the hegemony of dominant social identities: white, male, straight and able-bodied" (Anderson et al., 2020, p. 5). As a result, academics who identify as minoritized represent "less-than-ideal" academics, who do not resemble the preferred image of an academic. Instead, women of color in Australian institutions experience what Anderson et al. (2020) referred to as "headwinds" of individual and systemic bias and discrimination, racism, undue criticism, and a questioning of their competencies and qualifications, which threaten their wellbeing and actively hinder their career advancement. Similar experiences were reflected among faculty of color in Canadian universities including questioning of one's qualifications and competencies, feelings of exclusion by colleagues, and an overall persistent "unwillingness and almost complete denunciation of the effects of these racially charged environments on your health, wellness, and sense of wellbeing" (Daniel, 2019, p. 21).

Granted, one could perhaps argue that Black women and women of color represent a miniscule portion of the overall population numbers in these largely white populated countries. As a result, the representation relative to the population may be dismissed as proportional to their overall national demographic representation. However, the negative experiences Black women in these countries encounter are still problematic. Furthermore, in a country like South Africa, where Black women are in fact the majority, similar disparities are also observed (Mlambo, 2017). An analysis of faculty by gender indicated persistent over-representation of women in the lecturer, junior lecturer, or below junior lecturer ranks. In 2016, South African women represented 39.6% of associate professors and 27.5% of full professors, 45.1% of senior lecturers, and 53% of lecturers and junior lecturers (Mabokela & Mlambo, 2017). The intersection of race and gender in the South African context highlights persistent racial disparities, where white women comprised the majority, 53% of women faculty compared to African women who comprised only 14% of the faculty (Breetzke & Hedding, 2018).

The low representation of Black African faculty overall reflects the legacy of apartheid where higher education access was restricted for historically marginalized individuals, specifically Black people. The transition to democracy in 1994 brought new policies including affirmative action aimed at redressing historical inequalities and increasing Black women and men's participation in academia (Hlatshwayo, 2020). Despite these articulated policies, institutional culture remains largely unchanged as Black women academics remain marginalized, continue to be viewed as outsiders, and are largely treated as invisible (Mahabeer et al., 2018). Additionally, given the late access to higher education and academic positions, Black women in South Africa also experience infantilization where they are treated as late-bloomers, developmental academics who need grooming. "Which is indicative of the notion that the university does not trust that these academics can fulfil their roles without guidance" (Mahabeer et al., 2018, p. 36). Specifically, guidance from senior white colleagues.

Discussion

The preceding discussions highlight well-documented accounts of experiences of academics of African descent across various socio-political contexts. A recent article in the *Chronicle of Higher Education* titled, "Race on Campus: Why Faculty Diversity Remains Largely a Zero-Sum Game" (Patel, 2021), highlighted the representation of scholars of color in the U.S. has been largely stagnant over the past two decades. While concerns have been well articulated, there is stubborn resistance to offer meaningful resolution of these issues. Dar et al. (2020, p. 2) in their article, *The Business School is Racist: Act Up!,* make an "urgent call for scholars of colour to collectively act up to radically challenge the white supremacist nature of business schools, even as it plays out differently in local contexts." Australian scholars Anderson et al. (2020) asserted universities are both elite spaces that uphold colonial practice and can also be spaces of radical transformation. They argue, therefore, "the university occupies a unique position that can either reproduce inequality through the transmission of elitism and colonial knowledges or be a site of creative reimagining of what has happened in the past and what is possible in the future" (p. 939). Given the overwhelming potential for higher education institutions to be radical change makers, we challenge the higher education sector to move beyond the margins, collaborate beyond comfortable spaces, interrogate institutional cultures, structures, and policies, and foster cultures of inclusive excellence for Black women academics to thrive. In the following sections, we provide some initial recommendations for institutions to consider.

(Re)Defining Institutional Culture is a Two-Way Street

> More than three decades ago, Vincent Maphai (1989) asserted, most affirmative action programs operate from the assumption that Blacks are defective... Often no question is raised regarding the institution itself

> ... The Black is provided with a mentor who will help him adjust to the company. There is no remedial course for the company to adjust to Blacks.
>
> *(p. 18)*

This perception remains largely true in terms of how higher education institutions define the place and role of faculty from historically marginalized groups within them as *perpetual visitors* or *outsiders on the fringes*, who do not represent the *ideal academic*, and therefore are treated as individuals who do not fundamentally impact the culture of the university.

In recent years, many universities have created or enhanced their diversity, equity, and inclusion offices, with the primary focus on diversifying faculty, staff, and students and creating more inclusive institutional cultures. South African scholar Hlatshwayo (2020) reminded us that the calls for institutional transformation and decolonization of the academy are global in nature as these initiatives have begun around the world (Wamai, 2016). While these are positive efforts to be applauded, the creation of a singular administrative structure does not address deeply entrenched practices of marginalization (e.g., everyday racism; Essed, 1991) embedded in the day-to-day practices of how universities do their work. Institutional cultures that continue to interrogate and question the value of the scholarship of faculty of color; the legitimacy of such scholarship especially when focused on communities of color; overt and covert exclusion for informal networks; microaggressions from students and faculty colleagues, create alienating cultures that do not foster inclusivity. As Maphai further stated (1989, p. 21) "... affirmative action programs should focus on transforming the institutions, not merely Blacks and women within them."

Addressing the Revolving-Door Syndrome

The modest progress noted in the representation of women of African descent in the academy over the past two decades has been partly attributed to what some describe a revolving-door phenomenon (Lynch-Alexander, 2017; Parker et al., 2006), where academics from under-represented groups do not persist in higher education. This effectively means that institutions of higher education are making a limited appreciable difference in the inclusion of women and faculty of color as they are constantly replacing women and scholars of color who elect to leave the academy (Dernbach & Tan, 2021; Rollock, 2019; Sheth & Croom, 2021). Some scholars of color contend higher education institutions create environments where they are unable to represent their "total self." While they are sometimes valued for contributing to numerical diversity, universities fail to embrace and value the totality of their contributions, thus reinforcing the one-way expectation of assimilation to institutional norms. Women and faculty of color tend to have heavy service responsibilities, student mentorship, as well as outreach and engagement activities relative to peers' activities frequently under-valued in tenure and promotion decisions (Bartman, 2015; Britton, 2017; Rollock, 2019) especially at research-intensive institutions. Failure to actively address the revolving door by changing institutional culture to welcome Black women will mean institutions will continue to lose talented Black faculty.

The Leaky Pipeline: "We Cannot Find Qualified Blacks"

Two decades ago, Mabokela (2000) authored an article titled, *We Cannot Find Qualified Blacks: Faculty Diversification Programmes at South African Universities.* Drawing primarily on the experiences of Black faculty members at predominantly white South African universities, the author highlighted a pervasive argument for the lack of diversity across both South Africa and the USA. Increasingly, women represent the majority of students graduating with baccalaureate and Master's degrees in many high and middle-income countries; however, these graduation trends have not translated into a robust representation of women within academic ranks (Mlambo, 2017). For women, being the first, the only, or one of very few continues to be a fairly common but disheartening trend, especially at research-intensive universities. While most institutions of higher education, particularly in the global north, have diversity statements of one form or another, these have not translated into tangible impact toward change. Institutional committees still rely heavily on their own professional networks to recruit candidates, which often have limited access to other networks used by women and other members of under-represented groups. Additionally, members of search committees demonstrate interviewer bias by giving preference to applicants who reflect themselves, while being overly critical in their assessment of the qualifications and scholarly pursuits of women and scholars of color (Burden et al., 2005; Ceci & Williams, 2011). In addition to putting forward institutional commitments to diversifying faculty, these statements need to be supported with resources and accountability structures to ensure such statements become actions. In addition to ensuring hiring committees are represented by Black women or faculty of color, these committees should be set up with meaningful voting structures that allow for these faculty, who are often pre-tenure, to not have their decisions overridden by more senior white colleagues. Cluster diversity hires and deliberate mentorship can also provide a valuable community for junior faculty to support each other and to combat feelings of isolation.

Concluding Remarks

In this chapter, we have demonstrated both the distinct and shared experiences of women of African descent as they exist in academic spaces around the world. Jamaican Canadian scholar Andrea Davis (2018) asserted individual stories reflect the larger socio-political, economic, and historical ideologies and practices of spaces. The experiences highlighted in this chapter reveal the transnational nature of the oppression of Black women academics. While postcolonial feminism encourages us to question the homogenous perspective of Black womanhood, pan-African feminism reminds us that as Black women, when it comes to our experiences, the whole is greater than the sum of its parts.

While we assert higher education institutions have a key responsibility to make spaces welcoming for Black women faculty and other faculty of color, we also recognize the inherent power that lies in collective organizing among Black women, faculty of color, and our allies. As we process our individual and collective experiences, there exists an opportunity to collaborate and strategize as we advocate for change so that 20 years from now, we are not discussing Black women's plight in academia yet again.

References

Aiston, S. J., & Fo, C. K. (2020). The silence/ing of academic women. *Gender and Education, 33*(2), 138–155.

American Council on Education. (2017). *American college president study.* https://www.aceacps.org/summary-profile-dashboard/

Anderson, L., Gatwiri, K., & Townsend-Cross, M. (2020). Battling the "headwinds": The experiences of minoritised academics in the neoliberal Australian university. *International Journal of Qualitative Studies in Education, 33*(9), 939–953.

Assie-Lumumba, N. (2006). Empowerment of women in higher education in Africa: The role and mission of research. *UNESCO Forum Occasional Paper No. 11.* UNESCO.

Bartman, C. (2015). African American women in higher education: Issues and support strategies. *College Student Affairs Leadership,* (2), Article 5.

Bell, M. P., Berry, D., Leopold, J., & Nkomo, S. (2021). Making black lives matter in academia: A black feminist call for collective action against anti-blackness in the academy. *Gender, Work & Organization, 28*(S1), 39–57.

Breetzke, G. D., & Hedding, D. W. (2018). The changing demography of academic staff at higher education institutions (HEIS) in South Africa. *Higher Education Higher Education, 76,* 145–161.

Britton, D. M. (2017). Beyond the chilly climate: The salience of gender in women's academic careers. *Gender & Society, 31*(1), 5–27.

Burden, J. W., Jr., Harrison, L., Jr., & Hodge, S. R. (2005). Perceptions of African American faculty in kinesiology-based programs at predominantly white American institutions of higher education. *Research Quarterly for Exercise and Sport, 76*(2), 224–237.

Canada Education Board. (2018). *Gender inequities persist in Canadian post-secondary education and the workforce.* https://www.newswire.ca/news-releases/gender-inequities-persist-in-canadian-post-secondary-education-and-the-workforce-680243293.html

Catalyst. (2020a). *Women on Academia: Quick take.* https://www.catalyst.org/research/women-in-academia/

Catalyst. (2020b). *Women in the workforce India: Quick take.* https://www.catalyst.org/research/women-in-the-workforce-india/

Ceci, S. J., & Williams, W. M. (2011). Understanding current causes of women's underrepresentation in science. *Proceedings of the National Academy of Science of the United States (PNAS), 108*(8), 3157–3162.

Chakraborty, A. (2017). Can postcolonial feminism revive international relations? *Economic & Political Weekly, LII*(20), 51–55.

Corley, J. (2020, June 27). *Where are the women of color in academia.* https://www.forbes.com/sites/jacquelyncorley/2020/06/27/where-are-the-women-of-color-in-academia/?sh=122d96546401

Croom, N. N., (2017). Promotion beyond tenure: Unpacking racism and sexism in the experiences of black womyn professors. *Review of Higher Education, 40*(4), 557–583.

Daniel, B.-J. (2019). Teaching while black: Racial dynamics, evaluations, and the role of white females in the Canadian academy in carrying the racism torch. *Race, Ethnicity & Education, 22*(1), 21–37.

Dar, S., Liu, H., Martinez Dy, A., & Brewis, D. N. (2020). The business school is racist: Act up! *Organization*. https://doi.org/10.1177/1350508420928521

Davis, A. (2018). The black woman native speaking subject: Reflections of a black female professor in Canada. *Atlantis* Journal, *39*(1), 70–78.

Dernbach, B. Z., & Tan, E. (2021). 'I won't be the last Black woman to leave the college': At St. Olaf College, resignations of Black faculty and diverse staff leave students seeking answers. *Sahan Journal.*

Essed, P. (1991). *Understanding everyday racism: An interdisciplinary theory.* Sage.

Flaherty, C. (2016). *More faculty diversity, not on tenure track.* https://www.insidehighered.com/news/2016/08/22/study-finds-gains-faculty-diversity-not-tenure-track

Flaherty, C. (2020). *The souls of black professors. Inside higher education.* https://www.insidehighered.com/news/2020/10/21/scholars-talk-about-being-black-campus-2020

Frazier, K. N. (2011). Academic bullying: a barrier to tenure and promotion for African-American faculty. *Florida Journal of Educational Administration & Policy, 5*(1), 1–13.

Hlatshwayo, M. N. (2020). Being black in South African higher education: An intersectional insight. *Acta Academia, 52*(2), 163–180.

Jaschik, S. (2020). "*Lean semesters.*" Inside Higher Education. https://www.insidehighered.com/news/2020/10/16/author-discusses-her-new-book-black-women-higher-education

Jones, B., Hwang, E., & Bustamante, R. M. (2015). African American female professors' strategies for successful attainment of tenure and promotion at predominately white institutions: It can happen. *Education, Citizenship and Social Justice, 10*(2), 133–151.

Lynch-Alexander, E. (2017). Black minds matter: The call to retention of young Black academics (YBAs) in higher education. *International Journal of the Academic Business World, 11*(1), 31–35.

Mabokela, R. O. (2000). "We cannot find qualified blacks:" Faculty diversification programs at South African universities. *Comparative Education, 36*(1), 95–112.

Mabokela, R. O., & Green, A. L. (2001). *Sisters of the academy: Emergent black women scholars in higher education*. Stylus Publishing.

Mabokela, R. O., & Mlambo, Y. A. (2017). Access and equity and South African higher education: A review of policies after 20 years of democracy. *Comparative Education Review, 61*(4), 396–416.

Mahabeer, P., Nzimande, N., & Shoba, M. (2018). Academics of colour: Experiences of emerging black women academics in curriculum studies at a university in South Africa. *Agenda, 32*(1), 28–42.

Mama, A. (2006). Pursuing gender equality in the African university. *International Journal of African Renaissance Studies, 1*(1), 53–79.

Mama, A. (2017). The power of feminist pan-African intellect. *Feminist Africa, 22*, 1–15.

Maphai, V. (1989). Affirmative action in South Africa: A genuine option. *Social Dynamics, 15*, 1–24.

Marchand, M. H. (2009). The future of gender and development after 9/11: Insights from postcolonial feminism and transnationalism. *Third World Quarterly, 30*(5), 921–935.

McGregor, J. (2018). *The struggle for gender equality in tertiary education is a glass half-full story.* https://thespinoff.co.nz/society/19-09-2018/the-struggle-for-gender-equality-in-tertiary-education-is-a-glass-half-full-story/

Mlambo, Y. A. (2017). *Why not academia? The streamlined career choice process of black African women engineers: A grounded theory study.* PhD diss., Michigan State University.

Mohanty, C. T. (1988). Under western eyes: Feminist scholarship and colonial discourses. *Feminist Review, 30*, 51–80.

National Center for Education Statistics. (2018a). *Fast facts: Degrees conferred by race and sex.* https://nces.ed.gov/fastfacts/display.asp?id=72

National Center for Education Statistics. (2018b). *Fast facts: Race and ethnicity of college faculty.* https://nces.ed.gov/fastfacts/display.asp?id=61

Parker, S., Clayton-Pedersen, A., Moreno, J., Teraguchi, D., & Smith, D. G. (2006). *The revolving door for underrepresented minority faculty in higher education.* A research brief from the James Irvine Foundation Campus Diversity Initiative Project. http://hdl.handle.net/10244/50

Patel, V. (2021, February 23). *Race on campus.* Chronicle of higher education. https://www.chronicle.com/newsletter/race-on-campus/2021-02-23

Racine, L. (2003). Implementing a postcolonial feminist perspective in nursing research related to non-western populations. *Nursing Inquiry, 10*(2), 91–102.

Rollock, N. (2019), *Staying power: The career experiences and strategies of UK black female professors.* University and College Union. https://www.ucu.org.uk/media/10075/Staying-Power/pdf/UCU_Rollock_February_2019.pdf

Sheth, M. J., & Croom, N. N. (2021). Chronicles exploring hegemonic civility and the evisceration of academic freedom for critical womyn of color. In R. Dutt-Ballerstadt & K. Bhattacharya (Eds.), *Civility, free speech, and academic freedom in higher education: Faculty on the margins* (pp. 145–162). Routledge.

Turner, C. S., & Myers, S. L. Jr. (2000). *Faculty of color in academe: Bittersweet success.* Allyn and Bacon.

Walkington, L. (2017). How far have we really come? Black women faculty and graduate students' experiences in higher education. *Humboldt Journal of Social Relations, 39*, 51–65. https://www.jstor.org/stable/10.2307/90007871

Wamai, N. (May, 2016). *Decolonising the academy: Towards a global movement?* University World News. https://www.universityworldnews.com/post.php?story=20160524135416842

Winchester, H. P. M., & Browning, L. (2015). Gender equality in academic: A critical reflection. *Journal of Higher Education Policy and Management, 37*(3), 269–281. DOI: 10.1080/1360080X.2015.1034427

3

REIMAGINING BLACK FEMINIST EPISTEMOLOGY AND PRAXIS

Reflecting on the Contemporary and Evolving Conceptual Framework of One Black Faculty Woman's Academic Life

Sheila T. Gregory

I was asked by one of the editors to write a reflective piece revisiting my original work on Black faculty women in the academy (1999). The intent was to examine Black feminist epistemology and praxis from a more personal and contemporary perspective conceptualizing and re-positioning my academic narrative. It included how I redefined and realigned my teaching, research, and service, in a manner that illuminated my lived intersectional experiences, and interpretations of daily academic life, while meeting the new commitments to my expanded immediate family, continued mentoring of young people of color, social justice-related activities and my shared community advocacy. The chapter concludes with some lessons learned for faculty women who are also mothers or "other-mothers," navigating the tenure and promotion process, while sustaining their emotional and psychological well-being.

While I wrote this chapter, we were situated under unrivaled times. Our nation and the world were still recovering from the COVID-19 pandemic, with more than 83 million infected and 1 million deaths in the US and more than 526 million infected and 7 million deaths worldwide. We also witnessed a historic presidential election in the US, including our first woman of color in the White House, Vice President Kamala Harris, who was also an HBCU graduate. In 2013, the first hashtag, "#BlackLivesMatter" (BLM) started a global protest movement, after the senseless violence and death of Black and Brown people across this nation, sometimes at the hands of police, with often little to no justice. In 2020, with dozens of publicized reports and clear footage of these events, the nation and world took notice, and the emergence of the "Me Too" and "#Black Lives Matter" movements became global. The events of 2020 alone, led to some of the most sweeping changes our country has seen in some time, especially as it relates to race, sexual harassment, inequity, and social justice.

DOI: 10.4324/9781003184867-4

My hope is this chapter might inspire faculty women of color, not just in their quest for academic well-being and success, but also in dealing with the regrets from the past and finding peace in the journey where these experiences have led—prayerfully to greater authenticity and liberation.

Introduction

Thinking back over the past 30 years, I could not help but question if my choice of an academic career was too high a price for my young family? To what extent, if any, did it contribute to the demise of my first marriage? Did I sacrifice too much time away from my children when they needed my time and attention the most? My outline became increasingly extensive and more personal with raw narratives than I had originally outlined. In fact, I am thankful to the editors of this book, because I sent them a manuscript twice the length requested, after I could not cut it down any further. This has truly been a cathartic and healing experience.

My reflections found on these pages are by no means unique to only myself. Many women of color in the academy, particularly Black women who have similarly dedicated their lives and livelihood to form a village around our biological children and youth of color, are caught in the proverbial Catch-22. Following our hearts, with our minds, spirits, and hands, we work tirelessly creating opportunity, hope, and nurturing support for the survival and success of others, often invariably to our own detriment. Yet we persevere in "making do," often sacrificing our spirit, health, and best interests for those whom we perceive as not being able to do so for themselves. This "herstory" I dedicate to all those brilliantly talented and committed Black and Brown sisters and educators, like my mother, our "other mother" ancestors, and the editors and contributors in this book, who selflessly dedicated their lives to the betterment of others, most especially young Black and Brown women.

Early Life Lessons

My formidable schooling took place in the segregated city of Detroit, Michigan where I witnessed tremendous disparities between Black and white people, and the poor and the rich, which really made me question my purpose and whether what I wanted to do was something of which I could be proud. I was fortunate to have two parents who were highly educated, loved to travel, and took my siblings and me to many national and international places growing up. It really helped us to appreciate what we had been afforded. Even though we were not considered wealthy, we had what we needed. I learned early on the importance of strong role models and mentors, to help one navigate the unknown terrain that was plagued with landmines and quicksand. My parents are both very racially and socially conscientious, with a great capacity for empathy. In the early

1970s, for example, my mother was concerned about the subservient role of many women in society and supported the women's liberation movements. She was very active in numerous women's groups to promote their status. As late as the early 1970s, women could not obtain loans, credit cards, or bank accounts in their own names, without having their husbands or another male adult approve and co-sign for them. My mother felt it was unacceptable for women to be unfairly and unjustly discriminated against just because they were women and was determined to help remove this financial barrier. One of her strategies to fight for women's rights and gender equality, and against this financial subordination of women was to co-found and lead the first Feminist Federal Credit Union in Detroit, Michigan, with and for like-minded women. It was one of the first Feminist Federal Credit Unions in the USA and continued to be managed exclusively by women.

I reflect on the sacrifices of my mother and how she painstakingly and consistently made choices throughout her life, at a huge cost for her physical and psychological well-being, to sacrifice for her family. I remember when my mother was stressed, she would play, Australian musician Helen Reddy's song, *I Am Woman*. Some of the lyrics include:

> You can bend but never break me, 'cause it only serves to make me more determined to achieve my final goal. And I come back even stronger, not a novice any longer, 'cause you've deepened the conviction in my soul. Oh yes, I am wise, but it's wisdom born of pain. Yes, I've paid the price, but look how much I gained. If I have to, I can do anything. I am strong. I am invincible. I am woman.
>
> *(1972)*

Her experience taught me early on the importance of maintaining a strong emotional, psychological, and social well-being. I also realized these three elements tremendously influenced the way we think, feel, and act. In turn, it defined who we were, how we negotiated stress, and how we related to others. Over time, this can have a critical impact on our mental and physical health.

I knew as a young girl that being a mom was my greatest desire and it was molded by the childhood experiences of my mother and father, who fought so vigilantly to afford experiences for my siblings and me. In fact, I remember one day my eight-year-old son came home from school with a picture he drew in art class. The picture showed me in front of the computer, and I remember going to my room and breaking down into tears. At the time, I was a divorced assistant professor, striving for promotion and tenure, with two young children in elementary school. One of my strategies was to write after my children went to bed or before they awoke and spend quality time with them while we were together. I did make progress, but not as much as I had hoped. This remains an enormous regret in my life and a huge loss I can never get back or make-up to my beloved children. Parents in general and mothers, specifically, pray for our children to know they are loved unconditionally, and we treasure them always and do our best to provide the tools necessary to live a healthy, meaningful, rewarding, and happy life.

When my children were still young and I was an assistant professor in my first semester at the University of Nevada, Las Vegas, I was sitting in my office about to leave for a meeting when a young white woman knocked on my door and asked very politely, "Where is Dr. Gregory?" I said, "I am Dr. Gregory. What can I do for you?" She looked at me in disbelief and said, "No really, where is Dr. Gregory?" I said to her slowly, "I am Dr. Gregory. Is there something I can do to help you?" She stared at me, looked at my name on the door and my clearly displayed news article besides the entrance on the wall with my picture, and then replied, "That's ok. Sorry to bother you." Then she walked down the corridor. I was shocked. Even though I was the only faculty member of color in the department, I was one of four in the School of Education, but all the other faculty were men. This apparent racist interaction was more than what Critical Race Theory would call a "micro-aggression." Being the only female and woman of color in the department at the time, coupled with being only four African American faculty women in the School of Education, there remained this "double-consciousness" that was compounded by my age. I was also the youngest assistant professor in the entire School of Education, so I "stood out" because of my gender, race, age, and fluidity establishing this counter-narrative that attacked my intersectional experiences as less than the dominant Western discourse.

In the past five years, I have had the misfortune to suffer three concussions, two of which were serious enough to land me in the hospital and the last one was so severe, it required me to take a medical leave of absence because I literally could not stand up without falling. I'm not saying this was all attributed to my faculty work, but I am saying as a Black faculty woman, mother of two, daughter of elderly parents, and a single mother for 13 years at the time of these concussions, I cared for and about everyone else, to the detriment of my own well-being. I take full responsibility, but everyone and everything else came first. I realized I failed to sleep adequately, eat healthy, balance my life, exercise to the extent I should, and do the things I found enjoyable more than just on occasion. This failure led to my decline physically, mentally, and spiritually. I also suffered 2 TIAs—a transmit transient ischemic attack that temporary blocks blood flow to the brain. I thought I was suffering a stroke because the symptoms were very similar. For me coupled with my concussions, these were the straws that broke the camel's back. I vowed to pay more attention to self-care. This meant balancing all the commitments in my life, ensuring I'm doing something for myself, even if it's going to bed a little early, treating myself to a massage, or having my dog walk me each night. But most importantly for me, it's about saying no and sticking to it. In my professional life, I often feel as though I don't say no enough, because I don't want to be perceived as not pulling my fair share, regardless of my previous workload. At the same time, however, I realize my life is very fragile and if anything were to happen to me, it would be catastrophic for my family, because I have so many who depend on me for their care, including my 89-year-old mother, 91-year-old father, and 26-year-old daughter who suffers from multiple, complex medical challenges. I do have a wonderfully supportive husband whom I married four years ago, and he reminds me that I can no longer become overly stressed and taxed, lose too much sleep, or engage in anything not directly impactful to the ones we love. How we spend our time and money are directly related to who and what we care about.

After experiencing the COVID-19 pandemic, many of us are rethinking our lives and realigning our priorities, primarily focusing more on the family. Personally, I would fail to become my authentic self as a mother, daughter, wife, friend, mentor, teacher-scholar practitioner, educational leader, mentor, and community activist, if I did not remain reflective on my personal and professional life. I call myself taking back the power from within, each day, to ensure I do all I can to deepen my relationships with other people and with those whom I can truly impact the most. It is through my praxis as a social scientist and feminist researcher that I intentionally focus on my teaching, mentoring, and service because I find them going hand-in-hand with my passion and research contributions, through which I am uniquely able to utilize to significantly improve the lives of others. However, none of these things can come before my family and my loved ones. As we reflect upon epistemology, I hope you have a better understanding of my ways of knowing, feeling, being, and doing, as indicated in the deconstruction of my scholarship and praxis.

Many African American women have worked very hard to navigate this unfamiliar and often intimidating terrain to help encourage underserved undergraduate and graduate students and work within our own institutions to help develop and create a more inclusive and equitable work environment (Gregory, 1999). As we redefine our own success, it's important to envision the paths where we see ourselves in the future. While we are constantly pivoting as life happens, it is still important to have a plan. My mother used to always say, "failing to plan is planning to fail." We need to identify our praxis and how to create connections with other professionals, so we can continuously be responsive to their needs and help them reach their educational and professional pursuits.

Evolving Epistemological Frameworks

As I reflect on Black feminist epistemology and praxis, I recognize multiple methodological frameworks that have clearly described my professional and even to some extent, my personal trajectory. Patricia Hill Collins, *Black Feminist Thought* (1990) is arguably considered the early intellectual work on theorizing the web of social constructs—domination, social positioning, structural inequalities, and racism heard from the voices of Black faculty women as a collective and lived experience. In Collins' 2005 work, she described the politics of Black feminism as "being in one's honest body becomes an essential part of the force of life" (p. 289). These controlling images are still present today, so it remains important for those that follow to deconstruct these stereotypical ideas and notions that continue to plague the progress of Black faculty women in their academic, community work, activism, and general experiences.

Nearly 30 years after Collins' groundbreaking work, many scholars have taken up the torch and pressed on in contributions, such as Hull et al.'s (2015) *But Some of Us are Brave*; hooks' (1981), *Ain't I a Woman*; Crenshaw's (1996), *Critical Race Theory*; and Nash's (2019) *Black Feminism Reimagined.* In their collective works along with many others, these scholars have reintroduced the larger contemporary constructs, in terms of advocacy and activism within a contemporary Black feminist theory paradigm, inclusive of critical race theory, and realignment and expansion of intersectionality. Because academia continues to uphold institutionalized racist and sexist practices, although improvements have been made, it is critical to strengthen the counter-narrative that explains how Black faculty women renegotiate and reimagine academic success and achievement, as intentional and meaningful for themselves as individuals, and not from the capitalistic paradigm of wealth, power, and privilege. While outcomes may be similar, this newer lens through which academic women authenticate their lives, in turn demonstrate great resilience, strength, creativity, grace, empowerment, and liberation.

In the past three decades, I have surveyed and interviewed over a thousand faculty women of color (Gregory, 1994, 1995, 1999, 2001, 2005, 2006, 2016) nationally and internationally and have found that the academic workplace continues to isolate, marginalize, and ridicule faculty women of color in general, especially when it comes to navigating promotion and tenure. Much like the scholars mentioned earlier, a great part of my work has focused on the ways faculty women of color view their work experiences and negotiate their circumstances to meet the needs of their families, work and other obligations, and commitments. My first major research project was constructing a theoretical framework composed of economic, psychosocial, and job satisfaction theory (1994) to help explain the factors that affected the decision patterns of African American faculty women and their career mobility.

In another research study (2006), four years after receiving my doctoral degree, I spent nearly a month on the University of the West Indies (UWI) campuses in Jamaica, Barbados, and Trinidad-Tobago, interviewing senior faculty women who were esteemed colleagues and prolific writers and international researchers. These women embodied the type of scholar-practitioner I wanted to become. In hindsight, if Denzin and colleagues', *Handbook of Critical and Indigenous Methodologies* (2008) had been available at the time, I probably would have examined the raw data of the UWI faculty using a more global theoretical framework. This approach of problematizing the construction of race, gender, and class to spotlight greater attention to social justice and equity for Black women scholars is critical. In some regards, faculty status serves to intensify the dynamics of power and privilege, as these intersecting oppressions collide. At the same time, we know we cannot generalize the experiences of Black faculty women because of the great diversity among us. Yet, it is important we sustain solidarity and a critical mass, to help combat the "isms" and other forms of oppressions, such as sexual orientation and socio-economic positioning among many others (Crenshaw, 1996). This solidarity is also critical because Black faculty women must work hard at lifting one another up in their work around common interests, most specifically as it relates to scholarship, grants, teaching, committee work, and basic collective strategies often denied to them by others, especially due to their gender and race. These common goals can build critical bridges over brittle and often compromised foundations throughout the academic journey.

Lessons Learned

When I secured tenure, my parents told me it was now my obligation to stand up and speak out for those who did not have tenure, could not speak for themselves, or were marginalized, and I continue to take this commitment very seriously. At the same time, I recognized God had blessed me with two beautiful children whom I adored, and I needed to keep my eyes focused on their well-being, and now my elderly parents. As academic women of color, we are usually the primary caretakers of those around us and when it comes to family, it is an honor to care for those who have cared so lovingly for us. However, non-familial responsibilities must often take a back seat, when family needs are greater, and we should not be made to feel guilty about those decisions. God is obviously still working on me in that area, but I recognize my professional decisions have impacted my health on more than one occasion and I must protect my health by any means necessary for the betterment of my family and myself. In retrospect, I wish I had not taken on so much or continued to carry the weight that was not my burden to carry, in the name of collegiality and service to my institution, because the cost was too high. Wouldn't it be wonderful if hindsight was 20/20?

It is important to recognize that it is normal and healthy to reflect and reconsider your actions and time commitments as it relates to work and family obligations. Women in general, especially faculty, often seek roles that allow themselves greater autonomy and flexibility in their work and responsibilities. As I mentioned earlier, both of my parents were professors and many of my relatives were teachers, who significantly shaped my professional interests, as well as my commitment and self-asserted obligation to significantly contribute to practical research activities on strategies to attract, nurture, and support more women of color in the academy.

I wish to highlight some practices that have proved useful and reflective in my academic practice and personal life. Other strategies have come from my mother, father, other professional activities, and inspiring messages in my life. I have them recorded in my journal and pray I can properly cite them to give credit where credit is certainly due.

From my Mother, Tenicia Ann Banks Gregory

- Not everyone deserves to have a front-row seat in your life. Many of them need to be in the bleachers, while others need their view restricted.
- Don't give part-time people, full-time positions in your heart, mind, or spirit. They can often contaminate or infect the good in your life.
- Live your life with an intentional purpose and never give up your power to anyone.
- Use each action you perceive to be a failure as a learning opportunity to improve.
- Always be prepared to take advantage of unexpected opportunities that may cross your path, especially if they can significantly and positively impact the lives of others or empower them to improve their circumstances.

From my Father, Karl Dwight Gregory

- Reach back as you climb, cognizant that sometimes you may need to fall-back and push others up when needed.
- Maintain your physical health, remembering if you are not healthy, you cannot help others, or those depending on you.
- Increase your level of engagement with those who share your values, interests, and concerns to affirm your work and positive sense of self.
- Choose your battles and learn the difference between a battle and a war. Be cognizant of the consequences of the fight and whether it is worth your time, talents, and energies, given the circumstances and your path.
- God has a way of repeating the same challenge under different circumstances until we learn the lesson. Always seek your truth and learn your lessons from these experiences, so you are not doomed to repeat them.

From my Research, Professional, and Life Experience

- If you are alone and in doubt, talk to yourself as you would a person who you love dearly, who is going through what you are enduring. Your thoughts can be poison to your soul or nourishment for your spirit.

- The techno-world creates its own stress and need for immediate satisfaction, without patience or forethought required in life. Do not let it control your actions or your mood. There is a time and place for everything.
- Turn your obstacles into opportunities for thinking and doing things differently and better. The challenge is to anticipate them when possible, and always find a way or make one to achieve your goals and carve a path for others along your journey.
- We all need our space from everyone and everything. So don't feel guilty about taking the time you need to be alone. If need be, make appointments with yourself throughout the day, or go for a walk and sit under a tree. You will be amazed at how stress-free your mind will be and what the new surroundings can do for your creative thinking, problem solving, and peace of mind.
- Be sure to recognize the signs along your journey, so you might know which path may yield greater opportunity and satisfaction. Know your journey is yours alone and not everyone needs to know, understand, or agree with your choices or decisions. This is another example of liberation.

From the Bible

- To whom much is given, much will be required (Luke 12:48).
- I can do all things, through Christ which strengthens me (Philippians 4:13).

From Billie Holiday

- God bless the child that's got his own (1956).

Conclusion

From an interdisciplinary perspective, Bobbi Harro's Cycle of Liberation in *Readings for Diversity and Social Justice: An Anthology on Racism, Anti-semitism, Sexism, Heterosexism, Ableism, and Classism* (2000) is very important as we seek solace and peace with our lives of faculty work, as well as in our overall professional and personal lives, most especially during trying times. Most scholars remember the work of Paulo Freire in *Pedagogy of the Oppressed* first published in 1968 and provided the earliest foundation for research and scholarship on liberation. Harro's work, however, is more contemporary and talks about how to prepare to liberate yourself, the process, the challenging phases, and most importantly, how to reach out, build, coalesce, create change, and maintain to build and maintain your liberatory status (2000). She concludes by identifying the following five elements or "core" from the Cycle of Liberation: (1) the practice of love; (2) finding balance; (3) development of competence; (4) belief that we can succeed; (5) joy of our collective efficacy; (6) the knowledge that we are not alone; (7) commitment to critical transformation and finally; and (8) liberation as passion and compassion (p. 464). None of these are easy, but they should be considered as a part of your ongoing journey.

In summary, if you have ever seen the 1991 John Singleton film, *Boyz n the Hood*, you might recall the character of Doughboy, played by Ice Cube. Doughboy stated, "Either they don't know, don't show, or don't care," referring to what is happening in the Hood. His words are still relevant today in our society and even as some might argue in academia. Black faculty women in the academy have their ups and downs; however, the lows are often long and extreme, and the highs are sometimes momentary. I pray the final reflections below will help you survive and thrive in the academy (Gregory, 1999):

- Reflect on past and current practices to find ways to better align our research and service with our teaching and other work-related responsibilities;
- Seek professional and personal support wherever we can;
- Consider every small achievement a victory to keep motivated;
- Recognize whether we are fighting a battle or a war and proceed accordingly;
- Strategically utilize academic mentors for sage counsel as needed;
- Equip ourselves to be relevant and on the cutting edge in our fields at the national and international levels, through scholarly pursuits;
- Know who we are, what we stand for, and whose we are, so when stress and strife knock at our doors, we have the strength to face adversity, and;
- Chart a new path toward self-liberation, so the passion and joy we entered the academic with, continues to provide the peace and rewards in the future.

It takes great courage, strength, and commitment in the face of adversity, but this is nothing Black women have not overcome in the past, and it will certainly not stop us in the future.

References

Collins, P. H. (1990). *Black feminist thought: Knowledge, consciousness, and the politics of empowerment* (2nd ed.). Hyman Publishers.

Collins, P. H. (2005). *Black sexual politics: African Americans, gender, and the new racism* (1st ed.). Routledge.

Crenshaw, K. (1996). *Critical race theory publisher.* New Press.

Denzin, N., Lincoln, Y., & Linda, T. S. (2008). *Handbook of critical and indigenous methodologies.* Sage Publications.

Freire, P. (1968). *Pedagogy of the oppressed.* Seabury Press.

Gregory, S. (1994). *The economic and psychosocial factors which influence career mobility among African American female professors.* Dissertation: University of Pennsylvania, Philadelphia, PA.

Gregory, S. (1995). *Black women in the academy: The secrets to success and achievement.* University Press of America.

Gregory, S. (1999). *Black women in the academy: Secrets of success and achievement* (1st ed.). University Press of America.

Gregory, S. (2001). Black faculty women in the academy: History, status, and future. *Journal of Negro Education, 70*(3), 124–138.

Gregory, S. (2005). The role of black women educators, post 1960. In D. C. Hines (Ed.), *Black women in America: A historical encyclopedia*, Vol. 1–2. Oxford University Press.

Gregory, S. (2006). The cultural constructs of race, gender and class: A study of how Afro-Caribbean women academics negotiate their careers. *International Journal of Qualitative Studies in Education, 19*(3), 347–366.

Gregory, S. (2016). Foreword. In B. Marina & S. Ross (Eds.), *Beyond retention: Cultivating spaces of equity, justice, and fairness for women of Color in U.S. higher education* (p. xv–xvii). Information Age Publishing.

Harro, B. (2000). The cycle of liberation. In M. Adams, W. J. Blumenfeld, R. Castaneda, H. W. Hackman, M. L. Peters, & X. Zuniga (Eds.), *Readings for diversity and social justice: An anthology on racism, anti-semitism, sexism, heterosexism, ableism, and classism* (pp. 463–469). Routledge.

Holiday, B. (1956). *God bless the child.* Clef Records.

Hooks, B. (1981). *Ain't I a woman: Black women and feminism.* Pluto Classics.

Hull, G., Bell-Scott, P., and B. Smith. (2015). *But some of us are brave: Black women's studies* (2nd ed.). Feminist Press at CUNY.

Nash, J. (2019) *Black feminism reimagined after intersectionality.* Duke University Press.

Reddy, H. (1972). *I am woman. I am woman hear me roar album.* Capitol Records.

Singleton, J. (1991). *Boyz n the Hood.* Columbia Pictures.

4

MAIDS OF ACADEME IN HISTORICALLY WHITE INSTITUTIONS

Revisited Against the Backdrop of "Black Lives Matter"

Debra A. Harley

Throughout this chapter, I use the identification of Black to be inclusive of women of African descent. I refer to women of color to call attention to similarities shared with other people of color in historically white institutions (HWI). However, as many people of color share stigma and discrimination of the inseparable attitudinal and institutional effects of racism, I assert the experiences of Black women are not only different, but they are culturally and historically situated. "Historically, Black women have been one of the most isolated, underused, and consequently demoralized segments of the academic community" (Carter et al., 1988, p. 98). Yielding to these acknowledgments, Black women have always been agents of knowledge, both informally and formally. We have educated family members and friends sitting around the kitchen table; we did the same for slave owners, mistresses, and white women and their husbands around their kitchen tables. Education was served as bowls of wisdom and slices of knowledge.

The presence of Black women in higher education spans more than a century. Our movement into HWIs as dispensers of knowledge has not only constructed our work as prescribed in certain domains but has also clarified our labor as Maids of Academe (Harley, 2008). Black women in the academy continue to disproportionately work in service, mentoring, and respite care for students, faculty, and staff. In many ways, our responsibilities continue to grow, but our roles remain disproportionate within the university system. Bonomi (2020) reflected this dichotomous portrayal of Black women in the academy through five ways higher education can be hostile toward women of color, especially those in leadership roles.

First, women of color are *not reflected in leaders* (Bonomi). That is, 30% of college and university presidents are women, only 5% are people of color. In

DOI: 10.4324/9781003184867-5

top administrative roles, Black and Latinx women make up 52% of chief diversity and inclusive officers, while white men overwhelmingly occupy roles as chief financial officers. Black women and other women of color continue to be relegated to diversity-related positions. Second, women of color are put on a "*glass cliff*" (Bonomi). In other words, they are elevated to leadership roles when the institution is in crisis and when there is an increased risk of failure (e.g., Black Lives Matter [BLM] movement, racial unrest, and budget crisis). Third, Black women are nearly invisible within *full professorships* (NCES, 2019). If we are not promoted to such rank, our numbers are small in the pool of leadership candidates. In the academy, Black women faculty often pay the minority tax (i.e., extra responsibilities placed on minoritized faculty in efforts to achieve diversity; Balzora, 2021). Unfortunately, this type of work often is not acknowledged nor rewarded.

Fourth, women of color are *surrounded by white imagery* (Bonomi). The walls are filled with portraits and the yard with statues of white men with history and affiliation to the institution (presidents, deans, and alumni). These images send a loud and resounding message of how the institution views itself and who belongs there. Finally, women of color are subjected to public shaming as colleagues question their credentials or challenge their authority (Bonomi).

Each of these outcomes, notwithstanding whatever gains have been achieved, represents persistent inequalities at the intersections of race, gender, and class and remains at the forefront of current educational discourse and policies (Jones, 2006). Moreover, these persisting inequalities point to the failure of the equal opportunity framework that institutions list in all job announcements and activities, wherein they perpetuate the principle of the same rules for all people, the belief that equal outcomes could be secured. However, "this approach failed to recognize and address the structural basis of social inequities, and therefore [failed] to appreciate the need for changes to institutional cultures and structures" (Jones, 2006, p. 146). Clearly, HWIs must recognize the difference between their own protocol and performance to unearth their overt and covert resistance to removing Bonomi's (2020) hostilities to/against women of color in the academy.

The purpose of this chapter is to revisit the 2008 article, *Maids of Academe: African American Women Faculty at predominately White Institutions*, within the context of the BLM movement to understand how experiences in the academy shape the interpretation of Black women faculty regarding inequities and academic hostility. Throughout the chapter, I center (a) the intersections of Black women's identities; (b) how Black women faculty are seen as experts and work horses (maids) on issues related to Blackness and womanness yet simultaneously invisible in decision-making roles on policy and procedure; and (c) the role of advocacy and resiliency advice for persistence in the academy. By revisiting my 2008 article, I use my own story as a site of analysis and reflection on Maids of Academe and BLM. I analyze what, if any, change has occurred for Black women faculty in HWIs over time, and I draw attention to the BLM movement as a defining framework for promoting resiliency within and outside the halls of academia.

My Trajectory into and Within the Professoriate

After completing my doctorate at a HWI, I started my professional academic career 29 years ago at a teaching HWI; after one year, I moved to and have remained in a research extensive institution. I was the first and only Black faculty in my department at both institutions. That scenario played out for most of my career. Sadly, today HWIs are still achieving firsts with respect to the hiring of Black women faculty and administrators. Being the first (and only) comes with added expectations and being in that position is tiring; it gets old. At the time of my entrance into this role, affirmative action was at its height and Black PhDs were perceived as a commodity for hire, but not necessarily for inclusion and equity at HWIs. The Dean and the Provost at the research institution were committed to recruiting diverse faculty. Black women at HWIs often enter(ed) chilly and unwelcoming institutional cultures and environments wherein our presence was virtually invisible (Alfred, 2001; Moses, 1997). My first several years were rocky and fraught with landmines. I spent much of my time putting out fires and dealing with character assassination by my program chair (e.g., receiving negative reviews and them telling community agencies I was hired without recommendation). At the time, a good friend of mine (we completed our undergraduate and master's degrees together) was an assistant professor who had been hired three years before me in the same program but transferred to another department. He gave me some good advice: identify the enemies of the obstructer, disrupt the status quo, and let them deal with it. Not only was this valuable advice at the time, but I also still rely on it.

The program had large classes for a graduate program, and I did not receive any course content beyond a syllabus. Basically, all the courses I taught had to be redesigned or developed. It was clear from the syllabi it had been years since the courses were updated. As a new faculty member, all my courses were new preps that required substantial work and there was no teaching support (e.g., teaching assistant or course reduction). Regardless of our knowledge and expertise as Black women, we are too often relegated primarily to the realm of multiculturalism, both within and outside of our disciplines. I recall a department chair and colleagues would always direct questions to me about diversity – calling on my expertise as if such knowledge was not their responsibility. I guess they relied on my cultural capital and not my training since I received my doctoral training at an HWI. In other words, knowingly or unknowingly, my colleagues assumed I possessed knowledge in this area because of group membership, because clearly my doctoral training did not include content on multiculturalism and diversity.

Our visibility is magnified when our expertise on "Black issues" and situations having to do with racial difficulties arise. This expertise, however, is solution-focused, not grounded in an authority to make decisions. As the Maids of Academe, we are necessary in what McKay (1997) referred to as "a troubled peace" (p. 11). The landscape between 1992 and 2021 has not changed substantially. We continue to be defined in terms of numerical relevance or just enough of us for the institution to "seem" diverse; HWIs dare not surpass that magical formula or strive for more than the minimal. I continue to be surprised about the relative ease at which our numerical relevance is the goal. Yes, the current landscape is as much a quagmire as always because "the societal momentum generated by the Civil Rights Movement, the Women's Movement, and various alliances for social justice have yielded limited and unsustainable efforts" (Harley, 2008, p. 22). The current political and social climate is toxic; racism and sexism are ongoing practices embedded within the fabric of society. For example, nearly half of Black Americans experience racial discrimination when trying to rent an apartment or buy a home (Robert Wood Johnson Foundation, 2018), most Black adults have negative views about the country's racial progress, about half of Black people say being Black has hurt their ability to get ahead, and most Americans say Trump has made race relations worse (Pew Research Center, 2019).

Intersection of BLM and Black Women Faculty

Founded by Alicia Garza, Patrisse Cullors, and Opal Tometi, BLM is an international social justice movement in the United States, United Kingdom, and Canada – a call to arms, a resiliency movement, and a quest of self-preservation. The mission of BLM is "to eradicate white supremacy and build local power to intervene in violence inflicted on Black communities by the state and vigilantes" (https://blacklivesmatter.com). It signals condemnation of unjust killings of Black people by police and demands that society value the lives and humanity of Black people as much as those of white people (Encyclopedia Britannica, 2021). BLM has been around since 2013 but has seen a substantial shift in public opinion recently, with majority white participation. Many people have responded to and participated in the new wave for justice and denouncing devaluation of Black lives. On HWI campuses, BLM has also become a movement within a movement to decolonize the classroom, the grounds, administration, and structure of doing business.

Black faculty are dealing with dual pandemics (COVID-19 and racialized trauma) and Black women faculty have the added concern of gender, making our taxation a trivector (Gray & Brooks, 2021; McCoy & Lee, 2021; Walton et al., 2021). Black women faculty are called upon once again by university administrators not as activists, rather as servants (maids) to respond in this glass cliff situation (to clean up the mess). For Black women faculty, BLM provides another venue for voice and visibility. BLM is relevant in academia because of anti-Black sentiment for Black students and faculty, microaggressions, and denial of our racialized and gendered experiences in the academy (Bell et al., 2021). Against the backdrop of BLM, our voice and taxation in HWIs confront(ed) the consciousness of institutional leadership in a different way.

The role of gender in the BLM movement has raised questions about how Black women are valued. Fatty (2021) asserted,

> the overt and repeated lack of recognition toward Black female victims - and for its three queer, black, female founders – begs the question of whether this role of gender in the BLM movement is truly about all black lives, or rather just black male lives.
>
> *(p. 1)*

Fatty proports, the lack of support Black women face in general needs to change and the discrimination that already victimizes them only further perpetuates slave-related stereotypes that dehumanize us. These stereotypes impose the weight of being "superwomen," stronger than natural, and maids who are not vulnerable to life circumstances. Shammet (2020) explained the devaluation of Black women occurs from multiple perspectives. First, Black women are frequently overlooked by society, and we have almost gotten used to it. Second, our intersections of identities make it extremely difficult to determine where we fit. That is, Black men do not respect us because we are women, white women do not respect us because we are Black, and those who identify as heterosexual do not respect us if we are queer. Black women's lives matter because we have already been "actively" ignored by society (Fatty, 2021). "When [B]lack women are not acknowledged in their work or lived experiences, or even in their death, it makes them seem easily disposable;" easily victimized; and it becomes easier to ignore our needs (Shavonda Sisson, cited in Byers, 2020, para. 11). Overall, gender matters in BLM because "change cannot happen without all voices being heard" (Camille Mays, cited in Byers, 2020, para. 29), and ignoring Black women puts us at risk for greater harm.

Lessons Learned

My tenure in the professoriate resembles that of many other Black women faculty. My competence has been called into question, my scholarship neither read nor understood by those evaluating me, and my labor is taken for granted. For Black women, the Maids of Academe construction expects deference to our white and men counterparts and students, with the expectation that we will go about our maidly duties silently and compliantly. I want to reflect and discuss lessons I have learned; I hope they are received as pitfalls to avoid and roads to travel. My desire is not to sound hostile, but hopeful. My focus remains on how

I have changed and how I have responded from the intersection of my Blackness and womanness in this space for nearly three decades, and more recently against the backdrop of the BLM movement. My eyes are older, but my vision is still clear – I see little change in the chores of Black women [maids] in the academy. The Maids of Academe are still metaphorically performing childcare duties (teaching), fieldwork (research and scholarship), housework, cooking, and other duties (service) in ways and to the extent that our Blackness and womanness remain tied to representation (and exploitation) instead of inclusion.

Lesson One: Skinship Does Not Guarantee Kinship

I recall one event when Black faculty organized in response to comments by the university President about the low number of Black students accepted to the university saying, Black students have difficulty having the SAT score and GRE to get into the university. Of course, this information was inaccurate. As a group, Black faculty of concern (FOC), met with the President to voice our concerns about this as well as the status of Black faculty at the university. There were voices in solidarity as well as those of resistance. I learned a valuable lesson - just because we share skinship does not mean we share kinship. One of the cruel realities for Black faculty is to have Black faculty who are of senior rank and in a position of authority fail to identify with the struggle of Black faculty (and students). Nevertheless, a series of meetings led to a committee of the FOC developing a report containing strategies and recommendations to improve the climate, culture, and status of Black faculty. As one of the authors of that report, at the end of the workday on a Thursday afternoon I hand delivered the report to the office of the President (only after having delivered one earlier to the local newspaper). This did not sit well with the administration or board of directors. This was a calculated call by the committee and there was "hell" to pay. Eventually, a diversity officer position was created based on one of the recommendations.

I and other committee members were tenured at the time, but I wonder about the outcome of my academic career at the university if I had not been. I was promoted to the rank of professor and later became department chair. Subsequently, I hit the glass ceiling at the halfway mark of my time at the university. I continue to be highly taxed with little opportunity for upward mobility in administration. Then and now, I question whether my actions with the FOC played a role? Did my desirability decrease? Did I have desirability with this or successive administrations? Yet, my taxation remained high. What lesson(s) did I learn? I revert to the lessons I was taught as a Black child growing up in the rural south – "I am standing on the shoulders of many," "you cannot let the world define you," and "let what you do be something you can live with yourself." I am more interested in my own internal validation and letting my lessons be a tool for mentoring other faculty and students.

My presence in the academy is necessary because other women of color faculty and students need a reflection of themselves. My taxation is not only based on color, but also on gender and my status as "safe" for students and colleagues who need to express themselves because of gender identity, sexual orientation, disability, mental health status, and other intersections. I consider my persistence in the academy an opportunity to give back. As a product of a segregated elementary school education and a historically Black college and university (HBCU), the relevance of Black women educators reinforced this commitment. So, would I stand up and speak out yet again? The answer is a resounding yes. I learned to be okay with myself and will continue to teach that lesson to others. I see myself as an agent for social change and my role as a scholar as intersectional. However, as a Black woman in the academy, I do recognize my vulnerability and expendability, if not by tenure status and rank, certainly by race and gender.

Lesson Two: These Institutions Ain't Loyal

I learned from my taxation that I spent too much time doing my job. I fulfilled my responsibilities, but it did not allow time and energy to take advantage of and pursue opportunities for advancement elsewhere. I recall talking with other Black women faculty in the academy about our taxation. They too spoke about this realization; they found themselves not having time to review and apply for positions elsewhere. I do regret the taxation resulted in a personal sacrifice for me. Now, I teach and preach to others about the dangers of the persistent and repetitious inability to say "no" to taxation. As women of color, we often pay a high price for the loyalty penalty. The loyalty penalty is dangerous because as leadership changes, the next leaders do not know of your work or may not respect your contributions. In essence, it does not matter how loyal you are to the university, the university has no capacity to be loyal to you. I caution you that balance should be in the forefront and to pick your battles, not because of prestige but for impact, community, and relevance.

While revisiting my CV, I count my scholarship, teaching, service, and administration for my nearly three decades in higher education that have resulted in 22 courses developed and taught, 92 refereed journal publications, 85 book chapters, 5 books, and a series of book reviews, editorials, conference proceedings and presentations, and other non-refereed publications, and grant funding. While these were necessary for promotion and tenure, I am still unsure whether my work is known within my own institution. For example, of the numerous Deans I have seen come and go within the College, I recall only one who knew of faculty members' scholarship. She would mention your work to you, while other deans relied on you reporting your work to the department chair who would send an announcement about your work. Yet, administrators from other institutions would solicit my input or business and industry would request I conduct diversity trainings because they read my work.

Many colleagues do not read literature beyond their own discipline. I reflect on an invited article I wrote in 2001 about my experiences as a woman of color in the discipline. My department chair had no idea the article existed and a colleague in my program shared it with him. The article was not overly favorable of my experience and the chair wanted to challenge, as opposed to understand, my perceptions. When I was approached, I thought, "wow this is some shit." There was no thought given to my marginalization. So, neither one of them knew about my "Maids of Academe" article. Then reality set in. Of course, they did not know – it was published in the *Journal of African American Studies*. I am not sure they even knew the journal existed.

As I am on the downside of the academic mountain, I find my name still floating around as the "go to person." That is, go to Harley about tenure and promotion, for recommendations or contacts and connections, to be on or recommendations for certain committees, and to review and make recommendations on certain documents. I have a white colleague who is a friend (considered family) who always asks me to be on certain university-level committees. Even when I explained that I am overextended and frankly, tired of representing (minority tax), she continues to ask. I had to stop myself from saying, "of all people, why do you see me as being primarily responsible for representing the intersection of Blackness and womanness (tokenism)." I am not sure I responded that way, but this was indeed a teachable moment. This person considers herself aware and informed of minority taxation. What is the lesson here? For those close to us, our lives may intersect in some ways, and we are still worlds apart experientially. She thought by asking me to volunteer for these committees, she was helping Black faculty.

Lesson Three: Dear Black Men, Gender Matters

After spending much of my academic career dealing with racial, gender, and intersectional exclusion, I find on occasion I must deal with marginalization from Black men colleagues. That is, Black men colleagues accept the benefits of male privilege and double standards toward Black women faculty, and willful engagement in dismissiveness toward Black women faculty. I have had Black men colleagues explain (or more accurately, justify) their responses toward and positions taken about Black women faculty. Ironically, these positions were strongly aligned with exclusion, oppression, and marginalization of Black women faculty as espoused by the status quo. Unfortunately, this is an age-old problem within Black communities – the pitting of endangered Black men versus subjugated Black women.

As Black women, we find ourselves marginalized by Black men and white people, and we must reconcile practices of white superiority and Black hegemonic masculinity in the academy. A similar sentiment is evident toward Black women of BLM in which Black men tried to erase Black women who organized the movement. Amid controversy and internal dissention in the organization, these Black women stepped down from leadership roles. What is especially troubling about the optics as the voice and visibility of these Black women became more prominent, is how Black men became complicit in ignoring these Black women leaders' intersections of womanness, transness, queerness, and other identities. Anti-Black womanness (and misogynoir) manifests through actions that convey disdain, disgust, and disregard for these women's identity intersections. Ironically, the quote of a Black man, Rev. Al Sharpton, "with visibility comes vulnerability" (Eligon, 2021, p. 1), adds credence to this structured attack on these women.

Strategies to Apply Black Feminist Epistemology

The increasing presence of Black women in the academy, especially at HWIs, invites us to employ Black feminist epistemologies through which we can define our reality and tell our story. In doing so, we can develop productive strategies as scholars and educators and survive and grow as Black women. Black women in academe have shared experiences and similar strategies. Thus, I offer nine strategies that have helped me.

1. Learn the *unwritten and unspoken rules* of the game (e.g., the academy). Typically, we are informed of the requirement for promotion and tenure and expectations of citizenship in the academy. However, we are not given access to inner circle conversations wherein white colleagues, and to a certain extent, Black men colleagues ascertain necessary information. Black women are outsiders-within (Collins, 1986). That is, by nature of being at HWIs, we are allowed access (within), but outside of the unequal power structure (Baxley, 2012).
2. Establish *collaborations and cohorts*, realizing these may be with faculty at other universities and individuals in the community. It is important to realize those who can lend support may be community leaders. In addition, not all your support will come from people who look like you. You should recognize opportunity when it is presented and take it.
3. Seek out *mentoring*. As you seek out Black faculty and administrators for mentoring, realize their taxation. Black women faculty often find themselves as mentors for students, faculty, and staff regardless of race, gender, sexuality, class, and other social positionalities. We nurture, teach, and support those in search of help and direction, even sometimes to our own detriment. There may be times when they are unable to give you as much attention or support, but take what you can get, even in small doses. Remember that mentoring is a two-way engagement. You must maintain contact with your mentor and not always expect your mentor to do all the heavy lifting.
4. Go into your roles and responsibilities with your *eyes open*. Do not underestimate your taxation, real or perceived. Much of your taxation will be

through service and many activities will not be documented and credited as such. Therefore, be sure to negotiate your service to carry comparable weight with what you do. Often tasks are added throughout the year in service. Be sure to update and revise your distribution of effort to reflect all you do.

5 Look for ways to *capitalize on the intersection* of research, teaching, service, and/or administration. Be sure to let these areas support each other. Do not hesitate to dip and double dip whenever possible.

6 Black women's presence at HWIs is not new, but we are still members of the "others." *Own who you are and uplift the voices* of Black women faculty. This importance is underscored by Baxley (2012) who stressed, "navigating the role as a (legitimate) scholar and someone who is Othered is an unyielding balance that often goes unnoticed and unacknowledged in the dominant academic culture" (p. 47).

7 Take an *attitudinal temperature of the climate* in your program, department, and college. As with barometric temperature, the attitudinal temperature will fluctuate over time. You should monitor these changes, align them with the unwritten and unspoken rules, and adjust as necessary.

8 *Do not isolate* yourself in your discipline. Go, stumble across, and explore the halls and floors beyond your department to connect with others who are potential mentors. These individuals may be from different disciplines, have different pedagogical approaches, and hold different racial and gender identities. Your exploration is to find people who are catalysts for growth and professional development.

9 *Engage in continuous self-reflection and evaluation.* You are the keeper of your progress; therefore, review your progress independent of annual faculty reviews conducted by the college. Arm yourself with self-knowledge and adjust related to your performance and taxation. When you have your annual review, the best offense is to go in knowing where you stand. Thus, you are not caught off guard because of a lack of feedback or inaccurate feedback. Similarly, be wary of informal compliments because they are not documentation of what you have accomplished. Too often informal compliments derail you because you may think all is well and then you get blindsided. Self-reflection and evaluation may help you determine whether you should stay or leave. Remember, you are on a journey in the academy – where you start is not necessarily where you stay. Self-reflection can yield substantive self-advocacy.

Connecting Black Feminist Epistemology to BLM

BLM is about self-advocacy and resilience against acts of violence against Black people. In this sense, these strategies lend voice to self-preservation against academic vigilantes who seek to reinforce the marginalization of Black women in the academy and perpetuate the role of Black women as Maids of Academe.

These strategies are neither new nor unique, however, against the backdrop of BLM they are about universal connection and recognition that the identity of Black women in the academy is not individual. Contextually, these strategies bring the relevance of BLM within the academy "wherein anti-blackness is likely to be manifested as disdain, disregard, and disgust for Black faculty" (Bell et al., 2021, p. 29). Understanding how we as Black women faculty must close the circle in relation to disciplinary expertise, taxation, and intersectionality highlights that our lives matter in the academy and for the academy. Racism and sexism in the larger society reverberate in our lives in the academy, especially in HWIs. White supremacy, pervasive racism, and sexism continue to shape HWI institutions of higher education; they influence the ways overt and covert acts of harm and violence continue to adversely create inclusive spaces for Black women faculty. Just as students are using the tools, we teach in college classrooms to engage critically with the world around them (i.e., BLM; Wilson, 2015), so too must Black women faculty in our own display of historically informed and intersectional politics, demonstrate our ways of knowing, being, and narratives also matter.

Conclusion

Black women faculty in the academy must be aware of the politics of higher education and remain vigilant in our quest for professional growth. A career in the professoriate at HWIs for Black women involves exclusion and marginalization as central to our experiences. Yet, we persist and demonstrate resilience through our epistemologies, how we come to know, own, and share our experiences. The Maids of Academe continuously develop coping strategies to survive and thrive in academe in general, and HWIs in particular. Over decades, the plight of Maids of Academe has remained largely unchanged. That is, our roles and expectations are overwhelmingly assigned to specific race- and gender-based categories, and our numbers are still low compared to our white counterparts (to the point that our realization comes off as a perverse "luxury" (Ayana Jordan, as cited in Flaherty, 2020, para. 7). Against the backdrop of BLM, Black women as Maids of Academe continue to protest the unwritten protocol of marginalization.

References

Alfred, M. V. (2001). Success in the ivory tower. In R. O. Mabokela & A. L. Green (Eds.), *Sister of the academy: Emergent Black women scholars in higher education* (pp. 57–79). Stylus.

Balzora, S. (2021). When the minority tax is doubled: Being Black and female in academic medicine. *Nature Reviews Gastroenterology Hepatology, 18*(1). https://doi.org/.10.1038/s41575-020-00369-2

Baxley, T. P. (2012). Navigating as an African American female scholar: Catalysts and barriers in predominantly white academia. *International Journal of Critical Pedagogy, 4*(1), 47–64.

Bell, M. P., Berry, D., Leopold, J., & Nkomo, S. (2021). Making Black lives matter in academia: A Black feminist call for collective action against anti-blackness in the academy. *Gender, Work, & Organization, 28*(S1), 39–57. https://doi.org/10/1111/gwao.12555

Black Lives Matter. (n.d.). https://blacklivesmatter.com

Bonomi, A. (2020). Leading through resistance: Heels firm in the (ice!) cliff. In C. Rennison & A. Bonomi (Eds.), *Women leading change: Breaking the glass ceiling, cliff, and slipper* (pp. 149–162). Cognella.

Byers, P. S. (2020). Hidden in plain sight? Black female activists feel left out of BLM movement. *Milwaukee Neighborhood News Service.* https://milwaukeenns.org/2020/08/05/hidden-in-plain-sight-black-female--activists-feel-left-out-of-blm-movement/

Carter, D., Pearson, C., & Shavlik, D. (1988). Double jeopardy: Women of color in higher education. *Educational Record, 68,* 98–103.

Collins, P. H. 1986). Learning from the outsider within: The sociological significance of Black feminist though. *Social Problems, 33*(6), 14–32.

Eligon, J. (2021). Black Lives Matter has grown more powerful, and more divided. *New York Times.* https://www.nytimes.com/2021/06/04/us/black-lives-matter.html

Encyclopedia Britannica. (2021). *Black lives matter.* https://www.britannica.com/topic/social-movement

Fatty, A. (2021). Black lives matter or Black men matter: Gender and the movement for freedom. *Underground Railroad History Project.* https://undergroundrailroadhistory.org/black-lives-matter-or-black-men-matter-gender-and-the-movement-for-freedom/

Flaherty, C. (2020). The souls of Black professors. *Inside Higher Ed.* https://www.insidehighered.com/news/2020/10/21/scholars-talk-about-being-black-campus-2020

Gray, K. J., & Brooks, L. B. (20121). Give yourself permission to rest. *Genealogy, 5,* 17. https://doi.org/10.3390/genealogy5010017

Harley, D. A. (2008). Maids of Academe: African American women faculty at predominately white institutions. *Journal of African American Studies, 12*(1), 19–36. https://www.jstor.org/stable/41819156

Jones, C. (2006). Falling between the cracks: What diversity means for black women in higher education. *Policy Futures in Education, 4*(2), 145–159. https://doi.org/10.2304/pfie.2006.4.4.145

McCoy, H., & Lee, M. Y. (2021). Minority academics face dual pandemics of covid-19 and racism. *The World University Rankings.* https://www.timeshighereducation.com/opinion/minority-academics-face-dual- pandemics-covid-19-and-racism

McKay, N. Y. (1997). A troubled peace: Black women in the halls of the white academy. In L. Benjamin (Ed.), *Black women in the academy: Promises and perils* (pp. 11–22). University of Florida Press.

Moses, Y. (1997). Black women in academe. In L. Benjamin (Ed.), *Black women in the academy: Promises and perils* (pp. 22–37). University of Florida Press.

National Center for Education Statistics. (2019). *Full-time faculty in degree-granting postsecondary institutions, by race/ethnicity, sex, and academic rank: Fall 2015, fall 2017, and fall 2018.* Table 315.20. https://nces.ed.gov/programs/digest/d19/tables/dt19_315.20.asp

Pew Research Center. (2019). *Race in America 2019.* https://www.pwereserch.org/social-trends/2019/04/rce-in-america-2019/

Robert Wood Johnson Foundation. (2018). *Discrimination in America: Final summary.* https://www.rwjf.org/en/library/research/2017/10/discrimination-in-america-experiences-and-views.html

Shammet, T. (2020). The Black Lives Matter movement does not exist without black women. *The Commonwealth Times.* https://commonwealthtimes.org/2020/06/19/the-black-lives-matter-movement-does-not-exist-without-black-women/

Walton, Q., Campbell, R. D., & Blakey, J. M. (2021), Black women and COVID-19: The need for targeted mental health research and practice. *Qualitative Social Work, 20*(1–2), 247–255. https://doi.org/10.1177/1473325020973349

Wilson, J. (2020). How Black Lives Matter saved higher education. *Aljazeera America.* http://america.aljazeera.com/opinions/2015/12/how-black-lives-matter-saved-higher- education.html

5

THE BLACK WOMAN IS GOD

Cultivating the Power of a Disruptive Presence

Emerald Templeton

In Karen Seneferu and Melorra Green's 2016 art exhibit titled "The Black Woman is God," their central purpose was to disrupt the notion of a white, male deity by juxtaposing Black womanness to the highest spiritual form. Showcasing Black women artists, the enterprising factor in this work was that their contributions were given rightful recognition and attribution. Despite the dehumanization of and disregard for Black women in life and art, we were praised for the incalculable riches we bring. Similarly, this chapter seeks to agitate the idyllic height of white patriarchy in academe by elevating Black women and our contributions to the academy.

The misogynoir, or deep disdain for Black women, that permeates America's racist foundations is mirrored in higher education (Bailey, 2018). Stereotypes set the logic by and of which we are perceived and conceived. Monikers such as welfare queen and angry Black woman have been overused and refashioned into academese that deems us incompetent and unqualified beneficiaries of higher education (Evans, 2008; Gutiérrez y Muhs et al., 2012). Despite being the most educated group in America (National Center for Education Statistics, n.d.), Black women are the least valued, contending with gendered racism that has a unique bend and susceptibility to criticism reserved only for us (Evans, 2008; Harris-Perry, 2011). We bear the burden of care for others and frequently labor in unrecognized ways. Yet, we are not equally represented in executive leadership and faculty roles, nor are our contributions fully realized (Evans, 2008; Evans-Winters & Love, 2015; Gutiérrez y Muhs et al., 2012). However, the actuality of our presence disrupts what dominant society believes about us. Our very existence is radical and redefines the boundaries that confine academe.

DOI: 10.4324/9781003184867-6

Evans (2008) described the trials and triumphs Black women experienced while navigating the academy. She asserted, "[B]lack women academics have significantly contributed to the annals of human thought. This contribution must be taken seriously if higher education is to realize goals of academic excellence and to interact responsibly with other social institutions" (p. 2). To understand the rich contributions of Black women more fully to academe, one must be willing to explore our experiences, as well as our ways of knowing, doing, and being. Operating within our own contexts, Black women theorize, come to know, and find meaning in ways that reflect our lived experiences and often defy the stringent boundaries of traditional academic and formalized research practices (Dillard, 2000; Morton, 2020). Modeled in Black feminist epistemologies and praxis, these ways of knowing and doing present an alternative framework for changing the culture and transforming higher education.

Black Women in the Academy

Black women have a unique lens through which we view and then navigate the academy. Raced, gendered, and classed (Collins, 2000; Dillard, 2000; Evans, 2008; Evans-Winters & Love, 2015), we have negotiated a triple-threat of oppressive systems while moving through higher education, and even into the professoriate. Perlow et al. (2018) described the academy as perpetuating a "prescription to dominant Eurocentric/androcentric ideological, epistemological, methodological, and pedagogical traditions that are meant to maintain the hegemonic order" (p. 7). Black women have often been positioned at the bottom of that order in the academy, having our stories unheard, not believed, and the meanings changed (Collins, 2000). Students and faculty alike are exhausted by the heaviness of whiteness and patriarchy and have had to seek out community with other Black women who understand, honor, and respect our cultural epistemologies and praxis (Allen & Joseph, 2018; Dillard, 2000; Morton, 2020).

American institutions of higher education have been sites of exclusion and harm for Black women, reinforcing notions of a dominant white ideology that suggests who is deserving of access to knowledge and the production thereof (Collins, 2000; Evans-Winters & Love, 2015). However, Black women persist(ed) and have created our own spaces in the academy. From establishing our own educational institutions, Greek organizations, and support systems; to embarking upon many firsts in accessing and excelling in historically white institutions, Black women have exceeded the constraints of our presumed social location. We have a wealth of insight, knowledge, and experience from which we have contributed to academe, scholarship, and society (Evans, 2008; Evans-Winters & Love, 2015). Given this "legitimate site of knowledge" (Edwards et al., 2018, p. 86), we offer Black feminist epistemologies and praxis as lampposts to our paths in and through the academy.

Black Feminist Epistemologies and Praxis

Understanding of Black women's experiences must be situated within an understanding of gendered racism (Dillard, 2000; Evans-Winters & Love, 2015; Perlow et al., 2018). Because "Intersectionality is inextricably linked to an analysis of power" (Cho et al., 2013, p. 797), recognizing the political and structural inequalities with which Black women must contend is necessary. We have been systematically pushed to the margins and then out of institutions of higher education in violent ways. Concomitantly, we have been measured against a white, male standard. Nevertheless, Black women have fostered new ways of knowing, doing, and being borne out of our own "theorizing" and sensemaking around marginalization and liberation (Dillard, 2000). In this way, we can center and elevate those voices often silenced, operate within an understanding of our own contexts, and relish in our humanity.

Black women scholars have defined our process of knowing and doing such as *radical love* (bell hooks), *Black liberatory pedagogies* (bell hooks, Patricia Hill Collins, Audre Lorde), and *intersectionality* (Kimberlé Crenshaw). Common in these concepts is an extension of our ontologies, epistemologies, and praxis beyond the limitations and singular definition of the Ivory Tower, to our lived experiences in their full social, cultural, spiritual, and emotional representations (Morton, 2020). Centering the experiences and understandings of Black women, these concepts are rooted in the Black feminisms: Black Feminist Thought and Endarkened Feminist Epistemology.

Black Feminist Thought

Collins (2000) described Black Feminist Thought as "an activist response" to the oppression of Black women. An alternative view of ways of knowing, "Black Feminist Thought describes how knowledge is produced and validated by Black women" (Morton, 2020, p. 775). The main goals of Black Feminist Thought entail centering and legitimizing our ways of knowing, Black women as agents of their own knowledge and telling truths about "everyday, taken-for-granted knowledge" from Black women (Collins, 2000, p. 32). From this epistemological standpoint, Collins (2000) posited four assumptions:

1. Lived experiences serve as a criterion for meaning in which one invokes examples from their own narratives to impart wisdom.
2. Knowledge is developed via a dialogical process.
3. An ethic of caring that emphasizes individual expressiveness, the use of emotions in dialogues, and a capacity for empathy is important.
4. One must maintain an ethic of personal accountability to their knowing.

The intent of Black Feminist Thought is not to assume sameness among all Black-identified women, or to draw comparisons to other identity theories or forms of feminisms, but to provide an alternative framework for *what* is considered knowledge and *who* are considered knowledge producers. Collins (2000) stated,

> First, Black feminist thought fosters a fundamental paradigmatic shift in how we think about unjust power relations. By embracing a paradigm of intersecting oppressions of race, class, gender, sexuality, and nation, as well as Black women's individual and collective agency within them, Black feminist thought reconceptualizes the social relations of domination and resistance. Second, Black feminist thought addresses ongoing epistemological debates concerning the power dynamics that underlie what counts as knowledge.
>
> *(p. 273)*

This framework challenges the processes and practices by which knowledge is assumed and produced.

Endarkened Feminist Epistemology

Drawing heavily from Patricia Hill Collins' *Black Feminist Thought* and other feminist and spirituality theories, Dillard (2000) described Endarkened Feminist Epistemology as a non-hierarchical way of situating Black women's knowledge "in their cultural and historical contexts, to reclaim their personal and social roots or origins" (p. 672). The use of "endarkened" in naming this epistemology was done purposefully to contrast the presumed "enlightenment" of white feminism and to emphasize how Black women come to know (Dillard, 2000). Dillard (2000) described research as a responsibility and outlined the following six assumptions of Endarkened Feminist Epistemology: one must be able to define themselves in their own context; research is purposeful – intellectual and spiritual; an individual must be viewed in the context of community and come to know through dialogue; sensemaking happens as a result of lived experiences; knowledge production is historically and culturally bound; and finally, the dynamics of power must be considered in the determination of knowing and the knower. Endarkened Feminist Epistemology is like the third eye for marginalized identities, providing a particular way of seeing and knowing that is "historical, political, and cultural" (Dillard, 2000, p. 670).

Implications for Praxis: Using Black Feminist Epistemologies to Disrupt Supremacy

Much like the reality portrayed in Seneferu and Green's art exhibit "The Black Woman is God," the contributions of Black women to the field of higher education are rich yet unsung. Seneferu and Green's work masterfully depicted the wealth and beauty in our narratives without the overshadow of dominant white ideology. Such that art imitates life, the two theoretical frameworks presented herein parallel their guiding charge for uplifting Black women's ways of knowing and being, and in turn, disrupt white supremacy and patriarchy. A key tenet undergirding *Black Feminist Thought* and *Endarkened Feminist Epistemology* is the absence of our voices is detrimental, therefore listening to, honoring, and understanding our experiences contextually are integral to alleviating the harm of white supremacy and patriarchy. These epistemologies suggest a way forward in the academy that challenges what is known, and then, redefines the knower. John Camara noted: "Were Black women given the freedom to create and structure institutions in the image of the knowledge that they have gained implicitly, we could transform the world" (as cited in Edwards & Davidson, 2018, p. 19).

Black feminist epistemologies are rooted in drawing the margins into the center by amplifying the voices and underscoring the lived experiences of those narratives which do not reflect the dominant culture. Centering Black women has implications for who has a right to access and thrive in higher education, and in which ways. Catherine John Camara detailed incorporating a historical perspective by using pedagogical tools and curricular design that reflect aspects of African American culture such as literature, music, film, and poetry to expose students to systems of oppression that are raced, gendered, and classed, and the intersection thereof (as cited in Edwards & Davidson, 2018). Equally important is respect for the intellectual thought and knowledge of Black women. To disrupt the hegemony of whiteness and patriarchy, our experiences must be recognized as a site of meaning, our dialogue must be accepted as truth, we must be honored with care and compassion, and our values and worldview respected (Caldera, as cited in Collins, 2000; Dillard, 2000; Edwards & Davidson, 2018; Evans, 2008; Patton, 2009). Finally, Black women need opportunities to share and reflect on our individual and collective experiences (Allen & Joseph, 2018; Edwards & Davidson, 2018; Morton, 2020; Patton, 2009). Just as "The Black Woman is God" art exhibit served as a site of learning and growth for other Black women, Patton suggested "[as] scholars, and more importantly as Black women intellectuals, [our] mission must focus on empowering one another and fashioning [our] own identity through mentoring one another" (p. 517).

Concluding Thoughts

The phrase "The Black Woman is God," is not to suggest we are superior to others or to replace one oppressive power with another; the intent is to disrupt the notion of white supremacy. By turning the hierarchy of white hegemony on its head and positioning the Black woman in the foreground, this (re)conceptualization is an attempt to dismantle the ideological standpoint of white maleness as a measuring stick. The phrase is a call to action that proposes Black feminist epistemologies and praxis as a lens for (re)envisioning and transforming the academy. Instead of existing under a white gaze (Yancy, 2008), this approach allows Black women to be seen in the fullness of who we are.

References

Allen, E. L., & Joseph, N. M. (2018). The Sistah Network: Enhancing the educational and social experiences of Black women in the academy, *NASPA Journal About Women in Higher Education, 11*(2), 151–170. https://doi.org/10.1080/19407882.2017.1409638

Bailey, Moya. (2018). On misogynoir: Citation, erasure, and plagiarism. *Feminist Media Studies, 18*(4), 762–768. https://doi.org/10.1080/14680777.2018.1447395

Cho, S., Crenshaw, K. W., & McCall, L. (2013). Toward a field of intersectionality studies: Theory, applications, and praxis. *Journal of Women in Culture and Society, Signs, 38*(4), 785–810.

Collins, P. H. (2000). *Black feminist thought: Knowledge, consciousness, and the politics of empowerment* (2nd ed.). Routledge.

Dillard, C. B. (2000). The substance of things hoped for, the evidence of things not seen: Examining an endarkened feminist epistemology in educational research and leadership. *International Journal of Qualitative Studies in Education, 13*(6), 661–681. https://doi.org/10.1080/09518390050211565

Edwards, E. B., Esposito, J., & Evans-Winters, V. (2018). Does Beyoncé's Lemonade really teach us how to turn lemons into lemonade? Exploring the limits and possibilities through Black feminism. *Taboo: The Journal of Culture and Education, 16*(2). https://doi.org/10.31390/taboo.16.2.08

Edwards, K. T., & Davidson, D. (2018). *College curriculum at the crossroads: Women of color reflect and resist*. Routledge.

Evans, S. Y. (2008). *Black women in the ivory tower, 1850–1954: An intellectual history.* University Press of Florida.

Evans-Winters, V., & Love, B. L. (2015). *Black feminism in education: Black women speak back, up, and out (Black Studies and Critical Thinking).* Peter Lang.

Gutiérrez y Muhs, G., Niemann, Y. F., González, C. G., Harris, A. P., & Gonzalez, C. G. (2012). *Presumed incompetent: The Intersections of Race and Class for Women in Academia*. University Press of Colorado.

Harris-Perry, M. (2011). *Sister citizen: Shame, stereotypes, and Black women in America; for colored girls who've considered politics when being strong isn't enough*. Yale University Press.

Morton, C. S. (2020). (Re)centering the spirit: A spiritual black feminist take on cultivating right relationships in qualitative research. *Journal of College Student Development, 61*(6), 765–780.

National Center for Education Statistics. (n.d.). *NCES fast facts tool: Degrees conferred by race and sex*. https://nces.ed.gov/FastFacts/display.asp?id=72

Patton, L. D. (2009). My sister's keeper: A qualitative examination of mentoring experiences among African American women in graduate and professional schools. *Journal of Higher Education, 80*(5), 510–537. https://doi.org/10.1353/jhe.0.0062

Perlow, O. N., Wheeler, D. I., Bethea, S. L., & Scott, B. M. (2018). *Black women's liberatory pedagogies: Resistance, transformation, and healing within and beyond the academy.* Springer Nature.

Seneferu, K., & Green, M. (2016). *The Black woman is God*. http://www.theblackwomanisgod.com/2016-tbwig. [Virtual exhibition].

Yancy, G. (2008). *Black bodies, white gazes: The continuing significance of race.* Rowman and Littlefield.

SECTION II

Utility of Black Feminist Epistemologies, Research, and Praxis

6

WHAT BLACK CYBERFEMINISM TEACHES US ABOUT BLACK WOMEN ON COLLEGE CAMPUSES

Shawna Patterson-Stephens and Nadrea R. Njoku

Black women on college campuses are often misunderstood due to a lack of nuanced considerations for their lived experiences. Thus, the field of higher education remains miseducated about the realities of Black womanhood despite the progress gender, cultural, and legal studies have made regarding the intersectionality of socially constructed identities and corresponding oppressions (Collins & Bilge, 2016; Crenshaw, 1991). One aspect of society that requires more in-depth analysis is the virtual domain. As a white-assumed space rooted in white supremacist patriarchy and hegemonic notions of belonging, the media is an aspect of US infrastructure which perpetuates negative imagery to sustain disparities in academe. Black women are therefore (re)defining themselves within the confines of a hostile racially misogynist environment in a manner that propels agency and dispels mainstream conceptualizations of Black womanhood. The purpose of this chapter is to introduce Black Cyberfeminism as a framework for conceptualizing and analyzing Black women's virtual agency within postsecondary contexts. Through the lens of Black Cyberfeminism, we demonstrate how Black women in higher education navigate digital disparities and the virtual extension of self despite the white-assumed conceptualizations of media.

Marginalized groups use virtual platforms to cultivate community and consciousness-raising and the disapproved use of these narratives amongst media-based institutions is debated (Cottom, 2017). For example, Black women contend with how postsecondary institutions use their counterspaces, often constructed for the purposes of navigating systemic oppression and fending off isolation experienced in their academic spaces, to promote diversity to internal and external constituents. Inasmuch as Black women who tweet seek ownership of their content, Black women in higher education frequently find themselves advocating for autonomy over the counterspaces they have carved

DOI: 10.4324/9781003184867-8

out for themselves on campus and in the digital domain. Running parallel to one another, "tweet borrowing" and institutional appropriation are instances where institutions use their power to diminish Black women's voices and values. Black women on college campuses, particularly in predominantly white institutions, have long reported how they experience surveillance, tokenization, and targeted biased behaviors (Cooper et al., 2017; Harris-Perry, 2013). As in social media, Black women on college campuses have begun to leverage hypervisibility to make their lived experience legible to their surrounding community (Cottom, 2017). In this way, hypervisibility on physical campuses, juxtaposed with public virtual spaces, positions Black women to escalate their needs, outline resources they require, and diminish the compression which may otherwise occur on college campuses in the absence of bad publicity. For students, in particular, visibility on social media that should otherwise be reflected on campus reduces feelings of isolation and erasure (Cooper et al., 2017; Cottom, 2017).

Black Cyberfeminism

Black Cyberfeminism can be used to describe how Black women reposition their embodiment in higher education (Cooper et al., 2017). As Black women participate in higher education, they are constantly creating new knowledge. Cyberspaces have become platforms to explore both the joys and cognitive dissonance that emerge when Black women deposit their varied narratives. Black Cyberfeminism situates Black Feminist Thought in the digital domain, emphasizing the: (1) socio-structural oppression of technological and virtual spaces, (2) intersecting oppressions and privileges experienced in virtual spaces, and (3) distinctiveness of virtual Black feminisms. Black Cyberfeminism builds upon Black Feminist Thought by explicitly extending Black Feminist Thought into the digital domain (Cooper et al., 2017; Cottom, 2017; Richard & Gray, 2016). Both BFT and Black Cyberfeminism focus on occupying assumed white- and men-dominated spaces to reclaim misappropriated territories and propel critical social issues impacting Black women, including myriad forms of violence and assault (Cottom, 2017).

Black Cyberfeminism surfaces the intersection of identities within the context of power and privilege and applies this interplay to virtual spaces. Mainstream feminisms situated within the digital domain fail to acknowledge and complicate diverse modes of social identity. Moreover, they fail to capture how minoritized identities rub against an echo chamber of whiteness within the boundlessness of the digital sphere (Richard & Gray, 2016). For instance, the Facebook group was formerly known as "Pantsuit Nation" consistently centered on ideological viewpoints rooted in white womanhood, though it engaged a diverse membership. Black women frequently cited the group as a space that reified white supremacy and misogynoir, whereas white women often refused to recognize the role that the intersection of race and gender played in the 2016 presidential election. As within physical domains, Black Cyberfeminism articulates the ways women confront and circumvent the historical maneuvering of virtual spaces to exact the sociocultural and economic interests of the State. Black Cyberfeminism exposes default white cismanhood in virtual spaces and redirects hegemonic interpretations of Black womanhood as a method for reconfiguring white men-assumed space to suit the interests and needs of Black women. Assumed white cismanhood manifests in the digital sphere, which serves as a virtual representation of a broader society that actively works to exclude Black women (Richard & Gray, 2016). Thus, Black Cyberfeminism "encourages a privileging of women's perspectives and ways of knowing" (p. 123) in a manner that provides Black women with boundary-less space to resist white supremacist patriarchal infrastructures built within the physical domains of society. In other words, Black women employ internet technologies to extend their physical selves into the virtual realm to meet their distinct needs and purposes (Richard & Gray, 2016). Accepting the distinctness of minoritized digital feminisms therefore acknowledges the unique ways Black women use virtual technology to advance social change, activism, and extant feminisms within both physical and digital realms.

Black Feminist Thought Roots

The tenets of Black Cyberfeminism are a mode of analysis that advances the social location of Black women in higher education as a foundation for social change (Collins, 2000, 2004; Cottom, 2017; Richard & Gray, 2016). To grapple with Black Cyberfeminism you must understand Black Feminist Thought, as it creates a foundation for Black Cyberfeminism. The central tenets of BFT emphasize (1) the non-monolithic nature of Black womanhood, (2) intersectionality, (3) the outsider-within paradigm, and (4) the pursuit of social change (Collins, 2000).

While Black womanhood is non-monolithic, Black women share similar encounters concerning their response to the interplay of power and privilege pervasive throughout the world around them. The experiences of Black women vary, as their realities are shaped by the diverse nature of their backgrounds and intersectional identities. Exploring the lived experiences of Black women using an intersectional approach involves an understanding of how power and privilege continue to shift the positionalities of these identities throughout society – and thus, structural, cultural, and ideological realities – where these shifts converge with the interests of the State to maintain influence and control.

Exclusionary systems built on the disproportionate distribution of power and privilege continue to reinforce US institutions, even though the ways they function within contemporary contexts involve different manifestations of implicit and explicit bias (Collins, 2000; Crenshaw, 1991). Described as outsiders within, Collins (2000) emphasized how it appears Black women are included as part of systems, though they exist on the margins of society. They lack representation, power, and privilege in most US structures despite their high level of ingenuity and achievement (Collins, 2000, 2004).

Collins (2000) indicated the final tenet of Black Feminist Thought as utilizing the self-conceptualization of Black women to enact social change. In building upon their psychological armor, Black women develop a holistic, healthy self-concept that counters mainstream narratives contrived to diminish their existence as Black women. Collins (2000) asserted self-authorship should pave the way for a cohesive, systematic vehicle for improving the social location and material condition of Black women on a global scale, therefore, effecting change. To propel theory into action, Collins (2000) challenged Black women and proponents of Black feminisms to actively engage in centering the narratives and experiences of minoritized folx across different facets of US infrastructure as a step toward the adaptation of progressive legislation, policies, and social norms.

Black Cyberfeminism in Action

The bodies of Black women are politicized, evidenced of systemic, hegemonic modes of oppression pervasive in predominantly white systems, including media, where the social conceptualization of Black women's bodies is connected to storied tropes (Collins, 2004; Harris-Perry, 2013). Digital technologies provide Black women the capacity to "engage in new forms of contestation and in proactive endeavors in...different realms, from political to economic" (Sassen, 2002, p. 368). Black feminist scholarship has disrupted several themes related to Black womanhood, including respectability, strength, the performance of gender or femininity in popular culture, and the hypersexualization of Black women (Collins, 2004). Still, the ways Black women are presented in sociopolitical contexts lead to a recollection of typifications that are unrealistic and connected to the assumed value of their (gendered and racialized) flesh.

Through social media, Black women debunk myths and redesign the spatial composition of who participates and benefits from higher education. For example, hashtags such as #WhatDoctorsLookLike and #BlackGirlOnCampus consistently do the work of resisting notions that all doctors are white or that Black women do not participate in postsecondary education. Clicking on any of the hashtags recalls numerous posts highlighting how Black women consistently contribute to the academy.

In the same ways, Black women are reconfiguring white- and men-assumed space and shifting assumptions on who occupies space in higher education, they have also resisted and spoken truth to power through Black Cyberfeminism. In the digital domain, Black women articulate a voice that could be met with physical and professional harm if spoken on campus. In the same breath, they are finding an expanding community of allies and advocates to galvanize around their issues. Take, for example, the hashtags #BlackInTheIvory, #CiteASista, and #CiteBlackWomen. #BlackInTheIvory was a hashtag created by two Black women that galvanized thousands of academics to share their experiences as faculty in colleges and universities. These stories ranged from microaggressions to outright epistemic, intellectual, and emotional violence against Black people. Two hashtags with the same purpose have been #CiteASista and #CiteBlackWomen. Started by Black women either in graduate school or transitioning from student to scholar, each speaks directly against the appropriation and devalued prowess of Black women across all fields of study. Their betwixt status helped to frame their perspective as insider–outsider and thus these movements advocated for the intellectual credit to Black fem scholars by leveraging their cyber communities and influence. Black Cyberfeminism breaks down geographic walls to amplify beyond physical borders, producing multiple movements that hundreds of thousands of Black women and allies can support to move racial justice and equity forward in higher education. As with the hashtags mentioned above, there are numerous spaces where Black cyberfeminism takes place. Facebook groups, such as Binders Full of Women and Nonbinary People of Color in Academia, are other places where Black women "gather" to seek help, support, pose questions, or simply share moments of joy and pleasure. These groups have become landing spots for both emerging and seasoned professionals to identify and unmask. Similar spaces such as Instagram and Clubhouse also have variations of the examples mentioned above.

While the virtual environment is a space in which Black women actively resist misogynoir, it is the joy Black women express in these spaces that signifies a possible heterogeneous nature of Black womanhood. As with the social movements outlined above, Black women have found a large network of support across social media and the virtual working environment (e.g., webinars, virtual conferences, and podcasting). Within these spaces, they are given the platform to create mutual connections to celebrate their accomplishments and find humor in pain. Black women in higher education will continue to manifest virtual environments that transform around their evolving needs and perspectives. Researchers seeking to examine these phenomena will require critical theories and methodologies that allow for the analysis of authentic lived experiences among marginalized communities. As the relationship between Black women in academe and the digital domain advances, Black Cyberfeminism can serve as a foundational theoretical framing in examining the virtual agency of Black women.

References

Collins, P. H. (2000). *Black feminist thought: Knowledge, consciousness, and the politics of empowerment.* Routledge.

Collins, P. H. (2004). *Black sexual politics: African Americans, gender, and the new racism.* Routledge.

Collins, P. H., & Bilge, S. (2016). *Intersectionality.* Polity.

Cooper, B. C., Morris, S. M., & Boylorn, R. M. (2017). *The crunk feminist collection.* Feminist Press.

Cottom, T. M. (2017). Black cyberfeminism: Ways forward for intersectionality and digital sociology. In J. Daniels, K. Gregory, & T. McMillan Cottom (Eds.), *Digital sociologies* (pp. 211–232). Policy Press.

Crenshaw, K. (1991). Demarginalizing the intersection of race and sex: A Black feminist critique of antidiscrimination doctrine, feminist theory, and antiracist politics. *University of Chicago Legal Forum*, 1989, 139–167. http://chicagounbound.uchicago.edu/uclf/vol1989/iss1/8

Harris-Perry, M. V. (2013). *Sister citizen: Shame, stereotypes, and Black women in America.* Yale University Press.

Richard, G. T., & Gray, K. L. (2016). Gendered play, racialized reality: Black cyberfeminism, inclusive communities of practice, and the intersections of learning, socialization, and resilience in online gaming. *Frontiers: A Journal of Women's Studies, 39*(1), 112–148. https://doi.org/10.5250/fronjwomestud.39.1.0112

Sassen, S. (2002). Towards a sociology of information technology. *Current Technology, 50*(3), 365–388. https://doi.org/10.1177/0011392102050003005

7

UPROOTING THE PREVALENCE OF MISOGYNOIR IN COUNSELOR EDUCATION

Olivia T. Ngadjui

Black people must negotiate systemic racism while adhering to respectability politics to succeed professionally (Bailey, 2021; Coates, 2015). Misogynoir, a term coined by Moya Bailey emphasizes the mistreatment of Black trans and cis women by combining anti-Blackness and gender oppressive ideologies (Bailey, 2016, 2021; Bailey & Trudy, 2018; Trudy, 2014). Misogynoir includes harsh judgment and stereotypes placed on Black women and girls (e.g., being labeled "angry" during self-advocacy efforts or the minimization and denial toward assertions of suffering) that influence their health and sense of wellness (Bailey, 2016, 2021). Simultaneously, the counseling field advocates for diversity to promote culturally sensitive client care through the recruitment of Black, Indigenous, Asian, and people of color to both receive counselor education and to train future counselors (Meyers, 2017; Ngadjui, 2021).

Black Women Doctoral Student Realities within Counselor Education

This chapter draws from a larger grounded theory study, *Shaking Up the Room: The Process of Professional Identity Development of Black Doctoral Students in Counselor Education* (Ngadjui, 2021), to reveal the role of misogynoir in Black women doctoral students' navigation of counselor education programs at predominantly white institutions accredited by the Council for Accreditation of Counseling and Related Educational Programs (CACREP). As Black doctoral students comprise 25% of students in over 400 accredited counselor education programs in the United States, confidentiality was optimized by using pseudonyms for participants and intentional data analysis to focus on interview questions versus individual participants (Ngadjui, 2021). The study included five current and

DOI: 10.4324/9781003184867-9

past Black doctoral students from every region of the Association for Counselor Education and Supervision within the United States with an average age of 35 years (Ngadjui, 2021). Participants identified as a doctoral student, a doctoral candidate, a doctoral candidate nearing graduation, a recent graduate within the first year as a tenure track faculty, and a tenured faculty with more than ten years of experience (Ngadjui, 2021). Black doctoral women within the study ranged in their Black identity by identifying as Black/African American, Black/African American/African, and Black/Latina (Agyemang et al., 2005; Ngadjui, 2021; Omi & Winant, 2014).

Anais Nin's and Maya Drake's Examples of Mistreatment

Misogynoir (Bailey, 2016, 2021) arose as a theme in the study as participants described harmful experiences that influenced their meaning-making during their development as counselor educators (Ngadjui, 2021). Participants' experiences were impacted by microinvalidations (i.e., statements negating thoughts and feelings of marginalized individuals) by their non-Black counterparts and they were essentialized by faculty assumptions of their upbringing or demeanor (Ngadjui, 2021; Sue et al., 2008). For example, Anais Nin described how discriminatory statements made about their (lack of) ability at the intersection of her race and gender negatively impacted her pursuit of employment in counselor education (Ngadjui, 2021). Relatedly, Maya Drake discussed their faculty's essentialism by assuming Black women doctoral students ascribed to and/or experienced the same narrative in the department (Ngadjui, 2021). In other words, as faculty were making sense of their (mis)understanding of Black doctoral students, they were externally processing their (mis)perceptions onto Black women while increasing Black women's discomfort and marginalization.

Maya Drake also shared an interaction wherein a faculty member denied discriminatory behavior displayed by students that impacted Maya's ability to teach (Ngadjui, 2021). The faculty member labeled Maya Drake as angry and refused to advocate nor address the students' racially and gendered discrimination on her behalf. Anais Nin articulated how she was forced into isolation by non-Black peers in her department due to their inability (or refusal) to disrupt the mistreatment she was experiencing at the intersection of her race and gender. Their non-Black peers confirmed they intentionally kept their distance and thus perpetuated marginalization by not sharing opportunities with her (Ngadjui, 2021).

These instances of mistreatment of Black women in counselor education negatively impacted diversity initiatives and illuminated the prevalence of discrimination and anti-Black rhetoric, tainting the professional identity development of Black women in the field. This chapter provides foundational and necessary work for inclusion, not just diversity, in counselor education by (a) exploring the phenomenon of misogynoir, and (b) proposing considerations for counteracting misogynoir through a Black feminist lens to discontinue its perpetuation and harm to Black women.

Exploration of Misogynoir

Literature on misogynoir focuses on harmful media representation of Black women (Bailey, 2016, 2021; Bailey & Trudy, 2018; Trudy, 2014). These negative stereotypes perpetuate the mistreatment of Black women including hairstyle ridicule, domestic violence, social media bullying, and minimization of their pain (Bailey, 2021; Bailey & Trudy, 2018; Carter et al., 2018; Cooper, 2016; Gaines, 2018; Leath et al., 2021; Madden et al., 2018; Thompson, 2018; Trudy, 2014). Misogynoir can be perpetuated by Black men who privilege racism, white women who privilege sexism, and Black women who internalize anti-Blackness and misogyny (Bailey, 2021; Bailey & Trudy, 2018; Cooper, 2016; Crenshaw, 1989; Trudy, 2014). Other topics related to misogynoir include how Black women discuss their mistreatment, misogynoir on social media, and the creation of an instrument to build misogynoir awareness (Cook, 2020; Macías, 2015).

Bailey (2021) provided a detailed overview of misogynoir including earlier thoughts that led to the creation of the term as well as the visibility of misogynoir across society. Additionally, Bailey (2021) provided case studies showcasing the methods of resistance by Black trans and cis women to promote alternative representations of the media's disregard and erasure of Black women. Bailey (2021) further discussed the erasure of Black women in the media as it pertains to their safety and wellbeing including silence about violence against trans and cis Black women. The detailed account of Black women impacted by misogynoir included the media's depiction of Black women as criminals (Bailey, 2021).

Counteracting Misogynoir in Counselor Education through a Black Feminist Lens

Counteracting misogynoir in counselor education entails actively seeking knowledge to understand the plight of Black women and the challenges they encounter due to the intersection of anti-Blackness and misogyny (Bailey, 2021; Combahee River Collective, 1977; Crenshaw, 1989). Offering the term misogynoir during intensive interviews permitted participants to deeply and critically understand their ability to combat the harmful effects of internalizing race- and gender-based trauma (Hemmings & Evans, 2008). Utilizing intersectionality as a theoretical lens would promote an understanding of how privilege and marginalization function in Black women's lives (Collins & Bilge, 2016; Crenshaw, 1989). Another factor to consider entails the role of essentialism in inhibiting Black women's identities by imposing stereotypical archetypes such as the sacrificial mammy, fetishized jezebel, and angry sapphire

(Crenshaw, 1989; West, 1995). The lack of understanding about the Black experience in counselor education prompts non-Black peers to see and interact with Black women as extensions of these archetypes.

Finally, heightened understanding of how intersectionality impacts Black women can foster awareness and empathy about humanity (Collins & Bilge, 2016; Crenshaw, 1989). An example of considering the humanity of Black women entails listening to them, as in the case of the late Dr. Susan Moore who died due to invalidation of their pain in dealing with COVID-19 (Eligon, 2020). The validation of Black women's lived experiences with misogyny and racism can inspire anti-oppressive practices that consider intersections of identity among other groups (Combahee River Collective, 1977). The following reflective questions are provided for non-Black and Black individuals internalizing anti-Blackness and misogyny in counselor education to prompt consideration of equitable treatment toward Black women:

- What knowledge, assumptions, associations, or implicit bias do I have about Black women?
- What interactions have I had with Black women and how were they? How might they be influencing my interacting with my Black women identifying colleagues?
- How does my identity intersect with identities a Black woman may hold (e.g., race, gender, class, etc.)?

Conclusion

The prevalence of misogynoir in counselor education appears to be ambiguous and subtle because the ethics of counseling are human-centered through a Eurocentric lens of privilege (American Counseling Association, 2014; Baker et al., 2015; McCarthy, 2005). Faculty, administrators, and students must uproot misogynoir to center equity for Black women (Carter, 2007; Hemmings & Evans, 2018). This uprooting should entail intentional steps toward equitable treatment as misogynoir resides at the center of anti-Blackness and discriminatory practice (Bailey, 2016, 2021; Bailey & Trudy, 2018; Crenshaw, 1989; Trudy, 2014). Furthermore, the consideration of Black women in counselor education will result in better care of future counselors, counselor educators, clients, and society at large.

References

Agyemang, C., Bhopal, R., & Brujinzeels, M. (2005). Negro, Black, Black African, African Caribbean, African American or what? Labelling African origin populations in the health arena in the 21st century. *Journal of Epidemiology & Community Health, 59*(12), 1014–1018. https://doi.org/10.1136/jech.2005.035964

American Counseling Association. (2014). *ACA code of ethics*. Author.

Bailey, M. (2016). Misogynoir in medical media: On Caster Semenya and R. Kelly. *Catalyst: Feminism, Theory, Technoscience, 2*(2), 1–31. https://doi.org/10.28968/cftt.v2i2.28800

Bailey, M. (2021). *Misogynoir transformed: black women's digital resistance*. New York University Press.

Bailey, M., & Trudy. (2018). On misogynoir: Citation, erasure, and plagiarism. *Feminist Media Studies, 18*(4), 762–768. https://doi.org/10.1080/14680777.2018.1447395

Baker, C. A., Gaulke, K., & Smith, K. (2015). Counselor education cultural climate: Underrepresented master's students' experiences. *Journal for Multicultural Education, 9*(2), 85–97. https://doi.org/10.1108/JME-07-2014-0032

Carter, R. T. (2007). Racism and psychological and emotional injury: Recognizing and assessing race-based traumatic stress. *The Counseling Psychologist, 35*(1), 13–105. https://doi.org/10.1177/0011000006292033

Carter, R., Mustafaa, F. N., & Leath, S. (2018). Teachers' expectations of girls' classroom performance and behavior: Effects of girls' race and pubertal timing. *The Journal of Early Adolescence, 38*(7), 885–907. https://doi.org/10.1177/0272431617699947

Coates, T. (2015). *Between the world and me*. Spiegel & Grau.

Collins, P. H., & Bilge, S. (2016). *Intersectionality*. Polity Press.

Combahee River Collective. (1977). A Black feminist statement. In L. Nicholson (Ed.), *The second wave: A reader in feminist theory* (pp. 210–218). Routledge.

Cook, E. S. (2020). *Creation of the internalized misogynoir measure: A qualitative approach to designing an intersectional took for use with Black women* [Doctoral dissertation]. http://hdl.handle.net/2047/D20397589

Cooper, B. (2016). Connect the dots: Korryn Gaines, Skye Mockabee, and Joyce Queway. *Crunk Feminist Collective*. http://www.crunkfeministcollective.com/2016/08/03/connect-the-dots-for-korryn-gaines-skye-mockabee-and-joyce-queweay/

Crenshaw, K. (1989). Demarginalizing the intersection of race and sex: A Black feminist critique of antidiscrimination doctrine, feminist theory and antiracist politics. *University of Chicago Legal Forum, 8*, 139–167.

Eligon, J. (2020). Black doctor dies of covid-19 after complaining of racist treatment. *The New York Times*. https://www.nytimes.com/2020/12/23/us/susan-moore-black-doctor-indiana.html

Gaines, Z. (2018). A Black girl's song misogynoir, love, and Beyoncé's lemonade. *Taboo: The Journal of Culture and Education, 16*(2), 97–114. https://doi.org/10.31390/taboo.16.2.09

Hemmings, C., & Evans, A. M. (2018). Identifying and treating race-based trauma in counseling. *Journal of Multicultural Counseling and Development, 46*(1), 20–39.

Leath, S., Ware, N., Seward, M. D., McCoy, W. N., Ball, P., & Pfister, T. A. (2021). A qualitative study of Black college women's experiences of misogynoir and anti-racism with high school educators. *Social Sciences, 10*(1), 1–29. https://doi.org/10.3390/socsci10010029

Macías, K. (2015). *Tweeting away our blues: An interpretative phenomenological approach to exploring Black women's use of social media to combat misogynoir* [Doctoral dissertation]. https://nsuworks.nova.edu/shss_dcar_etd/25

Madden, S., Janoske, M., Briones Winkler, R., & Edgar, A.N. (2018). Mediated misogynoir: Intersecting race and gender in online harassment. In J. Ryan Vickery & T. Everbach (Eds.), *Mediating misogyny: Gender, technology & harassment* (pp. 71–90). Palgrave Macmillan.

McCarthy, J. (2005). Individualism and collectivism: What do they have to do with counseling? *Journal of Multicultural Counseling and Development, 33*(2), 108–117. https://doi.org/10.1002/j.2161-1912.2005.tb00009.x

Meyers, L. (2017). Making the counseling profession more diverse. *Counseling Today*, 32–48. https://ct.counseling.org/2017/10/making-counseling-profession-diverse/#

Ngadjui, O. T. (2021). *Shaking up the room: The process of professional identity development of Black doctoral students in counselor education* [Doctoral dissertation]. Idaho State University. Idaho State University Electronic Dissertations and Theses Database.

Omi, M., & Winant, H. (2014). Racial formations. In P. S. Rothenberg & K. S. Mayhew (Eds.), *Race, class, and gender in the United States: An integrated study* (9th ed., pp. 13–22). Worth. (Original work published 1986).

Sue, D. W., Nadal, K. L., Capodilupo, C. M., Lin, A. I., Torino, G. C., & Rivera, D. P. (2008). Racial microaggressions against Black Americans: Implications for counseling. *Journal of Counseling & Development, 86*(3), 330–338. https://doi.org/10.1002/j.1556-6678.2008.tb00517.x

Thompson, C. (2018). Misogynoir in Canada: Robyn Maynard documents the policing of Black lives in Canada. *Herizons, 32*(1), 21–23.

Trudy. (2014). Explanation of misogynoir. *Gradient Lair.* http://www.gradientlair.com/post/84107309247/definemisogynoir-anti-blackmisogyny-moya-bailey-coined

West, C. M. (1995). Mammy, sapphire, and jezebel: Historical images of Black women and their implications for psychotherapy. *Psychotherapy: Theory, Research, Practice, Training, 32*(3), 458–466. https://doi.org/10.1037/0033-3204.32.3.458

8

INTERSECTIONALITY METHODOLOGY AND THE BLACK WOMEN COMMITTED TO "WRITE-US" RESISTANCE

Chayla Haynes, Saran Stewart, Evette L. Allen Moore, Nicole M. Joseph, and Lori D. Patton

> I am invoked by our ancestry. Whenever I get discouraged about the work, and when I say the work, I'm talking about research, scholarship, and the academy, all of the emotional work. I call upon and think about all the Black women ancestors that did this before me.
>
> (E. Allen, personal communication, 2017)

We were Black women who wanted to write about Black women. Our shared story began in 2015 and started in the academy. We were all at different points in our careers and/or training. In a subsequent section of this chapter, we describe how we experience the academy, a context that sheds light on Intersectionality Methodology's (IM) contribution to higher education and social science research. Our connections to one another have been fostered over the years among us individually, in doctoral classrooms, in mentoring relationships, and in collaborative research, wherein we leaned on one another for sisterhood, togetherness, and support. After a while, our individual connections among us grew like a vine, bonding us more deeply to the legacy passed on by the Black women who raised us and strengthened our commitment to write *Black women into existence.*

In alignment with the Black feminist tradition, we organized and came together around a metaphorical "kitchen table" over a meal, while at a national education research conference. The conversation that followed was inspired by a single thought: "how might we expand the literature on Black women and present them (and us for that matter) intersectionally and with complexity, through scholarly collaborations that sustain us professionally and personally?" That thinking led us to establish the *Black Women Scholars Writing Collective* (the

DOI: 10.4324/9781003184867-10

Collective). The Collective takes up intersectionality in its endeavor to engage in *Write-Us* research (Austin, 1989). The Collective allows space for peer mentoring as resistance, thus promoting our research as a personal and political act. The work of the Collective happens individually and collaboratively among us. The research study that resulted as an introduction of IM (see Haynes et al., 2020) was our first collaboration. This chapter extends our first collaboration to present IM as a Black women onto-epistemological informed methodology and illustrate the ways in which our individual and collective philosophical approaches informed the research process to develop tenets of IM and interrupt white hetero cis-patriarchy (WHC-P).

Making the Personal Political: IM's Research Team

Both our collective and individual positionalities were interwoven within and throughout the study in a manner that "frames [the] social and professional relationships in the research field and also governs the tone of the research" (Sanghera & Thapar-Bjorkert, 2008, p. 553). The complexity of our identities as Black women scholars undergirds the power of our collective writing, and the lens through which we introduce IM to disrupt the WHC-P that perpetuates the intersectional subordination we, and most Black women and girls, confront in society. The academy especially in the United States, from our standpoint, is a WHC-P space that upholds the whiteness, maleness, and hetero cis-normativity that is often privileged, condoning the threat, or use of violence against Black people for all genders and sexual orientations (Evans-Winters, 2017). Specifically, we identify as five women scholars, who individually are Black, Black American, African American, and Black Caribbean. Our individual identities as mothers, religio-spiritual Black Christians, heterosexual, cisgender, immigrant, and scholars with disabilities allowed us to better apply intersectionality and examine its possibilities as a methodological approach. Our coming together was our way of establishing a network with the social capital we were not born with or entered the academy with, in comparison to our white cis-gender male counterparts. Our analytical prowess and the manner in which we coded were heavily influenced by the complex identity markers of our Black womanhood that are not unidimensional. Our positionality is not just how we identify ourselves but how others identify us, straddling multiple dichotomous roles, such as the oppressed and the oppressor, the insider and outsider, and the personal and political.

As Black women scholars, we stand at both the intersections of oppression and power in a society and academy rooted in WHC-P. We occupy and attempt to dismantle WHC-P as faculty and researchers in academic spaces, such as the PWI classroom and through citation politics that recenter white epistemologies. While we operate from the margins, the privileged aspects of our identities, like our "positions as 'scholars' set us apart to some extent from [some]

Black women about whom we write, and our work would be better if we acknowledged the distance and attempted to bridge it" (Austin, 1989, p. 545). Lastly, as Black women scholars and critical pedagogues, we acknowledge that education, like education research, is bound by identity politics and political struggle (Freire, 1985). Therefore, our engagement in intersectionality research and praxis is as much a political act as it is a personal one.

Intersectionality Methodology is Black Women Engaging in Write-Us Research

> It is time for Sapphire to testify on her own behalf, **in writing**, complete with footnotes. "To testify" means several different things in this context: to present the facts, to attest to their accuracy, and to profess a personal belief or conviction.
>
> *(Austin, 1989, p. 584)*

Black feminists use intersectionality to critique how racist, sexist, gendered, classist, stereotypical, and controlling images or tropes shape the ways white and non-white persons interpret our contributions, capabilities, and potential (Collins, 2000; Patton & Haynes, 2018). The *Black lady*, the *Mammy,* and the *Strong* or *Angry* Black woman are just a few of the harmful, controlling images used to diminish and demonize Black women and their labor. The interlocking identities of class, nationality, and sexual orientation, to name a few, are often hidden within the intersecting frames of race and gendered oppression. Black feminist legal scholar Regina Austin (1989) embraced the Sapphire trope in her article, *Sapphire Bound!* Austin called to action Black women and other minoritized women of color to make the personal political by engaging in write-us legal scholarship, and other research meant to remedy the societal race-based discrimination shaping their lives. In doing so, Austin prompted legal scholars who are Black women to recall the last time they were asked to "assess the hardships or struggles in their life in terms of being a woman, on top of being Black" (p. 540).

Austin (1989) used this line of questioning to illustrate how the basis of legal doctrine/policy implies Black women do not live in "integrated, undifferentiated, complete whole" lives, with "consciousness and politics"[1] of their own is racist and sexist (p. 540). Moreover, Austin challenged legal scholars to presume the strategies Black women employ to redress the societal ills that bear disproportionately on their lives for the benefit of all humanity would be inherently flawed because of the way that Black women are constructed in jurisprudence. Legal scholarship that reinforces such racist and sexist norms permits legal scholars to read Black womanhood as dispossessed, incapable of self-empowered, transformative leadership, and complex thinking.

The Sapphire trope depicts Black women as sassy, disrespectful, and ultimately disruptive (Patton & Haynes, 2018). Casting Black women as Sapphire is WHC-P's way of demonizing Black women for their ability to "mount scathing critiques of the sources of her oppression" (Austin, 1989, p. 541). Austin (1989) urged Black women to take on the role of "professional Sapphires" in write-us research and legal scholarship that is "forthright" in its "testimony" in which Black women declare "we are serious about ourselves" (p. 542).

The Black Women Scholars Writing Collective assumed the role of "professional Sapphires" in our 2020 study published in the *Review of Educational Research,* which examined how Crenshaw's intersectionality had been applied across its three dimensions (e.g., structural, political, and representational) by scholars who published empirical studies about Black women in higher education in the last 30 years (Haynes et al., 2020). Crenshaw's (1991) three-dimensional framework helps scholars like us, to evaluate the macro/micro level power relations that contribute to the intersectional subordination Black women, and similarly minoritized groups, experience. Structural intersectionality illustrates how multiple forms of structural oppression (e.g., racism, classism, and sexism) press down simultaneously to shape the everyday lives of Black women. With political intersectionality, Crenshaw (1991) asserted, Black women, because of their minoritized race and gendered status, among others, are situated within at least two subordinated groups, with often conflicting political agendas (e.g., racial justice agenda vs. gender justice agenda or class politics vs. race politics), contributing to their intersectional erasure. Finally, representational intersectionality illuminates how the exploitation of Black women's labor and bodies is rooted in racist, sexist, classist tropes or controlling images and stereotypes established in slavery and reinforced in mainstream media and societal discourse (Crenshaw, 1991).

Our intent to understand how scholars used their study findings to address Crenshaw's intersectionality was not only about bringing visibility to scholarship on Black women, but also about us understanding how we might learn to write about Black women in ways that create "enough static to interfere with the transmission of the dominant ideology and jam the messages that reduce our indignation, limit our activism, misdirect our energies, and otherwise make us the (re)producers of our own subordination" (Austin, 1989, p. 544). In our analysis, we discovered scholars who applied Crenshaw's intersectionality in their study of Black women in higher education employed a particular set of strategies, ultimately guiding research decisions they made regarding study design, methods, and analysis, which we coined as IM (Haynes et al., 2020). IM has four features that prompt researchers to: (1) centralize Black women as the subject, (2) use a critical lens to uncover the micro-/macro-level power relations, (3) address how power shapes the research process, and (4) bring the complex identity markers of Black Women to the fore.

Centralizing Black Women as the Subject

We learned scholars who took up intersectionality in their study of Black women centralized Black women, treating them as sources and/or producers of knowledge (Haynes et al., 2020). As knowledge sources/producers, Black women testify to their own experiences and without the need of corroboration, as WHC-P research paradigms or approaches insist upon. As knowers, Black women are treated in the research process as knowledge producers, capable of interpreting and telling their own stories. In short, centering Black women in research is to write about them in ways that show how the academy, the field, and/ or the researcher believes them, honors them, and highlights them. For example, to centralize Black women in a study on mental health would mean learning about the specific impact of Black women, their intersectional identities, and mental health rather than using an individual understanding of how race (e.g., experiences of Black Men), gender (e.g., experiences of white women), class, or sexual orientation (e.g., experiences of heterosexual individuals), etc. issues interact solely with mental health.

Using a Critical Lens to Uncover Micro/Macro-Level Power Relations

Critical, yet intersectional frameworks/theories help researchers critique the race, sexual orientation, gender, religio-spiritual, and socio-economic oppression that shape Black women's lives (Haynes et al., 2020). Black Feminist Thought, Endarkened Feminist Epistemology, Womanist Theology, and Critical Race Feminism are just a few of the critical lenses' scholars use to take up intersectionality in their study of Black women. Critical theories/frameworks also exist that support intersectional analyses from the standpoint of Black women's lived experiences outside of the United States. For example, Afro-Caribbean Feminist Thought (Stewart, 2019) has been used to explore the specific ways in which gender enables or necessitates post-colonial, African-Caribbean women's mobility, and the unexpected intimacies and experiences that emerge from these mobilities. Our analysis revealed that applying critical, yet intersectional lenses and research about Black women go hand-in-hand. Critical theories/frameworks elevate analysis, helping the researcher nuance their analysis in the study of Black women. Specifically, the scholars engaged in intersectional analysis use critical lenses to organize the research content, locate their research questions, and make judgments of their data (Haynes et al., 2020).

Addressing How Power Shapes the Research Process

Qualitative, quantitative, and mixed-methods research traditions are layered with intersectional subordination, mitigated, and reinforced at times by researcher reflexivity and positionality, along with researcher proximity to the intersectional subordination Black women experience (Haynes et al., 2020). For example, a white scholar studying Black women would ask themselves "who am I to do this research?," as a matter of interrogating how power, in this case, whiteness, shapes their, and the participants' experience in the research process, which that researcher would then address as part of their research design and analysis. Further, the multiple intersecting identities analyzed would explore the oppressed and oppressor dynamic of power and how that power influences the research study (e.g., a Black, middle-class, heterosexual woman recognizing their many power dynamics as a lens through which they view the coordinated research).

Bring the Complex Identity Markers of Black Women to the Fore

We noted applying a critical lens enables scholars to present analyses that capture Black women in the fullness of their humanity, rather than what Crenshaw called single-axis analyses (1991). Single-axis analysis tends to construct Black women as a monolith and can reinforce WHC-P. This permits institutional and state actors to respond to race-based discrimination and violence with one-dimensional, blanket approaches rather than with intersectional interventions (Haynes et al., 2020). Intersectional interventions take issue with campus and public policy that suggest all Black people, or people of color, experience racism in the same way (Patton & Njoku, 2019). For example, intersectional interventions reject norms that insist institutional, or state policies address the specific ways Black women experience systemic racism are too costly and time-intensive. Intersectional interventions reject broad-stroke policy analyses that prompt institutional leaders and state actors to be concerned with "how do we make this policy work" and instead urges them to ask and answer, "how do we make this policy work for Black women of different gendered-groups, sexual orientations, and class statuses?."

Our Hope for Intersectionality Methodology

"We have paid our dues, done more than our share of the doing and the dying, and are entitled to prosper with everyone else" (Austin, 1989, p. 539). Our engagement in this research showed us how to do as Austin (1989) instructed with IM. IM supports Black women's resistance and indignation of WHC-P and urges them to write with "empowered and empowering voices" (p. 543). IM posits this involves not only Black women testifying to their own experiences in research that situates them as sources and producers of knowledge, but it may also include intersectional interventions that resemble "grassroots"[1] efforts among "Sapphires by another name," who write collectively and generate research that addresses the societal and scholarly neglect Black women experience (Austin, 1989, p. 579).

IM, like intersectionality, operates from the standpoint wherein Black women's experiences are real, and thus their voices are legitimate. We invite Black women to expand on this research in ways that continue to illuminate and illustrate how Black women live intersectional lives, bringing visibility and nuance to the ways WHC-P shapes our lived experiences in, through, and outside of the academy. The accessibility of IM, like intersectionality, makes its application possible across academic disciplines/fields (e.g., education research, legal scholarship, or social science research) and research paradigms (e.g., qualitative, quantitative, and mixed-methods research). It is of particular importance to the lives of Black women that IM is embraced broadly and across academic disciplines/fields and research traditions. Applying IM prevents "the undoing of intersectionality" by scholars who simply use it as a buzzword (Harris & Patton, 2019, p. 365). IM provides Sapphire, and her allies and co-conspirators, with a guide to generate and evaluate the quality of research about Black women and train people to do the same (Joseph et al., 2021).

References

Austin, R. (1989). Sapphire bound. *Penn Law: Legal Scholarship Repository*, 539–578. https://scholarship.law.upenn.edu/cgi/viewcontent.cgi?article=2347&context=faculty_scholarship

Collins, P. H. (2000). *Black feminist thought: Knowledge, consciousness, and the politics of empowerment* (2nd ed.). Routledge. https://doi.org/10.4324/9780203900055

Crenshaw, K. (1991). Mapping the margins: Intersectionality, identity politics, and violence against women of color. *Stanford Law Review, 43*(6), 1241–1299.

Evans-Winters, V. (2017, October 7). *White male heteropatriarchy violence & mass trauma* [Blog post]. https://www.venusevanswinters.com/blog/white-male-heteropatriarchy-violence-mass-trauma

Freire, P. (1985). *The politics of education: Culture, power, and liberation.* Greenwood Publishing Group.

Harris, J. C., & Patton, L. D. (2019). Un/doing intersectionality through higher education research. *The Journal of Higher Education, 90*(3), 347–372.

Haynes, C., Joseph, N. M., Patton, L. D., Stewart, S., & Allen, E. L. (2020). Toward an understanding of intersectionality methodology: A 30-year literature synthesis of Black women's experiences in higher education. *Review of Educational Research, 90*(6), 751–787.

Joseph N. M., Haynes, C., & Patton, L. D. (2021). The politics of publishing: A national conversation with scholars who use their research about Black women to address intersectionality. *Educational Researcher, 50*(2), 115–126.

Patton, L. D., & Haynes, C. (2018). Hidden in plain sight: The Black women's blueprint for institutional transformation in higher education. *Teachers College Record, 120*(14), 1–18.

Patton, L. D., & Njoku, N. R. (2019). Theorizing Black women's experiences with institution-sanctioned violence: A #BlackLivesMatter imperative toward Black liberation on campus. *International Journal of Qualitative Studies in Education, 32*(9), 1162–1182.

Sanghera, G. S., & Thapar-Björkert, S. (2008). Methodological dilemmas: Gatekeepers and positionality in Bradford. *Ethnic and Racial Studies, 31*(3), 543–562.

Stewart, S. (2019). Navigating the academy in the post-diaspora: Afro-Caribbean feminism and the intellectual and emotional labour needed to transgress. *Caribbean Review of Gender Studies, 13*, 147–172.

9

ADVANCING AFRICAN DANCE AS A PRACTICE OF FREEDOM

Shani Collins and Truth Hunter

In *Homecoming*, Gyasi (2016) teleported us to a slave dungeon in Cape Coast, Ghana, in which we become silent witnesses to this historical trauma of the Transatlantic Slave Trade. As a result, we feel as if we are in the dungeons with these anguished enslaved African women crying a river of tears with them (Schramm, 2007).

> The smell was unbearable. In the corner, a woman was crying so hard that it seemed her bones would break from convulsions...These tears were a matter of routine. They came for all of the women. They dropped until the clay below them turned to mud. At night, Esi dreamed that if they all cried in unison, the mud would turn to river and they could be washed away into the Atlantic.
>
> *(Gyasi, 2016, pp. 28–29)*

As teaching artists, we were inspired by Gyasi's ability to evoke a deep feeling of connection to these enslaved African women, so we designed a repertory dance course to replicate the spirit of her work within our course curriculum at Connecticut College. A significant part of this course was our trip to a slave dungeon, but the one we visited was located on Goree Island in Senegal. We chose to take students to this historical site to initiate a process that we call *whole-hearted embodiment*. This personal investigation of the slave dungeon would enable students to move beyond the limits of what has been codified as intellect by western logics and translate their experiences into choreography that would be performed publicly. In this chapter, we show how bell hooks' ideas on education as a practice of freedom illuminate the theoretical under-pinning of our teaching practices, and we will also introduce the three essential

DOI: 10.4324/9781003184867-11

components of *whole-hearted embodiment* necessary for using dance as a practice of freedom.

Education as a Practice of Freedom

hooks' (1994) concept of education as a practice of freedom illuminated how the classroom experience can be a site for liberation. hooks acknowledged education has historically been used to enact social control, indoctrinate students with a particular ideology, and suppress radical thinking. Still, hooks saw the potential for education to be a political tool for unlocking freedom (hooks, 1994). Influenced by hooks' scholarship, we also believe dance education holds the same potential of enacting liberation. As such, we employed three core areas of hooks' work to shape our teaching and course curriculum: education as a political act, feminism and praxis, and integration of the mind and body.

Education as a Political Act

hooks shared as a Black woman producing scholarship in gender and women studies, she needed to make explicit that her work examined the Black experience from a feminist standpoint. hooks underscored education is not a neutral domain but a political space where she must explicitly state her position. Furthermore, hooks emphasized the importance of engaging in this process of self-actualization and role modeling it for students. hooks' concept of education as a political act empowered us to show up fully in our identities as Black women and to implement a curriculum that unapologetically centered the stories of people of the African diaspora.

Feminism and Praxis

hooks' deep concern with the practice of feminism is more than its title. She shared stories about the influence of Black women teachers in her childhood. She pointed out how they acknowledged her personhood, affirmed her intelligence, and challenged her to put her best foot forward. She recognized how they would not likely call themselves feminists, but their teaching methods supported the goals of feminism. hooks' influenced our teaching experience because feminism and praxis became centering anchors for our classroom experience. We did this by creating a supportive space where the humanity and the well-being of students were central to the learning process.

Integration of the Mind and Body

hooks acknowledged a western notion of dualism that purported students and teachers should only bring their minds into the classroom. hooks referred to this dynamic as a "disembodied spirit" that prevents the emergence of passion and creativity (p. 193). However, the practice of feminism enables pedagogy that nurtures the mind/body connection so love can organically emerge in the classroom experience. For our dance class, the integration of the mind and body became a consistent practice of learning how to use dance to heal the mind/body split so prevalent in many American classrooms.

hooks' concepts related to education as a practice of freedom have empowered us to see our teaching as a political act, grounded in feminist praxis with an unwavering commitment to the mind/body connection through dance education. While hooks' work greatly shaped our teaching and curriculum design, we also sensed we were conceptualizing what the practice of freedom could be for dance, specifically. Toward that end, we developed a framework from our reflections of what our course aimed to provide students.

Conceptualizing Whole-Hearted Embodiment

A Framework for Dance as a Practice of Freedom

For us, *whole-hearted embodiment* includes three components that support dance as a practice of freedom: (1) dance as a way to heal the body, (2) dance as a way to strengthen the body, and (3) dance as a way to express the body. In the subsequent sections, we will not only explain each component of our framework, but how our teaching conceptions and practices derived from our distinct ways of knowing as Black women dancers.

Dance as a Way to Heal the Body

In our studio practice, we paid particular attention to our breath as a sacred conduit to our freedom, noticing when it is shallow or when we are not breathing at all. Together we discovered breathwork is foundational to using dance as a way to heal the body. In West African dance technique, we often initiate movement from the bottom of our ribcage and in and around our solar plexuses. We practiced breathing in yoga poses, such as "full surrender" which allows our neck and hips to open up, release tension, and create space for more movement capacity. In these poses, we acknowledged any tension, emotional response, or injury we may have held in our bodies. When we listened to our bodies, we created more capacity in our ways of thinking that influenced how we showed up in a community with one another.

We learned we could use practices of the breath and the collective energy of our bodies as medicine to heal internalized forms of oppression, which hooks referred to as the enemy within (hooks, 2000). Furthermore, the healing process is made available when individual and collective voices are discovered, explored, valued, and written through the body. Dance as a way to heal the body is a component of *whole-hearted embodiment* that connects to hooks' concept of mind and body integration. We empowered students with tools and skills they can use to access their own healing in ways that probably would not happen in a traditional classroom setting. We intended for students in this class to transfer these practices over into their everyday lives so they could learn to come home to the body to enhance their well-being and resilience. As Black women, our teaching approach stemmed from our personal conviction that healing is a form of self-preservation while navigating a white hetero-patriarchal society, and for that reason, we empowered students with the tools to embody healing for themselves through African rooted dance and principles.

Dance as a Way to Strengthen the Body

For dance to become a practice of freedom, strengthening the body was crucial. We did this by setting personal and collective intentions, differentiating movement styles, and practicing West African dance techniques. We considered the studio dance practice a movement laboratory and a site for embodied learning. Intense training and conditioning were required to support the West African dance technique. We utilized a mirror to see the body and covered the mirror to focus on feeling only the body's sensations. We used standing exercises to warm up the body's joints, get our blood circulating, and practice proper alignment that could protect our bodies from injury. We taught students an essential sensibility to have in West African dance is to feel the earth underneath them with all their toes planted into the ground. We became more rooted in this practice by softening our knees and ankles and allowing ourselves to surrender to gravity. We practiced pushing off the ground for jumps and rebound dance movements. Exercises were designed to support groundedness and an ability to shift weight quickly.

All movements in our West African dance class were practiced with live drummers. The music and the movement are one. Students listened diligently to the music to decipher multiple rhythms, call and response from the drums, and demonstrate their bodies as musical beats as they feel the intrinsic quality and power the drums bring into space. Studio practice in this course functioned to establish foundational Africanist aesthetics in our bodies, developing skills for understanding differences between several African techniques and rhythms. Furthermore, dance as a way to strengthen the body is a component of *whole-hearted embodiment* that connects to hooks' emphasis on feminism and praxis. Within our classroom experience, we discovered ways to activate feminism by supporting students with learning how to own the power of their bodies through strengthening and conditioning. As Black women, we offered students more than a physical experience, we pushed them to think critically about the way dance has become overly sexualized within American culture by challenging them to reframe dance movement as a way to create agency and power in the mind, body, and spirit.

Dance as a Way to Express the Body

The choreographic process of the performance was a continuation of our liberation work. We intended for our performance to confront the silent histories of the African diaspora and rewrite them. Through a collaboration with students, we produced "*A(cross) the Water.*" The dance opens in an African village scene where three men of African descent are gathered, escorting two women, one seated on the shoulders of a young man as they all walk downstage through a path of light. The women dance, playing on the steps of Wala Sadon, krumping, mixed sensual women's dances that were choreographed to represent Mother Africa before colonization.

After a short blackout, the tone shifts abruptly, and we see the young man standing center-center facing the audience. He has dark skin, and he is wearing a black hoodie with a colorful African print patch on his back shaped in a circle. Walking toward us, we hear the text and voice of Oscar Brown Jr., "Bid 'em in." The dancers run in imminence, on and off the stage, slicing their arms through the space and scurrying on the ground. They are wearing black hoodies and black pants that revealed their skin through slits on the sides. Their piercing movement accented by the drums is juxtaposed as they rise up from the ground, their feet come together in fast steps on their tippy-toes, wrists bound together behind them while their heads hang to one side. They all move to the corner, and their bodies collapse in a pile, representing the horrors of the middle passage. Dancers represent Black bodies that were malnourished, debilitated by the heat, flesh torn apart, and family ties broken.

The next scene for the performance showcased Haitian warrior dances of resistance called Ibo and Nago. As the dance transitioned to its final scene of the prayer circle, dancers used improvisation and made choices within the choreographic structure. They allowed their bodies to demonstrate their ability to surrender, listen, and connect with each other on stage. Through the energy of improvisation, there is a sense of freedom stimulated by the spontaneous contact of their bodies in this scene. Our musicians supported the dancers in constructing the sound score, experimenting with different rhythms that would enhance this piece's narrative. Furthermore, dance as a way to express the body is a component of *whole-hearted embodiment* that connects to hooks' idea that education is political, and it is critical to make one's position known. In this class, we used choreography as a way to elevate silenced voices from the past and connect that historical experience to current-day police brutality and the killing of Black bodies. It was our mission to use our performance to educate. We showed students the performing arts could be used as a powerful platform to showcase counter-narratives.

In the previous sections, we discussed what we learned about embodied knowledge through dance. Based on our experience as teaching artists, we have learned it is essential to be an active participant in our teaching and learning. Through rethinking, rewriting, and centering the body, we model for and teach students how to surrender to the intrinsic nature of African dance. The practice of embodiment can facilitate radical transformation, deep connection, and emotional and intellectual insights because it enables us to connect the mind and body (Rendón, 2010). This connection creates new possibilities that would be difficult to develop, operating solely from the mind or the body. We asked students to consider human feelings and sensations as tools that unlock the deeper meaning of the dance "*A(cross) the Water.*" As Black women, we felt it was our duty to create a deeply meaningful performance based on students' experiences at Goree Island in Senegal. This allowed us to live up to the calling that our ancestors put forth to pass down knowledge from one generation to another.

Advancing African Dance as a Practice of Freedom

At the end of the book *Homecoming*, a young African American man named Marcus visits the slave dungeons in Cape Coast, Ghana. Without knowing it, he steps into the room where his ancestors cried a river of tears, and suddenly he becomes sick to his stomach. Marcus, in his bodily discomfort, flees from the scene and he pushes open "the door of no return." In doing this, he symbolically rebels against the oppressive violence of the space. He did something his ancestors could not, he physically and mentally broke free. This part of the book exemplifies the Ghanaian principle of Sankofa, which is connected to the proverb that means to go back and get it (Seeman, 2010). This timeless wisdom of Sankofa encompasses the process of *whole-hearted embodiment,* in which we took students on a dance journey to the past to create new ways of seeing in the present. We believe African dance is a portal into understanding African culture, philosophy, and cosmology, which can help to expand our worldviews (Primus, 1996). Therefore, we intend to continue to use African dance and performance as a way to dismantle racist ideas projected on people of African descent, and with this intention in mind, we hope our concept of *whole-hearted embodiment* will be in service to the legacy of hooks' vision of using education as a practice of freedom.

References

Gyasi, Y. (2016). *Homegoing: A novel.* Vintage.

hooks, b. (1994). *Teaching to transgress: Education as the Practice of freedom.* Routledge.

hooks, b. (2000). *Feminism is for everybody: Passionate politics.* Pluto Press.

Primus, P. (1996). African dance. In K. Welsh Asante (Ed.), *African dance: An artistic historical and philosophical inquiry* (pp. 3–11). Africa World Press.

Rendón, L. I. (2012). *Sentipensante (sensing/thinking) pedagogy: Educating for wholeness, social justice and liberation.* Stylus Publishing, LLC.

Schramm, K. (2007). Slave route projects: Tracing the heritage of slavery in Ghana. In F. De Jong and M. Rowlands (Eds.), *Reclaiming Heritage: Alternative Imaginaries of Memory in West Africa* (pp. 71–98). Left Coast Press.

Seeman, E. R. (2010). Reassessing the "Sankofa symbol" in New York's African burial ground. *William & Mary Quarterly, 67*(1), 101–122.

10

SPIRIT MURDER

Black Women's Realities in the Academy

Ebony J. Aya

In *We Want to Do More Than Survive*, author Bettina Love (2019) articulated the reality of Black students in K-12 education. Love explained that in addition to physical crimes against Black children, they also experience spirit murder – or racism that literally kills the spirit. The concept of spirit murder is rooted in the work of Patricia Williams (1987), who defined the phenomenon as racism that results in more than just physical pain, "it is a crime, an offense so deeply painful and assaultive" (p. 129). Expanding on Williams' definition, Love (2019) stated, "racism robs dark people of their humanity and dignity and leaves personal, psychological, and spiritual injuries" (p 38). Love (2019) cited concrete examples of what spirit murder looks like in the lives of dark children, which includes Black girls and boys being physically harmed for refusing to hand over their cell phones, taking a carton of milk (that came with their free lunch), and for refusing to cut their natural hair. The purpose of this chapter is to explore the ways spirit murder has manifested in Black women's realities as they pursue graduate education and entry into the professoriate.

Berry (2018) expanded Williams and Love's thinking with a focus on the experiences of Black women, emphasizing spirit murder as a crime that "lives at the intersections of race and gender" (p. 118). The predicament Black women face can also be called gendered racism, a term coined by Essed (1991) to describe "a type of racial and gender oppression that interconnects to create a distinct, and often more challenging, experience for women who simultaneously occupy multiple subordinated positions" (Spates et al., 2020, p. 585). These crimes against Black women occur throughout society; Black women and girls are subjected to incarceration, violence, and demeaning stereotypes because of gendered racism (Young & Hines, 2018). Unable to avoid the predicament that befalls Black women, these same crimes of race and gender show

DOI: 10.4324/9781003184867-12

up in academia in particular ways that analogize the murder of Black women by police. Young and Hines (2018) stated Black women who condemn white supremacy in academia,

> are witnessing their integrity, careers, and scholarship being questioned, while they are simultaneously being targeted and in the crossfire of racist incidents that parallel the senseless murdering of black women in society.... Black women are being murdered or unjustly removed so that their stories can never be heard.
>
> *(p. 20)*

Generett and Cozart (2011/2012) affirmed the battles we fight outside of academia on behalf of others often mirror the battles we fight within academia for ourselves. *In Sisters of the Academy*, Woods (2001) identified one of those hurdles for Black women was not being able to find and sustain mentors who were willing to see them through the doctoral process. At times, the struggle is related to so few Black women or other faculty of color available to provide support to Black women doctoral students. However, the barrier is also connected to the reality that Black women doctoral students seldom find support for their research interests. They are "accused of not having objectivity or of being too close to the topic to conduct quality research" (Woods, 2001, p. 113). This reality has yielded inappropriate advice for Black women to deemphasize the racial and gendered aspects of their research (Woods, 2001).

Similarly, Generett and Cozart (2011/2012) noted despite more Black women earning doctoral degrees, their research is dismissed as irrelevant to the knowledge base (academic discipline) and not generalizable. According to Generett and Cozart, this results in Black women doctoral students losing trust in themselves and their ability to break down barriers. It also leads to Black women doctoral students denying their way of knowing, a knowing deeply connected to spirit and culture, to appear smart (Shadid, 2015). This denial of Black women's way of knowing and experiences is what Spivak (1988) and Collins (2019) call epistemic violence, practices of silencing used to undermine and invalidate the ideas of marginalized people. Shadid (2015) confessed to the epistemic violence she encountered daily "when words like spirit and faith became unacceptable explanations within serious academic inquiries" (p. 64).

Black women doctoral students also experience spirit murder because of isolation from others (Berry, 2018). Ongoing racial and ethnic bias against Black women doctoral students perpetuates a lack of belonging and tokenism in predominantly white institutions (Wingfield, 2015). Carroll (2015) suggested the limited number of Black women within academia ends up forcing them into small communities where they must fend for themselves. Ultimately, this isolation affects academic performance, with some Black women being placed on academic probation (Wingfield, 2015) or withdrawing from their programs altogether.

Black women doctoral students face significant barriers in securing positions in higher education after matriculation. In a recent *Inside Higher Ed* article, Zawadi Rucks-Ahidiana (2021) stated, "in 2019, 1,832 Black women received Ph.Ds. Of those, 522 had an academic job placement. Just 2.7 percent of all academic job placements in 2019 were of Black women with Ph.D.s" (para 2). Rucks-Ahidiana highlighted the absence of Black women in higher education also extended to non-tenure track faculty and part-time faculty. Despite the recent emphasis on cultural diversity and inclusion, academia is not enacting its commitment to retaining, advancing, and loving Black women doctoral students who seek to become faculty and administrators. This is particularly true for faculty speaking out against racism and white supremacy (Young & Hines, 2018), including Nikole Hannah-Jones who was initially denied tenure at the University of North Carolina Chapel-Hill. Despite her Pulitzer Prize, Hannah-Jones was denied a position she was qualified for because of push-back from conservatives who categorized her work as propaganda (Robertson, 2021). Love (2019) identified this type of pushback as white rage as a reaction to the prospect of Black advancement.

Impact of Spirit Murder on Black Women's Health

Black women endure gendered racism as a result of spirit murder. Black women experience a disproportionate amount of mental and physical stress (Spates et al., 2020). This increased stress leads to Black women experiencing health challenges at rates not shared by the rest of the US population. These challenges include but are not limited to infant and maternal mortality, cancer, diabetes, high blood pressure, and other diseases (Spates et al., 2020). Additionally, the effects of gendered racism as well as other "isms" (i.e., classism, heterosexism, and ableism) strips Black women of opportunities for equal access to health care (Smith, 2015).

To combat stereotypes and controlling images associated with Black women (i.e., Jezebel, Sapphire, and Mammie; see Collins, 2001), many Black women embody the Strong Black Woman (SBW) trope as a badge of honor (Walker-Barnes, 2017). Though the SBW trope was conceptualized by Black women to resist oppression and emphasize strength and resilience, it has simultaneously limited Black women's ability to speak up concerning health challenges and have those concerns taken seriously by others. Walker-Barnes (2017) asserted,

> many StrongBlackWomen find themselves caught in a cycle of socialization, stress, and distress in which their adherence to the archetype results in poor mental and physical health outcomes, decreased use of health-promoting behaviors, and increased risk of early termination from treatment.
>
> *(p. 46)*

Ultimately, the stress leads to Black women experiencing breakdowns which increase the probability of early death including suicide (Walker-Barnes, 2017).

Black women across all institutions and sectors in society experience these health disparities; pursuing and earning an advanced degree do not protect them from struggles, institutionalized oppression, or gendered racism as Black women. Research conducted utilizing the Gendered Racism Microaggression Scale on Black women in the United States confirms Black women's lived realities despite educational attainment. Of the 231 participants, 62% had earned a graduate degree or higher and reported having significant mental and physical health challenges because of gendered racism (Lewis et al., 2017).

Where Do We Go from Here?

Despite barriers, Black women doctoral students, faculty, and administrators experience, they are still expected to endure the "murdering of their spirits" with patience, finesse, and in nonthreatening ways (Carroll, 2015). This explains the double standard that often befalls Black women in academia, where they are simultaneously disregarded and heralded for their strength. Wingfield (2015) explained some of the dichotomies, "You are a strong Black woman/ you are weak...You don't matter/you do matter...you are professional/you are unprofessional...you are competent/you are incompetent" (p. 83). Drawing on Dillard's framework of Endarkened Feminist Epistemology (EFE), Wingfield suggested because of the subjectivity Black women in academia face, they must "reconcile these dichotomies to develop a strong sense of individual agency to counter racism and sexism" (2015, p. 84).

In *Learning to (Re)member the Things We've Learned to Forget*, Dillard (2012) asked "How do we (re)member as a way of talking back to the power of these seductions, resisting them, and recognizing our own power in the process" (p. 16). Dillard's emphasis on (re)membering as a way forward for Black women not only describes the abuses Black women doctoral students and faculty endure but also offers prescriptive ways to move forward. Dillard (2012) confessed (re)membering it is not easy work.

> Seduction creates powerful sites of amnesia, often masked as nostalgia, colorblindness, or "universal" theories and cultural production that have created very strong frames in the individual and collective cultural memories of systems of education, of societies and nations of the world.
>
> *(p. 17)*

Black women are oftentimes seduced to forget because (re)membering the abuses we have sustained in academia is painful. Thus, the duty of (re)membering necessitates a spiritual consciousness to root us to something that gives us the tenacity to move forward when the pain of (re)membering becomes seemingly unbearable. The hope, as Dillard suggested, lies in the possibility of being full human beings as African peoples, moving beyond DuBois' concept of double consciousness to a "broader vision in which our consciousness as Black people includes analysis of how our minds, bodies, and spirits situate us as individuals within a collective and are known to us through the collective" (p. 18).

Dillard also emphasized EFE's concept of (re)membering to heal ourselves. Sacredness and spirituality are core components of EFE and pivotal in the process of (re)membering. Drawing from the scholarship of Black feminists including Anna Julia Cooper, Alice Walker, and bell hooks, each of whom readily elevated the importance of connectivity to a higher power, Dillard noted the requirement to "bring a spiritual vision and sacred practice to bear" (p. 75) in our work.

Spirituality and sacred practice are both protective factors for Black women in the academy dealing with spirit murder. Dillard (2016) posited, "Our very souls need to honor the wisdom and spirituality of transnational Black women's ways of knowing and being in inquiry" (p. 407). Spirituality is the consciousness and the sacred is the practice of that consciousness. The sacred is practiced through individual and collective rituals. Davis (2008), who like Dillard affirmed the historical and spiritual resources Black women must draw from to push back against our experiences, emphasized how (re)membering her ancestors in a vision helped her finish her dissertation when she was ready to give up,

> I was visited as in a dream by three enslaved Black women. They came to me collectively, but each of them spoke individually. The first woman said. 'Little daughter, you must not give up. You have got to be here to tell our stories. You have been trained to tell the world about us .... Chile, you got to hang on. just fo' a little while longer, it ain't gon' be long now. Whatever you do. dontcha* get turned around, girl. You come too far now.'
>
> *(p. 180)*

Cannon and Morton (2015) discussed the God-consciousness that helps Black women overcome the challenges we face. Historically, Black women in the academy have been made to feel as if we need to leave some of ourselves at the door to be accepted. But when Black women can tap into that God-consciousness, we derive the strength we need to persevere.

> Having conversations about my spirituality in the context of the academy helped me negotiate my spirituality and counter any self-imposed marginalization. Instead of keeping my spirituality private, I used my spirituality as a lens to guide my graduate student work.
>
> *(Cannon & Morton, 2015, p. 148)*

Conclusion

In this chapter, I highlighted how Black women in academia experience spirit murder because of gendered racism and the effect it has on our mental and physical health. Spirituality and sacred practice, as articulated through Dillard's Endarkened Feminist Framework, can deepen our ability to push for abolition in education – in both the K-12 and higher education contexts. Love (2019) emphasized,

> Abolitionist teaching...seeks to resist, agitate, and tear down the educational survival complex through teachers who work in solidarity with their schools' community to achieve incremental changes in their classrooms and schools for students in the present day, while simultaneously freedom dreaming and vigorously creating a vision for what schools will be when the educational survival complex is destroyed.
>
> *(p. 89)*

To ultimately address how (and the extent to which) Black women are marginalized in higher education, we must tackle the roots of spirit murder and dismantle the educational survival context. (Re)membering who we are through grounded sacred practice enables us to dream about what that future will look like and shows us how to get there.

References

Berry, T. R. (2018). *States of grace: Counterstories of Black women in the academy.* Peter Lang.

Brown-Glaude, W. R. (2010). But some of us are brave: Black women faculty transforming the academy. *Signs, 35*(4), 801–809. https://www.jstor.org/stable/10.1086/651035

Cannon, M. A., & Morton, C. H. (2015). God consciousness enacted: Living, moving, and having my being in him. *Western Journal of Black Studies, 39*(2), 147–156. http://search.ebscohost.com.ezp1.lib.umn.edu/login.aspx?direct=true&AuthType=ip,uid&db=aph&AN=109380558&site=ehost-live

Carroll, C. M. (2015). Three's a crowd: The dilemma of the Black woman in higher education. In A. Hull, P. Bell-Scott, & B. Smith (Eds.), *All the women are white, all the Blacks are men, but some of us are brave: Black women's studies* (pp. 115–128). The Feminist Press.

Collins, A. C. (2001). Black women in the academy: An historical overview. In A. L. Green & R. Mabokela (Eds.), *Sisters of the academy: Emergent Black women scholars in higher education* (pp. 29–41). Stylus Publishing.

Collins, P. H. (2019). *Intersectionality as critical social theory.* Duke University Press.

Davis, O. I. (2008). A visitation from the foremothers: Black women's healing through a 'performance of care'—From African Diaspora to the American Academy. *Women's Studies in Communication, 31*(2), 175–185. https://doi.org./10.1080/07491409.2008.10162530

Dillard, C. B. (2012). *Learning to (re)member the things we've learned to forget.* Peter Lang.

Dillard, C. B. (2016). Turning the ships around: A case study of (re)membering as transnational endarkened feminist inquiry and praxis for Black teachers. *American Educational Studies Association, 52*(5), 406–423. https://doi.org/10.1080/00131946.2016.1214916.

Essed, P. (1991). *Understanding everyday racism: An interdisciplinary theory.* Sage Publications.

Generett, G. G., & Cozart, S. (2011/2012). The spirit bears witness: Reflections of two Black women's journey in the academy. *Negro Educational Review, 62/63*(1–4), 141–165, 265. http://iibp.chadwyck.com.ezp2.lib.umn.edu/toc/05481457/62631420112012.htm

Lewis, J. A., Williams, M. G., Peppers, E. J., & Gadson, C. A. (2017). Applying intersectionality to explore the relations between gendered racism and health among Black women. *Journal of Counseling Psychology, 64*(5), 475–486. http://dx.doi.org.ezp1.lib.umn.edu/10.1037/cou0000231

Love, B. (2019). *We want to do more than survive: Abolitionist teaching and the pursuit of educational freedom.* Beacon Press.

Robertson, K. (2021, May 19). Nikole Hannah-Jones denied tenure at University of North Carolina. *New York Times.* https://www.nytimes.com/2021/05/19/business/media/nikole-hannah-jones-unc.html

Rucks-Ahidiana, Z. (2021, July 16). The systemic scarcity of tenured Black women. *Inside Higher Ed.* Retrieved July 30, 2021, from https://www.insidehighered.com/advice/2021/07/16/black-women-face-many-obstacles-their-efforts-win-tenure-opinion

Shadid, K. T. (2015). Eating from the tree of life: An endarkened feminist revelation. In V. E. Evans-Winters & B. Love (Eds.), *Black feminism in education: Black women speak back, up and out* (pp. 61–70). Peter Lang.

Smith, B. (2015). Black women's health: Notes for a course. In A. Hull, P. Bell-Scott, & B. Smith (Eds.), *All the women are white, all the Blacks are men, but some of us are brave: Black women's studies* (pp. 103–114). The Feminist Press.

Spates, K., Evans, N., James, T. A., & Martinez, K. (2020). Gendered racism in the lives of Black women: A qualitative exploration. *Journal of Black Psychology, 46*(8), 583–606. https://doi.org/10.1177/0095798420962257

Spivak, G. C. (1988). Can the subaltern speak? In C. Nelson & L. Grossberg (Eds.), *Marxism and the interpretation of culture.* University of Illinois Press.

Walker Barnes, C. (2017). When the bough breaks: The strong black woman and the embodiment of stress. In S. Y. Evans, K. Bell, & N. K. Burton (Eds.), *Black women's mental health: Balancing strength and vulnerability* (pp. 43–56). SUNY Press.

Williams, P. (1987). Spirit-murdering the messenger: The discourse of fingerpointing as the law's response to racism. *University of Miami Law Review, 42*(1), 127–158. https://heinonline.org/HOL/P?h=hein.journals/umialr42&i=137

Wingfield, T. T. (2015). (Her)story: The evolution of dual identity as an emerging Black female scholar. In V. E. Evans-Winters & B. L. Love (Eds.), *Black feminism in education: Black women speak back, up, and out* (pp. 81–92). Peter Lang.

Woods, R. L. (2001). Invisible women: The experiences of Black female doctoral students at the University of Michigan. In A. L. Green & R. Mabokela (Eds.), *Sisters of the academy: Emergent Black women scholars in higher education* (pp. 105–115). Stylus Publishing.

Young, J. L., & Hines, D. E. (2018). Killing my spirit, renewing my soul: Black female professors' critical reflections on spirit killings while teaching. *Women, Gender, and Families of Color, 6*(1), 18–25. https://www.muse.jhu.edu/article/698585

11

SISTA CIRCLES WITH SISTUH SCHOLARS

Socializing Black Women Doctoral Students

Tiffany J. Davis and April L. Peters

Diversifying the professoriate remains a critical task as the academy strives to reflect a more racially diverse nation. Despite Black women's greater access to and success in postsecondary education, they remain woefully underrepresented among full-time faculty, comprising just 3% of all full-time faculty at degree-granting institutions (National Center for Education Statistics, 2020). Given these challenges of expanding professional and academic opportunities for Black women, it is critical to understand and interrogate the pipeline to the professoriate; thus, the importance of exploring Black women's doctoral experiences is central.

In this chapter, we share an example of how Black feminist epistemologies (BFEs) can be interwoven with academic praxis. To help readers understand our impetus in creating the SistUH Scholar Initiative, we begin by articulating our personal journeys into the professoriate. We then provide an overview of SistUH Scholars and outline the BFEs that inform the initiative. We conclude by providing some lessons learned and strategies to help readers apply BFEs within praxis.

Tiffany's Journey into the Professoriate

I am a student affairs educator by training, thus when I began my doctoral program at The University of Georgia, I had executive-level administrative aspirations. My professional experiences until then focused on supporting the postsecondary transition and success of historically underserved student populations, namely, racially/ethnically minoritized, first-generation, and low-income students. As a Black woman professional engaged in diversity work, I navigated toxic work cultures, confronted racist and sexist behavior, and

DOI: 10.4324/9781003184867-13

experienced a lack of professional role models and mentors with similar racial and gender identities. Yet, I wanted to be at the table where decisions were being made and as a Black woman, I was sure the Ph.D. would afford me the *legitimacy* I needed for an invitation to the table to be a key decision-maker.

I chose a doctoral program that would provide a strong administrative focus yet had an intentional approach to expanding students' applied research and teaching capacity because I wanted there not to be any room for questioning my expertise and training. For example, we were required to serve as master's level teaching assistants and participate in collaborative research teams throughout our time in the program to demystify the process of research and develop strong methodological skills. My research team focused on student success initiatives and staff experiences at historically Black colleges and universities. I gravitated to qualitative research methodology; its focus on understanding experience, illuminating stories, and developing theory resonated with me. Therefore, I chose to complement my Ph.D. with a graduate certificate in Interdisciplinary Qualitative Research which required a foundational course that introduced theoretical frameworks and emphasized their importance in anchoring research studies. Yet, I learned BFEs outside of my formal curriculum. Having earned a post-master's graduate certificate in organizational behavior and change in addition to my master's degree in college student personnel, student development, person–environment, and organizational theory comprised my theoretical toolkit. I learned about BFEs through collaborative research opportunities with other Black women scholars and exposure to professional conferences, such as Association for the Study of Higher Education (ASHE) and American Educational Research Association. In learning these epistemologies, they not only reflected my lived experience, but also served as the conduit for my understanding of how these epistemologies can be used in transformative ways to explore important questions central for the thriving, advocacy, and liberation of Black women in the academy – personal and research interests and commitments that deepened during my time as a doctoral student.

I just completed my ninth year in the academy on the non-tenure track. I did not plan for an academic career, and I was not mentored into the role. I do believe, however, I had key socialization experiences that contributed to my being prepared for the role, albeit identity neutral to a fault. Thus, as a faculty member, advisor, and mentor, I invested in ensuring Black doctoral women are provided spaces that acknowledge their full, authentic selves and allow them to be appropriately socialized for the professoriate.

April's Journey into the Professoriate

I began my career as a teacher. I was alternatively certified and assigned a "mentor," who only had one year of teaching experience under her belt when she was assigned to mentor me. While we became good friends, I did not receive any significant mentoring in my tenure as a teacher. My journey took me to different positions as an educator as well as through a Ph.D. program, where I focused on the intersecting experiences of race and gender for an early career African American woman principal. In my doctoral program, I had the opportunity to develop a cognate area based on my interest. As a result, I took classes in several areas outside of the college (as was required) and culled together a cognate that I termed Black Women's Studies. In classes in African American/African Studies, Sociology, and Women's Studies, I encountered BFEs. This provided me with validation and space to understand myself and my research interests. I was able to engage in readings that were at once eye-opening and seemed to speak to and for me from the depths of my soul.

Subsequently, I became a high school principal. This experience crystallized the research I read about Black women school leaders in many ways. I experienced the ways my intersecting identities impacted my leadership practice even when I was not initially aware of it. For instance, I was keenly aware of the intersection of race and gender, but I was a young principal, and as a result, I became aware of the intersection of age along with race and gender in the role of principal. Eventually, I left K-12 for a career in academia. Again, for me, the experience of mentoring was interesting, and often, challenging. I had a formal mentoring committee to support me through tenure and promotion. However, that committee was reconstituted several times (of necessity) and ultimately, I had to find mentoring in other spaces. I remember a dear mentor saying to me once, "you are mentoring your mentors." My initial years in academia were an assortment of professional accomplishments, racial microaggressions, and outright racism intersected with sexism. I considered leaving the profession on many occasions and at one point received a very nice offer to leave and become a consultant. Ultimately, I remained and took a more agentic outlook on my career, by changing institutions, running for president of our national organization, and taking on several leadership positions at my new institution.

In addition to these things, I also cultivated a village of like-minded Black women academicians, many of whom do similar research. We have supported one another, talked each other off the ledge, advised each other, written letters of recommendation, fellowshipped together at conferences, roomed together at conferences, presented together, provided each other insight, and published together. Without my village, my trajectory in the professoriate would be different.

As a result of this corpus of experiences, I dedicated not only my research to mentoring and support of early career Black women but also my efforts. In addition to the SistUH Scholar program, I also informally mentor several pre-tenure women of color faculty across the country. I believe mentoring should be deliberate and so in each case, I have approached potential mentees and asked them if they wanted/needed some support. My driving philosophy has been to offer "the me I needed" to Black women as they journey through the challenges of academia.

The SistUH Scholar Initiative

Our trajectories into the academy reveal our interconnected realities related to insufficient mentorship and multiple oppressions due to our salient identities as Black women, as well as our synergistic commitments to supporting the socialization of Black women into the professoriate. Thus, the SistUH Scholar Initiative (Davis et al., 2022) was developed to serve as a culturally relevant space for Black doctoral women to support their success in the graduate program, provide mentoring and co-mentoring opportunities, and socialize them toward careers in the professoriate. As the only two Black faculty members within our educational leadership department that overwhelmingly enrolls students of color and had a critical mass of Black women doctoral students, we knew we wanted to take a more engaged approach.

To begin, the SistUH Scholar Initiative was simultaneously a grassroots initiative – in response to needs articulated by Black doctoral women in the department – and our intentional approach to group mentoring and socialization. Furthermore, SistUH Scholar assisted us in achieving alignment between our scholarly and service commitments. In planning conversations, we were clear about the core inclusions and key outcomes of the pilot program: (a) we wanted to provide a consistent space for authentic dialogue, mentoring, and co-mentoring to take place through monthly gatherings; (b) we wanted to explicitly frame this experience through understanding Black women's experience and positionality through a scholarly book club; (c) we wanted to provide opportunities for deeper processing of the monthly topics through reflective diary entries; and (d) we wanted to enhance participant's sense of *scholarhood* (Porter et al., 2018) through collaborative writing and publishing opportunities.

In sharing an overview of SistUH Scholar, we will also intertwine the Black Feminist Epistemologies (BFEs) that informed our program design, specifically Crenshaw's (1988, 1991) Intersectionality, Collins' (1989) Black Feminist Thought, and Dillard's (2000) Endarkened Feminist Epistemology. In this next section, we describe such epistemologies and then discuss how they are applicable to our program components: sista circles, scholarly book club, reflective diaries, and collaborative writing and publishing opportunities.

Crenshaw's Intersectionality

Legal scholar Kimberlé Crenshaw (1988, 1991) coined the term intersectionality to address the "inadequacy of antidiscrimination law to address employment barriers and undo racism and sexism that directly influenced Black women in particular" (Agosto & Roland, 2018, p. 258). Influenced by both the tenets of Critical Race Theory (Bell, 1995) and Black Feminist Thought (Collins, 1989), Crenshaw described the multiplicative negative impact of racism, sexism (and other forms of oppression) experienced by Black women. Intersectionality has been applied as a lens to understand the experiences of Black women in many fields (Moorosi et al., 2018), including postsecondary education. Intersectionality provides a space for Black women that is neglected in white, Western feminism, and in anti-racism (Davis, 2008; Jordan-Zachery, 2007).

Moreover, it not only provides a conceptual tool to understand Black women's experiences but also serves as a means of liberation (Jordan-Zachary, 2007). Intersectionality acknowledges the multiplicative experiences of oppression of race and gender, but also the intersections of social class, sexual orientation, and other facets of identity that are marginalized.

"In essence, intersectionality articulates a politics of survival for Black women" (Jordan-Zachary, 2007, p. 256). Further, using intersectionality provides researchers an epistemological means to both examine the group and the individual and simultaneously honor the uniqueness of both (Witherspoon & Arnold, 2010). This concept is therefore central to the epistemological understanding of Black women's experiences.

Collins' Black Feminist Thought

Overlapping intersectionality as a methodological and epistemological tool for understanding Black women's lived experiences is BFE. Jean-Marie (2004) informed, "Black women's Afrocentric epistemology deconstructs dominant ideologies that justify, support, and rationalize the interests of those in power" (p. 44).

Patricia Hill Collins (1989) developed BFT to explain how Black women's ways of knowing are strongly connected to their spirituality and/or activism (Collins, 1989; Peters & Nash, 2021). BFT articulates both an Afrocentric consciousness and a feminist standpoint (Collins, 1989). Collins (1989) posited, "since Black women have access to both the Afrocentric and the feminist standpoints, and alternative epistemology used to rearticulate a Black women's standpoint reflects elements of both traditions" (p. 756).

This perspective is specifically centered on the experiences of being both Black and woman. Peters and Nash (2021) asserted,

> BFT acknowledges Black women's activism is characterized by both a struggle for group survival – Black women's efforts to challenge oppression; and a struggle for institutional transformation – Black women's large-scale efforts to unite with communities and institutions to engage in systemic change.
>
> *(p. 9)*

The following four tenets provide an understanding of the contours of BFT.

Concrete Experience as a Criterion of Meaning. The first tenet of BFT is concrete experience as a criterion of meaning. Black women make meaning from their lived experiences. These experiences are reflective of their intersectional experiences of race, gender, and class marginalization. They use these experiences to theorize and make meaning of their lives. They also provide Black women with credibility for making knowledge claims (Collins, 1989). Black women often prefer their own knowledge claims grounded in concrete experience over mastery of "white masculinist epistemologies" (Collins, 1989, p. 760).

Use of Dialogue in Assessing Knowledge Claims. The second tenet of Black Feminist Thought is the use of dialogue. Collins (1989) indicated knowledge is validated through connectedness and dialogue. Several aspects of African American culture reveal the importance of dialogue. The oral tradition of storytelling and passing along history, amplified during slavery, connects culturally to the discourse of dialogue. Further, dialogue is manifest through the call and response "discourse mode" (Collins, 1989, p. 763). Other manifestations of the use of dialogue occur with storytelling. Collins (1989) elucidated "women tend to ground the epistemological premises in the metaphors suggesting speaking and listening" (p. 765).

Ethic of caring. The concept of care has been written about widely across research focused on women (Bass, 2009; Collins, 1989; Noddings, 1984; Sernak, 2004; Witherspoon & Arnold, 2010). Noddings' (1984) work on care informs us that it is "relational, reciprocal, situated, and requiring commitment" (Sernak, 2004, p. 74). Noddings further suggested that caring has cultural implications. Black women's invocation of an ethic of caring evolves from a history of kinship networks which were "adapted from the African ethos, serving to enable enslaved communities to cope with the exploitation and oppression of slavery" (Sernak, 2004, p. 78). Post slavery, Black women continued kinship networks developed at churches, women's organizations, Civil Rights organizations, and other activist activities. From their caregiving, they engaged in mothering and other mothering to become leaders in their communities (Collins, 1989; Sernak, 2004).

Ethic of Personal Accountability. The final tenet of Black Feminist Thought is an ethic of personal accountability. This tenet suggests that people must be accountable for their knowledge claims. In other words, Black women's knowledge production emanates from personal experiences. Further, Black women are expected to support the validity of their claims based on personal responsibility.

Dillard's Endarkened Feminist Epistemology

Endarkened Feminist Epistemology developed by Dillard (2000) is influenced by the strengths of various feminist and spiritual frameworks (Colompos-Tohtsonie et al., 2020; Dillard, 2000; McClish-Boyd & Bhattacharya, 2021; Wright, 2003). Dillard (2000) employed the term Endarkened Feminist Epistemology to contrast the common feminist term enlightened, which means new insight, and to create a new form of articulating new feminist insights (Dillard, 2000; McClish-Boyd & Bhattacharya, 2021). The six contours of Endarkened Feminist Epistemology are articulated below.

Self-definition forms one's participation and responsibility to one's community. This means that all views conveyed, and actions implemented within an educational context arise from personally and culturally defined set of beliefs that render the researcher responsible to the members and well-being of the community from which the definitions arise (Dillard, 2000).

Research is both an intellectual and a spiritual pursuit, a pursuit of purpose. Drawing on a spiritual tradition, the concern is not just an intellectual pursuit, the production of knowledge, but also with uncovering and constructing truth as the fabric of everyday life (Dillard, 2000).

Only within the context of community does the individual appear and, through *dialogue*, continue to become. This assumption means that dialogue is important in conducting research and assessing knowledge. The value in sharing unspoken experiences and being connected to be understood and finding the truth (Dillard, 2000).

Concrete experiences within everyday life form the criterion of meaning, the matrix of meaning-making. The experiences and acts of African Americans or people of color that occur in everyday life are critical to make sense of actions, expressions, experiences, and community life are studied. At the same time, attempting to understand and explain the wisdom contained in those meanings. Thus, knowledge and wisdom are two components of knowing that are important for endarkened feminist epistemology (Dillard, 2000).

Knowing and research extend both historically in time and outward to the world; to approach them otherwise is to diminish their cultural and empirical meaningfulness. Endarkened feminist epistemology acknowledges and works against the absent presence of women of color from the development of rules which historically guided educational research, the system of knowledge production within higher education, and the meanings of the legitimacy of the research process (Dillard, 2000).

Power relations, manifest as racism, sexism, homophobia, etc., structure gender, race, and other identity relations within research. Endarkened Feminist Epistemology is vigilant and persistent to understand and experience the realities of Black women by uncovering the confluence of multiple identities (Dillard, 2000).

In short, each epistemological paradigm informs and contributes to a deeper understanding of Black women's lived experiences. Intersectionality (Crenshaw, 1988, 1991) examines the power dynamics that produce injustice, while Endarkened Feminist Epistemology (Dillard, 2000) examines the experiences of Black women as they interact or overlap without calling white male supremacy as the dominate force driving the lived experiences (Dillard, 2000; Haynes et al., 2020). Endarkened Feminist Epistemology articulates the realities of

Black women within the historical and current context of oppression (Dillard, 2000). Black Feminist Thought (Collins, 1989) and Endarkened Feminist Epistemology continue to address systems of oppression (Dillard, 2000; Jacobs, 2019). Yet, the difference is the focus of the participant within the study, the community versus the individual. Black Feminist Thought (Collins, 1989) provides a framework for investigating the ways race, class, and gender are created and experienced by communities, involving both men and women (Jacobs, 2019), while Endarkened Feminist Epistemology is grounded in individual experiences (Dillard, 2000).

Sista Circles

Collins' (1989) Black Feminist Thought was used to inform the adoption of sista circle methodology (Johnson, 2015) as an avenue to organize monthly gatherings that allowed the Black doctoral women to express their journeys through graduate school and aspirations toward the professoriate with other Black women as a source of bonding and empowerment. In outlining a history of sista circles, Johnson (2015) wrote,

> As traditionally defined, sista circles are support groups formed among Black women of the same community, profession, or organization that build upon friendships or networks already existing between Black women. Sista circles were the foundation of the Black women's club movement of the late 1800s. During this era, Black women transformed sista circles into formalized Black women's clubs. Black women's clubs provided a space for Black women to discuss the issues that impacted them and ways to uplift the Black race.
>
> *(p. 44)*

An emerging qualitative method, sista circle methodology exists at the nexus of a mentoring support group and a research methodology, thereby legitimizing mentoring as research. Our monthly sista circles were grounded in dialogue and we sought to explore and understand our individual and common racialized and gendered experiences of academia through discussions and activities centered around research, publication, the dissertation process, doctoral program completion benchmarks, career aspirations, and professional development pertinent to faculty position acquisition. "Sista circles provide a unique support for Black women whose shared experiences enable conversations marked by the offering of advice and wisdom" (Johnson, 2015, p. 45). We served as primary facilitators of the group, posing questions, and encouraging participation. During our monthly sessions, we also celebrated each other's milestones and professional achievements.

Scholarly Book Club

While our purpose was to honor the individual experience of our Black women doctoral students, BFEs guide us to consider and understand the experiences of Black women broadly and connect with a larger communal experience. Thus, we decided to engage in a scholarly book study of Melissa Harris-Perry's (2013) *Sister Citizen: Shame, Stereotypes, and Black Women in America* to interrogate Black women's positioning in society and how that related to our experiences in the academy. We provided copies of the book to each woman, set up a summer reading schedule, and provided biweekly discussion forum threads that allowed each of us to reflect on the confluence of our multiple identities. For example, we posed, "What are some of the distorted images, stereotypes, or expectations that you acknowledge have influenced your life and ability to 'stand straight despite the crooked world' (p. 32) in which you live? How have you managed to 'stand straight'?" and "MHP argues the 'internal, psychological, emotional, and personal experiences of Black women are inherently political' (p. 5). Do you agree? How does this show up in your life? How does this manifest within doctoral education?" We began these reflections in the discussion forums and continued them within our sista circles.

Reflective Diaries

Diary methods of data generation allow researchers to gain longer and more regular insight into participants' lived experiences. In writing diaries, the women will have more autonomy to share their experiences, stories, and perspectives in ways that are authentic for them (Meth, 2003). We asked the women to keep a diary outside of these meetings to help encourage deeper reflection on their scholarly and professional identity journeys outside of our sista circles. We provided structured prompts for the women that complemented the topic of our circles and asked the women to provide their thoughts, feelings, and examples of critical experiences and memories. For example, "Describe an experience you have had as a doctoral student where your intersecting identities were salient for you. What happened? How did you respond? What are your reflections on this incident since then?" and "There is ample research about the impact of "Imposter Syndrome." Have you experienced this? How has this influenced your notions of the self as a scholar? What have you done to address "Imposter Syndrome?"

Collaborative Writing and Publishing Opportunities

BFEs confirm that the system of knowledge production within higher education marginalizes the voices and experiences of women of color; therefore, we wanted to ensure that our experience together would be captured and contribute to the extant literature related to Black women's experience in the academy. Our primary research questions included: (1) How do Black women make sense of their scholarly and professional identities during doctoral education? and (2) How do Black women doctoral students describe their supports and barriers in negotiating their scholarly and professional identities?

The SistUH Scholar data collection occurred between December 2018 and May 2020 with nine participants and generated nine sista circles session transcriptions, eight participant diary entries, and a six-week scholarly book club discussion forum. In an upcoming book chapter (Davis et al., 2022), we co-authored first-person narratives alongside two SistUH Scholar participants related to mentoring experiences in the academy and how this group helped us to retain each other.

Applying Black Feminist Epistemologies: Lessons Learned

Our research on Black women doctoral students provided several insights. The sista circle methodology (Johnson, 2015) provided safety in the discussions where the researchers and participants shared lived experiences of the intersectionality of race and gender and other identity planes, researchers provided mentoring and support to the participants, and every member of the circle had a voice – an opportunity and an expectation to participate. This methodology, grounded in BFEs, provided the researchers an opportunity to share and learn from the participants. As a result, we identified two key "learnings" related to the importance of articulating an intersectional Black identity and the desire for more guest facilitators.

Importance of Articulating an Intersectional Black Identity

Identity is complex and research has illuminated the power of race and gender concordance in mentoring relationships (Bertrand Jones et al., 2013; Davis et al., 2022; Pope & Edwards, 2016). "The act of sharing one's story and drawing a connection to other Black women who have similar experiences is powerful and can aid the understanding of the many challenges people face" (Clemons, 2019, p. 13). Therefore, the group make-up should be done thoughtfully and should be balanced with inclusivity. Some individuals have a different relationship with Blackness than others, so selection criteria matter. While we reject Black women as a monolith, we also recognize the value of having Black women who can speak to and understand their lived experiences considering their multiple oppressions. A major learning of this research is that campus structures are racist and exclusionary. The sister circle discussions often focused on the historical structures that pre-existed Black women's opportunities to enroll in postsecondary education. Further, many of the supports in place tend to reify the demographics of students and faculty. Our sista circle conversation was not only a means to focus on our common and overlapping epistemological perspectives, but also a space of resistance and support.

More Guest Facilitators

Our in-person monthly sista circles transitioned to online gatherings given the COVID-19 pandemic. However, this afforded us the opportunity to ask Black women PhDs outside of UH to join us in dialogue with the women via Zoom conferencing. By inviting diverse Black women to share space with the Black doctoral women, this increases the likelihood of interacting with and learning from Black women with other, and possibly dissimilar, multiple identities.

Conclusion

The creation of the SistUH circle program utilized the sister circle methodology and this was a unique and special means of providing support to a vulnerable student population BY a vulnerable faculty population. Our grounding in BFEs provided a foundation for our use of the sista circle methodology (Johnson, 2015), including the various components of the SistUH Scholars program. We were most interested in providing structured support and mentoring to Black women doctoral students that honored our culture, intersecting identities, lived experiences, and ways of knowing. We accomplished this by acknowledging and simultaneously learning about our intersecting identities as well as connecting explicitly and implicitly to the tenets of Intersectionality (Crenshaw, 1998, 1991), Black Feminist Thought (Collins, 1989), and Endarkened Feminist Epistemologies (Dillard, 2000). BFEs articulate ways of knowing for Black women grounded in lived experiences, personal accountability, the seamlessness of research and personal/spiritual experiences, and the strength of caring for others. The SistUH Scholars program participants embraced these tenets by sista circle discussions which focused on the personal, professional, spiritual, and research interests of group members; a scholarly book study that provided the space to discuss the intersecting identities of race and gender (as well as other identity planes); the reflective diaries which provided a space to for participants to speak to their "scholarhood," as well as the ways in which they experienced their intersecting identities; and research collaboration which provided (and continues to provide) a space to explore and reflect upon the totality of our common experience.

References

Agosto, V., & Roland, E. (2018). Intersectionality and educational leadership: A critical review. *Review of Research in Education, 42*(1), 255–285. https://doi.org/10.3102/0091732X18762433

Bass, L. (2009). Fostering an ethic of care in leadership: A conversation with five African American women. *Advances in Developing Human Resources, 11*, 619–632.

Bell, D. (1995). *Who's afraid of critical race theory?* [Lecture essay]. https://heinonline.org/HOL/LandingPage?handle=hein.journals/unilllr1995&div=40&id=&page=

Bertrand Jones, T., Wilder, J., & Osborne-Lampkin, L. (2013). Employing a Black feminist approach to doctoral advising: Preparing Black women for the professoriate. *The Journal of Negro Education, 82*(3), 326–338.

Clemons, K. M. (2019). Black feminist thought and qualitative research in education. *Oxford Research Encyclopedia of Education*. https://doi.org/10.1093/acrefore/9780190264093.013.1194

Collins, P. H. (1989). The social construction of Black Feminist Thought. *Signs: Journal of Women in Culture and Society, 14*(4), 745–773.

Colompos-Tohtsonie, M. T., Walter, S. L., Avila, K., & Militz-Frielink, S. (2020). Exploring the heartbeat of the Black family: Observations through the lens of endarkened epistemology. *Black History Bulletin, 83*(2), 19–29.

Crenshaw, K. (1991). Mapping the margins: Intersectionality, identity politics, and violence against Women of Color. *Stanford Law Review, 43*(6), 1241–1299.

Crenshaw, K. W. (1988). Race, reform, and retrenchment: Transformation and legitimation in antidiscrimination law. *Harvard Law Review, 101*, 1331–1387.

Davis, K. (2008). Intersectionality as buzzword: A sociology of science perspective on what makes a feminist theory successful. *Feminist Theory, 9*, 67–85.

Davis, T. J., Peters, A. L., White, C. L., & Wilson, M. S. (2022). SistUH Scholars: Black women faculty-doctoral student mentoring relationships. In B. T. Kelly and S. Fries-Britt (Eds.), *Building mentorship networks to support Black women: A guide to succeeding in the academy*. Routledge.

Dillard, C. B. (2000). The substance of things hoped for, the evidence of things not seen: Examining an endarkened feminist epistemology in educational research and leadership. *International Journal of Qualitative Studies in Education, 13*(6), 661–681. https://doi.org/10.1080/09518390050211565

Harris Perry, M. V. (2013). *Sister citizen: Shame, stereotypes, and Black women in America*. Yale University Press.

Haynes, C., Joseph, N. M., Patton, L. D., Stewart, S., & Allen, E. L. (2020). Toward an understanding of Intersectionality methodology: A 30-year literature synthesis of Black women's experiences in higher education. *Review of Educational Research, 90*(6), 751–787.

Jacobs, F. (2019). Black feminism and radical planning: New directions for disaster planning research. *Planning Theory, 18*(1), 24–39.

Jean-Marie, G. (2004). Black women administrators in historically Black institutions: Social justice project rooted in community. *Journal of Women in Educational Leadership, 2*(1), 39–63.

Johnson, L. S. (2015). *Using sista circles to examine the professional experience of contemporary Black women teachers in schools: A collective story about school culture and support* [Unpublished doctoral dissertation]. University of Georgia.

Jordan-Zachery, J. S. (2007). Am I a Black woman or a woman who is Black? A few thoughts on the meaning of intersectionality. *Politics and Gender, 3*(2), 254–263.

McClish-Boyd, K., & Bhattacharya, K. (2021). Endarkened narrative inquiry: a methodological framework constructed through improvisations. *International Journal of Qualitative Studies in Education, 34*(6), 534–548. https://doi.org/10.1080/09518398.2021.1871981

Meth, P. (2003). Entries and omissions: Using solicited diaries in geographical research. *Royal Geographical Society, 32*(2), 195–205. https://doi.org/10.1111/1475-4762.00263

Moorosi, P., Fuller, K., & Reilly, E. (2018). Leadership and intersectionality: Constructions of successful leadership among black women school principals in three different contexts. *Management in Education, 32*(4), 152–159. https://doi.org/10.1177/0892020618791006

National Center for Education Statistics. (2020). *Characteristics of postsecondary faculty.* U. S. Department of Education. https://nces.ed.gov/fastfacts/display.asp?id=61

Noddings, N. (1984). *Caring: A feminine approach to ethics and moral education.* University of California Press.

Peters, A. L., & Nash, A. M. (2021). I'm Every Woman: Advancing the Intersectional Leadership of Black Women School Leaders as Anti-Racist Praxis. *Journal of School Leadership, 31*(1–2), 7–28.

Pope, E. C., & Edwards, K. T. (2016). Curriculum homeplacing as complicated conversation: (Re)narrating the mentoring of Black women doctoral students. *Gender & Education, 28*(6), 769–785. https://doi.org/10.1080/09540253.2016.1221898

Porter, C. J., Davis, T. J., & Boss, G. J. (2018, December 13). My sister's keeper: Advancing scholarship and sustaining one another through an academic writing (life) group. *Medium – National Center for Institutional Diversity.*

Sernak, K. S. (2004). Slaves no more: The caring power of African-American female leaders. *Scholar Practitioner Quarterly, 2*(3), 71–97.

Witherspoon, N., & Arnold, B. M. (2010). Pastoral care: Notions of caring and the Black female principal. *The Journal of Negro Education, 79*(3), 220–232.

Wright, H. K. (2003). An endarkened feminist epistemology? Identity, difference, and the politics of representation in educational research. *International Journal of Qualitative Studies in Education, 16*(2), 197–214. https://doi.org/10.1080/0951839032000060626

SECTION III

Black Feminist Praxis Enacted

Journeying Toward Reappointment, Tenure, and Promotion

12

#BLACKINTHEIVORY

Utilizing Twitter to Explore Black Womxn's Experiences in the Academy

Christina Wright Fields and Katrina M. Overby

As Black womxn activist scholars ourselves, we engage in a form of resistance by making our experiences visible. In this chapter, we explore how Black womxn engaged in hashtag activism or "discursive protest on social media united through a hash tagged word" (Yang, 2016, p. 13). We explored narrative agency to interrogate how these comments and retweets associated with a specific hashtag represented Black womxn's numerous personal stories and lived experiences.

As such, we create spaces to share our truths to illuminate the prevalence of racism and sexism in the academy. We build upon the foundation of many Black womxn scholar–activists (e.g., Sojourner Truth, Ida B. Wells, and Ana Julia Cooper) who unapologetically centered Black womxn's lives, epistemologies, and ontologies within their praxis for survival and liberation. Specifically, we root our interpretations and articulations of our lived experiences through a Black feminist theoretical lens. Evans-Winters (2019) asserted in her book *Black Feminism in Qualitative Inquiry: A Mosaic for Writing Our Daughter's Body*:

> Black Feminism is a critical social theory born out of the lived experiences and struggles of Black women living at the intersections of race, class, and gender oppression. Indubitably, Black feminism as a tradition of Black women's intellectual thought is devalued and marginalized in qualitative methods courses and textbooks. Conversely, White men scholars are apotheosized as founders of qualitative inquiry in general and White women as "doers" of feminist qualitative research.
>
> *(p. 17)*

DOI: 10.4324/9781003184867-15

To that end, we claim stake in this space as "doers" of Black feminist intellectual qualitative knowledge production and push back against the marginalization of our voices. We lean on our sister-scholar Evans-Winters (2019), who stated,

> Moreover, Black feminism as a standpoint theory, also offers original suppositions into how Black women are able to confront the social world order, while being simultaneously vulnerable and resilient in the face of systematic inequality, including marginalization in the academy.
>
> *(p. 18)*

We commune with other Black womxn intellectuals who do the work of dismantling systemic racism built into the fabric of the ivory tower while demystifying our experiences in the academy.

Black girls and womxn are often positioned uniquely as they are constantly negotiating issues of race and gender in a society primarily dominated by whiteness. Historically, the academy has worked to silence Black voices (hooks, 1989), challenge or refute our knowledge or scholarship (Collins, 2000), and make it burdensome to be accepted, respected, and recognized (Collins, 2001). As Black womxn, we understand the importance of speaking and sharing our knowledge, particularly in spaces where we were never meant to succeed or survive. We continue Collins' (2000) work of developing "a distinctive Black women's standpoint...by utilizing alternative ways of producing and validating knowledge"' in the academy (p. 252). By acknowledging Black womxn's experiences as valuable representations of knowledge, we share our narratives to describe how we influence systemic and institutional change for and alongside Black womxn.

Background of Found Poems

We used poetry to describe and articulate our experiences with navigating predominantly white institutional spaces. We shared our narratives by creating a found poem. Found poems utilize words or phrases from an existing text (i.e., songs, articles, poems, and social media) (Butler-Kisber, 2020). More specifically, we used a pure found poem approach, in which the words of the specific text remained as they appeared in the hashtags. As poets, we collectively decided where to indicate line breaks in our found poem. Our poem, Sawubona—I SEE You, allowed us to "create new self-definitions that validate a Black womxn's standpoint" by disrupting the assumptions and notions of what it is to be a Black womxn in the academy (Collins, 1989, p. 750). We authentically interrogate our socialization into and through the academy, by engaging readers with our differing experiences, interpretations, and reactions with being proud Black womxn educators and activist scholars (via the found poem).

Exploring Narrative Agency through #BlackInTheIvory

To create our found poem, we examined the hashtag #BlackInTheIvory. Social media provides Black womxn a platform to share their narratives and develop a community wherein Black womxn can connect. Utilizing these platforms allows Black womxn to share their complexity of identity while affirming their lived experiences unapologetically and authentically with one another, thus validating their ways of knowing. We engaged in the narrative agency to understand how Black womxn make use of social media as a transformative and liberatory space to give voice to their personal narratives. Yang (2016) described a narrative agency in hashtag activism as "the capacity to create stories on social media by using hashtags in a way that is collective and recognized by the public" (p. 14). As such, the stories accumulated using #BlackInTheIvory illustrated a collective identity unique to Black womxn in the academy, thus in need of further exploration and consideration.

The #BlackInTheIvory movement has been active since its inception on June 6, 2020. Created by faculty member Dr. Shardé M. Davis and doctoral student Joy Woods, the platform was designed to provide a countering space for Black academics to share their lived experiences in the academy as they tackle anti-racist practices in predominately white spaces. Similar to other hashtag conversations, such as #ShutDownSTEM and #ScholarStrike, the hashtag followed national conversations about combating anti-Black racism and white privilege in higher education.

#BlackInTheIvory continues to unearth the injustices and challenges via macro and microaggressions, faced daily by Black academics and make them visible for many non-Black scholars. This hashtag movement was integral in starting conversations among colleagues and administrators about their institutional practices. We selected #BlackInTheIvory as our text for the found poem because these tweets are personal narratives, and we intentionally center and validate the lived experiences, stories, and perceptions of Black womxn in the academy. Evans-Winters (2019) explained, "Black women as researchers, and the researched, bring our lived realities into the research project" (p. 17). #BlackInTheIvory resonated with us as we had countless discussions following this moment among ourselves and other Black scholars due to the similar obstacles, barriers, and challenges we collectively encountered as we climbed the academic ladder. As qualitative researchers, we intentionally center the voices and narratives of Black womxn scholars, as we are actively challenging institutions to confront their racist and oppressive practices more than ever in recent years.

Our qualitative approach began as we selected a three-day window (June 6–8, 2020), the first three days of the hashtag, and we randomly selected tweets from any public profile that contained the hashtag on Twitter. The tweets we reviewed included personal accounts from Black womxn in academia (professors and graduate students) and their calls to action to acknowledge and dismantle racist white supremacist ideologies and structures within higher education institutions. The tweets were a combination of pictures and words. As we read multiple tweets (see Table 12.1), we noticed many Black womxn faced both blatant and covert racism and sexism in the academy; they shared how they were subjected to alienation, cultural insensitivity, tokenism, and being labeled as "troublemakers." As these womxn reckoned with the "weight of both White invisibility and Black visibility" they were perceived as expendable leaving many of them to be unacknowledged, unrewarded, underfunded, and unnoticed (Harley, 2007, p. 23). Next, we intentionally reflected and interrogated how key phrases and words from the #BlackintheIvory tweets correlated to our own personal and collective stories and lived experiences (i.e., encounters with institutional racism, microaggressions, bias, and oppression) within the academy.

TABLE 12.1 Sample of Tweets from #BlackintheIvory June 6–8, 2020

Tweet	Handle
I don't want a seat at a table that was never meant for me. I want to be a part of building a new table.	@AprilSwodobaMD
This #BlackintheIvory is not just a Twitter trend. These are real stories, and they are affecting our livelihoods. We are undervalued and overlooked if we are let in at all.	@jenniferejoness
So much anti-blackness in academia revolves around only admitting and promoting "the least threatening Black" or "the right kind of Black"—the tokens.	@alwaystheself
Being "that Black girl in that lab" yet having to introduce yourself to people five separate times before they remember who you are. Hyper-visible yet invisible.	@singingshoes21
Dear Academia, Recognize: POC profs "are asked by institutions, colleagues and peers to do work that is uncompensated, unacknowledged and unrewarded. It's been called the Black tax or brown tax." E.g., Diversity committees, mentoring, etc.	@ayanaeliza
Representation matters. Period.	@DrNeblett
We are calling for radical change in systems all across this country, that includes the system of the academy. If #BlackintheIvory has proven nothing else, it has illustrated that this is a SYSTEM wide problem. And no place is safe. Not a one.	@smileitsjoy
If you're white & are incredibly uncomfortable w/ reading, seeing, and hearing our stories of racism and anti-Blackness via #BlackintheIvory Imagine feeling like that every day of your life. Y'all don't even know the half of it. Don't turn away & forget. Sit with it & do better.	@DrShardeDavis

Having brilliant Black mentees decide NOT to become academics because they see how bad you are treated and don't want to subject themselves to the same.	@DrNiCole
Told that I was ruining the "tone" of the lab because I didn't smile and laugh enough. #BlackintheIvory	@J_I_Benjamin
I embrace being #BlackintheIvory. However, my stories of my blackness in the Ivory would shame every strain of the academy—my own and everybody else's. Being #BlackintheIvory means there are no safe spaces—sometimes, not even your mind.	@aasewell
Being told "you'll need to do something about your hair so that it's professional." Working at my desk in my office & being asked "can you come empty the trash?." Getting the question "did you came up with this?" during the Q&A of my research talk. #BlackintheIvory	@DrRubidium
My 1st year of grad school I got an email labeled "College Classroom Etiquette," from a TA. She said I was louder than the other students. That I was in a graduate course with PhD students from different departments & that I was college not high school (1/2) #BlackintheIvory	@thememoryworker
Remember that Black person you didn't hire, couldn't recommend, wouldn't tenure, didn't admit, because they weren't *just* perfect? They were almost right but not stellar enough? Twice as good for half as much is racism too. #BlackintheIvory	@AmeliaNGibson
Being paraded around during recruitment so faculty can convince prospective students that the department "values diversity" #BlackintheIvory	@Black_Ecologist

Sawubona—"I SEE You"

Our found poem (see Table 12.2) presented a dialogic engagement; a critical inquiry into the intersections of womxnhood and racial representation in the academy. Through poetry, we interrogated our racialized and gendered identities and explored how we navigated, negotiated, and learned how to thrive from our respective standpoints. The poem served as a creative, healing, and liberating space to illustrate how we as Black womxn faculty reflect, (re)imagine, and embody our praxis. Evans-Winters (2019) argued,

> Oversight of Black women's contributions to qualitative research can be attributed to scholars not knowing or willing to acknowledge Black people are scientists and theorists, lack of awareness of Black women as producers of knowledge, and a tradition of racial and gender exclusion in the academy. *(p. 17)*

Thus, validating and acknowledging our own ways of knowing and our lived experiences, in this case, tweets engaged in the #BlackInTheIvory movement challenged those who excluded Black womxn's theoretical contributions.

We engaged in a series of steps to synthesize and select the tweets that created our found poem. First, we individually identified 15 tweets that resonated with us, and then we compiled them into a table. Next, we reviewed the table collectively to distinguish key phrases within those tweets. Lastly, we purposefully and strategically rearranged these phrases to create a found poem, Sawubona—I see you. In this poem, We SEE ourselves and each other.

No place is safe. Not one! Black womxn in the academy are collectively mentally exhausted. *Undervalued and overlooked.* They are often marginalized on multiple levels and in a multitude of spaces, including outside of their academic institutions. Safe spaces for Black womxn are limited beyond their communities and sometimes seek refuge in each other. *Representation matters. Period.* As we are excluded from decision-making conversations, we are often left exposed and unprotected from institutional racism. *I want to be a part of building a new*

TABLE 12.2 Found Poem— "Sawubona—I SEE You"

Not just a Twitter trend, real stories affecting our livelihoods.
So much anti-Blackness in the academy.
Only admitting and promoting the "least threatening Black" or "the right kind of Black"—the tokens.
Undervalued and overlooked.
Twice as good for half as much is racism too.

Brilliant Black academics how bad you are treated.
Being told "you'll need to do something about your hair so that it's professional."
Told that I was ruining the "tone" because I didn't smile and laugh enough.
A TA said I was louder than the other students.
Being paraded around during recruitment.
Hyper-visible yet invisible.

There are no safe spaces.
Do work that is uncompensated, unacknowledged, and unrewarded, it's called the Black tax or Brown tax.
Representation matters. Period.
I don't want a seat at a table that was never meant for me. I want to be a part of building a new table.

We are calling for radical change in systems all across this country, that includes the system of the academy.
No place is safe. Not one!
Uncomfortable...hearing our stories of racism and anti-Blackness. Sit with it & do better.

table. Yet, Black womxn are building their own spaces and "tables" to thrive and heal. #BlackInTheIvory allowed Black womxn to find support for personal and academic challenges they encountered in the academy. Black womxn resisted,

> against lack of support and full inclusion at the institution, they resist singular stories and flatted differences in the classroom, they resist standards of beauty thrust upon them, they resist policies, structures, histories, and legacies that mar higher education institutions.
>
> *(Stewart, 2019, p. 25)*

Brilliant Black academics how bad you are treated: Denied tenure, received biased student evaluations, encountered hostile work environments, and experienced micro and macro aggressions. Despite these challenges, they continued to still affirm the importance of their presence in the academy and the work they produced in their respective fields. *Uncomfortable…hearing our stories of racism and anti-Blackness. Sit with it & do better.*

This chapter highlights the anti-Blackness specifically faced by Black womxn in the academy via #BlackInTheIvory and utilizes poetry as a creative expression in which to re-shape and re-envision our collective narrative agency. *Not just a Twitter trend, real stories affecting our livelihoods.* We recognize the struggle for Black womxn's voices to be lifted in the academy is not new or over. Yet, we stand in solidarity as our collective narratives push beyond asking for a "seat at the table" to forging new rooms that center Black womxn's knowledge as essential to the growth and sustainability of the academy. Knowledge is power. Our knowledge is valuable.

References

Butler-Kisber, L. (2020). Poetic inquiry. In E. Fitzpatrick & K. Fitzpatrick (Eds.), *Poetry, method and education research: Doing critical, decolonising and political inquiry* (pp. 22–40). Routledge.

Collins, P. H. (1989). The social construction of black feminist thought. *Signs, 14*(4), 745–773.

Collins, P. H. (2000). *Black feminist thought: Knowledge, consciousness, and the politics of empowerment* (2nd ed.). Routledge.

Collins, P. H. (2001). Black women in the academy: An historical overview. In R. O. Mabokela & A. L. Green (Eds.), *Sisters of the academy: Emergent black women scholars in higher education* (pp. 29–41). Stylus Publishing

Evans-Winters, V. E. (2019). *Black feminism in qualitative inquiry: A mosaic for writing our daughter's body*. Routledge.

Harley, D. (2007). Maids of academe: African women faculty at predominately white institutions. *Journal of African American Studies, 12*, 19–36. https://doi.org/10.1007/s/12111-007-9030-5

hooks, b. (1989). *Talking back: Thinking feminist, thinking black*. South End Press.
Stewart, T. J. (2019). "Where we are, resistance lives": Black women, social media, and everyday resistance in higher education. *JCSCORE, 5*(2), 1–31. https://doi.org/10.15763/issn.2642-2387.2019.5.2.1-31
Yang, G. (2016). Narrative agency in hashtag activism: The Case of #BlackLivesMatter. *Media and Communication, 4*(4), 13–17. https://doi.org/10.17645/mac.v4i4.692

13

REPURPOSING MY STATUS AS AN OUTSIDER WITHIN

A Black Feminist Scholar-Pracademic's Journey to Becoming an Invested Indifferent

Nicole M. West

While there has recently been a marked increase in scholarly literature exploring the experiences of Black women faculty and higher education administrators, missing from the analyses are the perspectives of Black women who have navigated the journey from full-time administrator to full-time academic. In addition, while recent articles describe the transition from faculty to administrator (Foster, 2006; Glick, 2006; Griffith, 2006; Palm, 2006) and administrator to faculty (Firmin, 2008; Kniess et al., 2017; Martin III, 2020; McCluskey-Titus & Cawthon, 2004), only one study was found that examined the transition of student affairs practitioners into tenure-track faculty positions using a critical cultural theory (Perry et al., 2019). Findings in the Perry et al. (2019) article highlighted the impact of marginalized cultural group membership on the transition from roles in student affairs to academic affairs. Given these findings and the myriad challenges Black women faculty encounter, these gaps in literature should be further explored to suggest culturally and theoretically grounded strategies that might aid Black women in academia.

Black Women and (Black) Feminism in Higher Education

Black women in a variety of academic and administrative roles in higher education continue to leverage critical cultural theories such as Black feminist thought (BFT), Critical Race Theory, Critical Race Feminism, Hip Hop Feminism, and Womanist theory to both illuminate and contextualize their experiences in the academy (Croom & Patton, 2011/2012; Evans-Winters & Love, 2015; Porter et al., 2020; West, 2019). Coker et al. (2018) used BFT in an autoethnographic study to situate the experiences of four Black women enrolled and employed in higher education regarding their academic development, gravitation

DOI: 10.4324/9781003184867-16

toward higher education, and leadership. According to these scholars, "due to the complex intersectionality of the lives of Black women, they must often assess how race and gender, in particular, play a role in their experiences and interaction with others" (Coker et al., 2018, p. 49). While not explicitly grounded in BFT, Womble's (1995) discussion of her transition from a teaching institution to a research institution is one of the earlier scholarly works that illuminated the complexity associated with Black women faculty members' transition experiences in higher education. In describing her journey, Womble (1995) outlined common challenges that might be encountered by any faculty member moving to a new institutional type, but more importantly, she highlighted specific and nuanced issues that African American women faculty face during these kinds of transitions, which reflected several BFT tenets. Similarly, Porter et al. (2020) extended Collins' (1986) conceptualization of Black women's outsider within status and suggested "Black women in full-time, contingent faculty positions actually hold an outsider-outsider-within status" (p. 680).

Black Women as Outsiders within Academia

Black women in higher education continue to experience the double-edged sword of finally having access to predominantly white institutions (PWIs), but not actually being welcomed and included in the culture of these institutions as students, faculty, and/or administrators (Howard-Hamilton, 2003; Patitu & Hinton, 2003; West, 2015). In her widely cited paper, *Learning from the Outsider Within: The Sociological Significance of Black Feminist Thought*, Collins (1986) asserted Black women academics' outsider within status is rooted in and reminiscent of early Black women domestic workers' exploitative experiences with white families. Black women were invited inside of white homes as "the help", trusted to provide care for their white families, and remembered affectionately in their white employers' memoirs, but were still treated as outsiders (Collins, 1986). Similarly, contemporary Black women are participating at all levels within academia and are often tokenized for their double (and sometimes triple or multiple) minority status (Buchanan, 2020; Dickens et al., 2020), but continue to be marginalized and isolated, which contributes to their severe underrepresentation as students, faculty, and administrators (West, 2020).

As a means of disrupting deficit-oriented analyses of Black women's experiences and perspectives, Collins (1986) reframed their status as marginalized intellectuals in the academy as an epistemological tool that can be used to generate distinctive analyses of their interconnected, subordinate cultural group identities. Further, Collins (1986) outlined the relationship between three themes that characterized the specialized body of thought produced by and for Black women and suggested this unique perspective had the potential to move academia at large toward the actualization of a more humanistic enterprise. Collins (1986) attested Black feminists' proximity to the interlocking nature of oppression, coupled with the agency they demonstrate in redefining and valuing themselves and rearticulating the relevancy of their culture is what uniquely situates them for the task of "encouraging and institutionalizing outsider within ways of seeing" for other marginalized groups in academia (p. S29). Thus, in this chapter, I make use of Collins' (1986) assertion to illuminate the ways Black women's unique vantage as outsiders within academia may be used to derive alternate praxiological approaches to aid in navigating the challenges they (and other marginalized intellectuals) face in higher education. To this end, I use scholarly personal narrative (Nash & Bradley, 2011) to explore the following research question: How did a Black American woman in student affairs leverage BFT vis-à-vis her outsider within positionality while navigating the journey of becoming a faculty member?

Data Collection and Analysis

I used scholarly personal narrative (SPN; Nash & Bradley, 2011) in this study to unearth the ways I employed Collins' (1986, 2000) BFT as a Black American woman who transitioned from a full-time student affairs administrative position to a full-time, tenure-track faculty position in a student affairs master's program. Data were gathered and analyzed in Spring 2021, which was my sixth semester at Missouri State University, a large, public, comprehensive doctoral PWI in the Midwest region of the USA. Data included social media posts I authored on Facebook and Twitter between Summer 2018 and Spring 2021 that were related to my research question. These date delimitations were used because they marked the period between my first semester as a full-time faculty member and the final semester before I submitted my materials for tenure and promotion to Associate Professor[1] *(see West, 2021 for a detailed account of my transition experience)*.

First, I conducted a preliminary review of posts I made on Facebook and Twitter between Summer 2018 and Spring 2021 and isolated posts related to the focus of the study. In addition to the text contained in each post, hashtags, photographs, and memes was particularly useful in applying initial or open codes (Saldaña, 2011) to the data set, which consisted of 238 Facebook posts and 82 Twitter posts (i.e., tweets). Retweets and shares were only included in the initial data set if they had been shared with new text I authored in addition to the original tweet or post. Some of the more common hashtags that appeared in the data set included #greatwestmigration, #publishorperish, #facultylife, #blackwomeninhighered, and #blackfeministscholarpracademic. During the next round of data analysis, I engaged in Saldaña's (2011) *process coding*, which involved using *inductive coding* to sort the initial codes into categories and *deductive coding* to identify themes from those categories related to the purpose of the study, which focused on how I used BFT, specifically my status as an outsider within, in my journey from student affairs administrator to a faculty member.

Findings

Analysis of data in this study resulted in the following themes, which are described in more detail below: leveraging simultaneity, becoming an indifferent outsider, becoming invested within, and embracing a Black feminist scholar-pracademic identity.

Leveraging Simultaneity

The most salient part of my journey from administrator to a faculty member is the way I intentionally leveraged simultaneity to reconceptualize my status as an outsider within higher education. Although I began articulating this idea in a previous paper (West, 2019), I was not fully cognizant of the ways I was enacting the BFT practice of consciously rejecting artificiality imposed either/or binaries and embracing a both/and epistemological stance. I had been drifting in and out of this consciousness for several years while grappling with the myriad of contradictory realities associated with my lived experiences as a Black woman administrator employed in higher education. However, it was my transition to a tenure-track faculty position in the Fall of 2018, coupled with the Summer of 2020 rife with its obvious and actualized disregard for Black lives, particularly when those lives manifested in women's bodies, that demanded a more dogmatic and consistent reliance on this approach.

In the wake of the murders of Ahmaud Aubery, Geroge Floyd, and Breonna Taylor, I responded to one of my Facebook friend's posts to articulate the complexity of embracing seemingly contradictory viewpoints, perspectives, and/or realities (see Figure 13.1). In response to her post, I acknowledged that as someone without a Black son, I could not imagine the anguish of Black mothers who regularly feared for their sons' safety. However, I simultaneously noted that as the sister of a Black man and auntie of a precious Black boy, I wholeheartedly identified with the fear that their lives were always in danger. As another example, I also used the post to argue for the appropriateness of *both* civil protest *and* unbridled anger among Black Americans in response to the national epidemic of anti-Black, state-sanctioned police violence.

As I channeled my anger about the wholly unjustified and unrecompensed murder of Breonna Taylor into an unapologetic and passionate absorption with "all things Black women" *and* liberating apathy with regard to most other things, I realized I could leverage this same "both invested and indifferent" simultaneity to assuage the cognitive dissonance I was experiencing as a Black woman faculty member who loved the work I was doing, but had serious reservations about the interlocking systems of oppression under which I was laboring. The freedom to embrace seemingly antithetical realities opened up axiological space that empowered me to imagine new possibilities related to my positionality in the academy. Vis-à-vis my outsider within status, I discovered

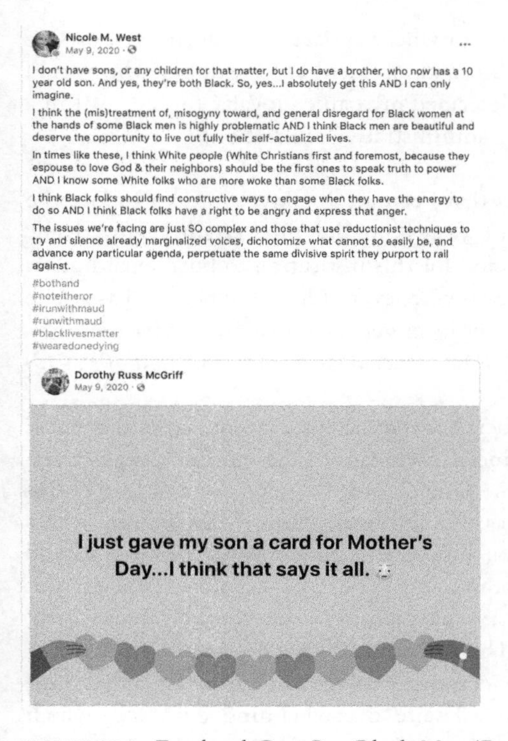

FIGURE 13.1 Facebook Post Re: Black Men/Boys

an enhanced position of resistance and identity by situating myself as *both* consumingly invested in my work as a faculty member *and* indifferent regarding the context in which I performed that work. I adopted an entrenched position of spending my time within being deeply invested in what I found meaningful, which overwhelmingly centered Black women, while leveraging my status as an outsider to be purposefully, overtly, and obstinately indifferent to individuals, ideals, philosophies, policies, structures, and systems that did not value and center Black women, but rather harmed them.

Becoming an Indifferent Outsider

As a relatively new faculty member, coming to terms with Collins' (1986) characterization of my standpoint as a Black woman outsider within academia, yet using that positionality to embrace indifference has been incredibly liberating. Becoming an indifferent outsider has provided me with the psychosocial distance I needed to establish healthy emotional boundaries regarding my life as a Black woman faculty member, which drastically contrasts with my experiences as a former student affairs administrator who was deeply connected to postsecondary education as if it were an animate object that I loved but who would not or could not love me back. I described my pained loyalty to one PWI in a journal entry after being denied an administrative promotion:

> I still know deep in my heart that I cannot disallow my heart to love the land...and try as I have to walk away if not literally, certainly figuratively, You fan the flame of my passion for this institution to burn even hotter. Over the past few days, months, years even, I have felt betrayed as a wife who has lost the affection of her lover yet can't leave, can't give up.
>
> *(N. West, personal communication, April 30, 2013)*

As a tenure-earning faculty member, however, I consciously chose to actively lack interest in a system that routinely marginalized the culture, perspectives, and contributions of Black women. This conscious act served as a line of demarcation that protected me from overvaluing and thus overinvesting in this system of higher education, which only seemed to promise promotion and prestige for some. My posture of indifference is not a casual lack of concern, but rather a militant dismissal, dare I say vehement rejection, of the value, worth, and credibility of the opinions held by those who do not champion Black women's causes. Since the ivory tower continues to constrain Black women's full participation in higher education—despite overwhelming evidence, which suggests that doing so is detrimental on a variety of individual and systemic levels—why should I exert so much emotional and mental labor trying to conform to a system that was never designed for me, to move that system toward a more just version of itself? It finally dawned on me—there is no such thing as a "more just version" of a system not designed to be so in the first place.

Another way I repurposed Collins' (1986) characterization of Black women's outsider within status was by relying on my newfound indifferent outsider praxiological standpoint to openly address issues related to diversity, equity, inclusion, and social justice, especially those I believed salient to Black women. As a Black woman, early career faculty member nearing the submission of my application for promotion and tenure, this was a crucial, albeit risky, task associated with my professorial identity as a Black feminist scholar-pracademic. However, being an outsider-and-indifferent gave me the courage to passionately challenge institutional practices that diminished the experiences of Black women students, faculty, and staff/administrators—which were the primary foci of my research agenda—with little regard for how my perspectives would be perceived or received. In addition to resigning from my position as program coordinator due to a salary inequity issue my university was unwilling to address, I documented the reason behind my decision to do so in a clearly articulated email to the students and faculty in my academic program. Although this

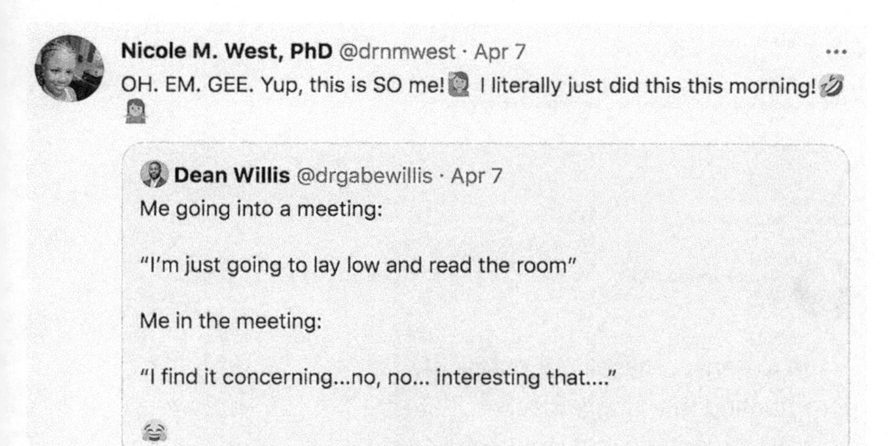

FIGURE 13.2 Tweet Re: Laying Low in Meetings

was a personal example of speaking up for myself, I also became much more vocal in speaking out against subtle and overt forms of racist sexism/sexist racism directed at Black women on campus. As illustrated in Figure 13.2, one of my retweets humorously illustrated the internal struggle I often experienced as an indifferent outsider participating in campus meetings where, often, I was compelled to speak out.

The courage I discovered to openly address issues affecting Black women on my campus also emboldened me to engage in public critique of the epidemic of racialized violence and police brutality against Black Americans that continued to escalate during the Summer of 2020. I was especially vocal about the unjustified police homicide of Breonna Taylor. I began a series of semiregular posts on Facebook between June 25 and September 24, 2020, using the hashtags #sayhername, #breonnataylor, #justiceforbreonna, #wearedonedyingtoo, and #signedblackwomeneverywhere. Among these Facebook posts was one that encouraged others to flood the Jefferson County Commonwealth's Attorney, Thomas B. Wine, with calls demanding the arrest and prosecution of the police officers who were responsible for Breonna's untimely death; another post I shared provided a link that automatically drafted an email to Mr. Wine demanding the same. In addition to these posts, I continued to use my Facebook timeline over the next several months to call attention to the widespread disregard for the safety of Black women in the USA and to disrupt the ways Black women's responses to these gross injustices were weaponized against them, especially in the propagation of the "angry Black woman" trope (see Figure 13.3).

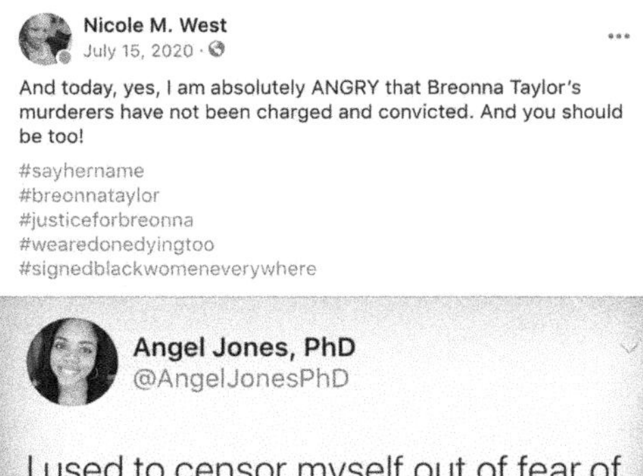

FIGURE 13.3 Facebook Post Re: Angry Black Woman

Becoming Invested Within

A direct corollary of establishing my positionality as an indifferent outsider was the freedom to use my location as a scholar within the academy to explore my passion for investing myself in work that centered Black women. I realized I could use my position within, and the resources associated with my role as a faculty member, to develop and highlight interim persistence strategies Black women in higher education could employ to materially improve their experiences as outsiders within the academy (West & Bertrand Jones, 2018). From this new vantage—which was void of the need to receive validation from a system I finally accepted did not have the capacity to give it—I discovered an even greater passion for working to materially enhance the experiences of Black women in higher education and clarified "my why" as I shared in the Tweet in Figure 13.4. I began caring less about earning the academy's respect and more about how to put material resources such as graduate school admissions and fellowships, publication and grant opportunities, faculty appointments, administrative promotions, and equitable compensation into the hands of qualified Black women. I began focusing even more narrowly and unapologetically on

FIGURE 13.4 Tweet Re: This is My Why

how I could use my position within to engage in research, teaching, and service that benefitted Black women.

In line with Collins' (1986) characterization of Black women academics as outsiders within, my "'marginality' has been an excitement to creativity," which has resulted in a greater sense of purpose and focus (p. S15). This deepened commitment to my positionality as an invested scholar within the academy opened me up to the "type of intellectual ingenuity, which is stimulated by both the pain and exhilaration of my journey as a Black woman in higher education" (West, 2019, p. 372). As a research-to-practice extension of my work on professional counterspaces (West, 2017), I developed several innovative initiatives to benefit Black women on my campus and in the broader higher education community. One of those projects was a self-emancipatory, diversity and inclusion strategy and critical action research methodology—known as a *Participatory Action Research Counterspace* (PARC)—which I created to positively impact the experiences of multiplicatively minoritized groups, like Black women, in majority settings, like PWIs. Preliminary findings of a PARC I implemented on my campus for a group of Black women students, faculty, and administrators during the 2020–2021 academic year, indicated that these spaces: (a) provided

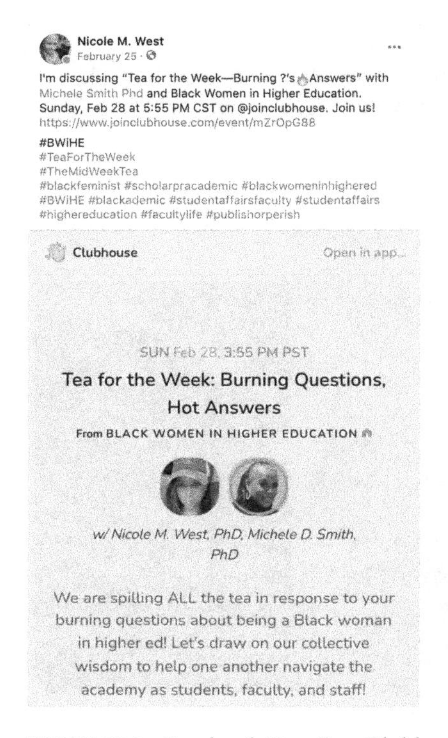

FIGURE 13.5 Facebook Post Re: Clubhouse Room

a critical participatory action research-oriented community, (b) employed self-emancipatory strategies that enhance the experiences of co-researchers, (c) centered the intersectional lived experiences and perspectives of co-researchers, (d) facilitated the development of counterhegemonic standpoints, and (e) illuminated practices that redress oppression of multiplicatively minoritized/marginalized cultural group(s) in majority settings (West, 2022).

I have also collaborated with several Black women colleagues beyond my campus and discovered a way to extend my work on professional counterspaces for Black women in higher education by exploring the use of a new audio-only, drop-in, social media app called Clubhouse. As one of the administrators of the Black Womxn in Higher Education club on Clubhouse, which currently has 13,000+ followers, I have been able to provide a virtual network of professional support and development for a much larger audience of Black women in higher education. We have used this virtual professional counterspace to moderate weekly co-working sessions and to facilitate dialogue among Black women administrators and faculty about the wide range of issues they face in higher education (see Figure 13.5).

Embracing a Black Feminist Scholar-Pracademic Identity

One of the most powerful outcomes that resulted from repurposing my outsider within status was the way I leveraged my positionality as an invested indifferent to conceptualize and fully embrace my professorial identity as a faculty member, which also impacted me personally.

I had begun to articulate my identity as a Black feminist scholar-pracademic as:

> a critically engaged researcher with a great mixture of administrative and academic talent that has accrued as a result of the unique vantage and corollary benefits and burdens associated with being an outsider within higher education, who is unapologetically pro-Black women, and leverages their strengths and contributions to improve the experiences of Black women in higher education.
>
> *(West, 2021, p. 8)*

However, I could not have imagined how embracing a "within-and-invested and outsider-and-indifferent" stance would empower me to live a more genuine version of myself in *and* outside of the academy. I was finally absolved of feeling the need to temper my passion for tackling issues specifically related to Black women in the academy, which resulted in an even stronger connection between my life as a faculty member and my social persona. As illustrated in Figures 13.6 and 13.7, almost all my social media posts related to my professional accomplishments included some reference to my positionality as a Black feminist scholar-pracademic.

Using Collins' (1986) outsider within positionality to reconceptualize myself as a Black feminist scholar-pracademic also helped me prioritize showing up as my authentic self in ways I had previously been too afraid to. On several occasions, including the one I described in Figure 13.8, I brought to consciousness the ways I had been liberated from caring about the arbitrary opinions of others, especially those rooted in the hegemonic bedrock of the academy. Interestingly, in this post, I drew an explicit connection between my liberation from respectability politics masquerading as professionalism in the academy and the murder of Breonna Taylor. These micro-acts of resistance felt like a responsibility I owed a cause bigger than myself, but that simultaneously set me free too.

Another Facebook post I shared captured the essence of my repurposed, yet continually evolving status as an administrator turned academic who is an invested indifferent (see Figure 13.9). In this post, somewhat scantily clad in workout clothes with steely determined eyes, it was resolved: I was ready to do the work I loved and was going to do so from an authentic and empowered standpoint—on my own terms, in my own skin, succeeding and excelling with little regard for what the academy thought about me and my Black sistas.

FIGURE 13.6 Tweet Re: NASPA Teaching Award

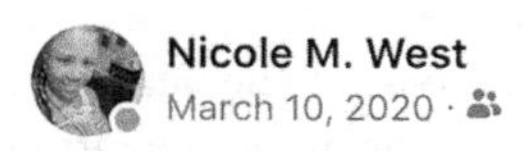

Excited to share another one of my research publications! This one has also been a long time coming, right Dr. W Jea Henry?! Mom (Dorothye West), thank you for your excellent proofreading again; the check is in the mail! 😜 #blackademic #scholarpracademic #blackfeministthought #publishorperish

TANDFONLINE.COM

A Contemporary Portrait of Black Women Student Affairs Administrators in the United States

FIGURE 13.7 Facebook Post Re: Contemporary Portrait Publication

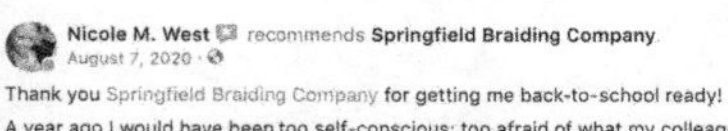

FIGURE 13.8 Facebook Post Re: Springfield Braiding Company

FIGURE 13.9 Facebook Post Re: Feelin' the Skin I'm In

Lessons Learned

Undoubtedly it was the intentional self-reposturing of myself as an academic who was deeply invested in my work as a Black feminist scholar-pracademic, yet ragingly indifferent regarding the hegemonic systems of the ivory tower within which I was doing that work, that enabled me to see how Collins' (1986) articulation of Black women's outsider within status assisted me in successfully transitioning from administrator to academic. Based on my analysis, there are four primary takeaways that could benefit Black women transitioning (or employed) within higher education: (1) give yourself permission to embrace antithetical perspectives and realities, which provides you with (2) the psychosocial distance needed to create appropriate emotional boundaries related to your work, which empowers you to (3) passionately pursue the work you care about and find meaningful, and (4) articulate a coherent professorial identity.

A critical milestone in my transition from administrator to faculty member was the conceptualization and clarification of, and commitment to my identity as a Black feminist scholar-pracademic. These developmental tasks would have been significantly delayed if I had not come to an understanding of how Black feminists often must leverage simultaneity, or as Morgan (1999) put it, be "brave enough to fuck with the grays" (p. 59). As exemplified in my discussion of this first theme, rejecting subjectively imposed binary schemas and consciously resisting the pressure to choose one option over another—especially when there was viability in both options—opened possibilities of thought that were previously inaccessible. This approach enabled me to distinguish and explore the complexities and nuances of my reality as a new, tenure-earning, Black woman faculty member. I realized I could *both* love *and* hate, fully embrace *and* vehemently reject, various aspects of my positionality in the academy, which aligns with Walkington's (2017) conclusion that most of the documented persistence strategies used by Black women faculty and graduate students occur at an individual level. Collins (2000) articulated the personally powerful liberation that results from employing a Black feminist both/and conceptual standpoint to "[reconcile] what we have been trained to see as opposites" (p. viii).

Coming to terms with the fact that I loved the work I was doing, as well as the women on whose behalf I was working *and* was often debilitated by the context in which I was doing that work, helped me draw clear emotional boundaries around aspects of my existence as a Black woman faculty member on the tenure-track. Collins (2000) pointed out the importance of Black women self-defining and publicly expressing their love for one another as an act of resisting oppression. She noted, "if members of the group on the bottom love one another and affirm one another's worth, then the entire system that assigns that group to the bottom becomes suspect" (Collins, 2000, p. 170). Thus, with reckless abandon, I pursued an even more intimate relationship with my mission to enhance the experiences of Black women in the academy and simultaneously adopted an intentionally indifferent attitude toward anything (and anyone) that did not move that cause forward. This psychological repositioning helped me lean even harder into my identity as a Black feminist scholar-pracademic and enlivened my vigor to enact my research as praxis, on campus and beyond. Ultimately, I am hopeful my carefully allocated passion and indifference will lead to a positive impact in the academy, whether my contributions are valued at present or not. More importantly, what I care about deeply is that Black women students, faculty, and administrators in higher education are better off because of my work.

The most significant outcome I have experienced in this transition, and in my analysis of it, is developing a greater capacity to explore a more authentic and coherent version of myself as a higher education scholar independent of the opinions of others. Creating emotional distance between myself and those people, values, beliefs, and practices that marginalize Black women helped me to see them for what they were—highly subjective, and often flawed, ideological constructions that existed to be challenged. In some cases, this also meant critiquing how I integrated these ideas into my own schema about what it meant to be a Black woman and more specifically, a Black feminist. Once I decided to attach significantly less emotional value, if any at all, to the ways *others* problematized, misrepresented, misunderstood, and oversimplified my existence as a Black woman, the more freedom I experienced to imagine a more robust conceptualization of myself as a Black feminist scholar-pracademic. The findings of this study suggest Black women (and other marginalized groups of) faculty and administrators may enhance their experiences by intentionally invoking a Black feminist (or other critical cultural) standpoint to bolster themselves along their professional journeys.

Note

1 I included posts I authored during Summer 2018 as it was my first semester of transitioning to this faculty position since I was able to secure and began working on a new faculty grant that semester.

References

Buchanan, N. T. (2020) Researching while Black (and female). *Women & Therapy, 43*(1–2), 91–111.

Coker, A. D., Martin, C., Culver, J., & Johnson, C. (2018). Black women's academic and leadership development in higher education: An autoethnographic study. *Periferia, 10*(2), 44–46.

Collins, P. H. (1986). Learning from the outsider within: The sociological significance of Black feminist thought. *Social Problems, 33*(6), S14–S32.

Collins, P. H. (2000). *Black feminist thought: Knowledge, consciousness, and the politics of empowerment* (2nd ed.). Routledge.

Croom, N., & Patton, L. (2011/2012). The miner's canary: A critical race perspective on the representation of Black women full professors. *Negro Educational Review, 62/63*(1–4), 13–39.

Dickens, D., Jones, M., & Hall, N. (2020). Being a token Black female faculty member in physics: Exploring research on gendered racism, identity shifting as a coping strategy, and inclusivity in physics. *The Physics Teacher, 58*, 335–337.

Evans-Winters, V. E., & Love, B. L. (Eds.). (2015). *Black feminism in education: Black women speak back, up, and out.* Peter Lang.

Firmin, M. (2008). Transitioning from administration to faculty: Addictions to break. *Journal of Practical Leadership, 3*, 144–148.

Foster, B. L. (2006). From faculty to administrator: Like going to a new planet. In R. J. Henry (Ed.), *Transitions between faculty and administrative careers* (New Directions for Higher Education, No. 134, pp. 49–57). Jossey-Bass.

Glick, M. D. (2006). Becoming "one of them" or "moving to the dark side." In R. J. Henry (Ed.), *Transitions between faculty and administrative careers* (New Directions for Higher Education, No. 134, pp. 87–96). Jossey-Bass.

Griffith, J. C. (2006). Transition from faculty to administrator and transition back to the faculty. In R. J. Henry (Ed.), *Transitions between faculty and administrative careers* (New Directions for Higher Education, No. 134, pp. 67–77). Jossey-Bass.

Howard-Hamilton, M. F. (2003). Theoretical frameworks for African American women. In M. F. Howard-Hamilton (Ed.), *Meeting the needs of African American women* (New Directions for Student Services, No. 104, pp. 19–28). Jossey-Bass.

Kniess, D., Benjamin, M., & Boettcher, M. (2017). Negotiating faculty identity in the transition from student affairs practitioner to tenure-track faculty. *College Student Affairs Journal, 35*(1), 13–24.

Martin, Q., III. (2020). Look before you leap: Making the transition from administration to faculty. *International Journal for Academic Development*, 1–6.

McCluskey-Titus, P., & Cawthon, T. W. (2004). The grass is always greener on the other side of the fence: Making a transition from student affairs administrator to full-time faculty. *NASPA Journal, 41*(2), 317–335.

Morgan, J. (1999). *When chickenheads come home to roost: My life as a hip-hop feminist.* Simon and Schuster.

Nash, R. J., & Bradley, D. L. (2011). *Me-search and re-search: A guide for writing scholarly personal narrative manuscripts.* IAP.

Palm, R. (2006). Perspectives from the dark side: The career transition from faculty to administrator. In R. J. Henry (Ed.), *Transitions between faculty and administrative careers* (New Directions for Higher Education, No. 134, pp. 59–65). Jossey-Bass.

Patitu, C. L., & Hinton, K. G. (2003). The experiences of African American women faculty and administrators in higher education: Has anything changed? In M. F. Howard-Hamilton (Ed.), *New directions for student services. Meeting the needs of African American women* (Vol. 104, pp. 79–93). Jossey-Bass.

Perry, A. L., Dean, S. R., & Hilton, A. A. (2019). New faculty transitions and obstacles: An auto-ethnographic exploration. *Journal of the Professoriate, 10*(2), 43–72.

Porter, C. J., Moore, C. M., Boss, G. J., Davis, T. J., & Louis, D. A. (2020) To be Black women and contingent faculty: Four scholarly personal narratives. *The Journal of Higher Education, 91*(5), 674–697.

Saldaña, J. (2011). *Fundamentals of qualitative research*. Oxford.

Walkington, L. (2017). How far have we really come? Black women faculty and graduate students' experiences in higher education. *Humboldt Journal of Social Relations, 39*, 51–65.

West, N. M. (2015). In our own words: African American women student affairs professionals define their experiences at PWIs. *Advancing Women in Leadership Journal, 35*, 108–119.

West, N. M. (2017). Withstanding our status as outsiders-within: Professional counterspaces for African American women student affairs administrators. *NASPA Journal about Women in Higher Education, 10*(3), 281–300.

West, N. M. (2019). Another lesson from the outsider within: The transcendent relevance of Black Feminist Thought. *Journal of Student Affairs Research and Practice, 57*(4), 371–384.

West, N. M. (2020). A contemporary portrait of Black women student affairs administrators in the United States. *Journal of Women and Gender in Higher Education, 13*(1), 72–92.

West, N. M. (2021). Embodying Black feminist epistemology to make green grass grow: The transition from administrator to academic for a Black woman in student affairs. *The Journal of Diversity in Higher Education.* https://doi.org/10.1037/dhe0000375

West, N. M. (2022, March). Defining the contours of a Participatory Action Research Counterspace developed by, for, and about Black women in higher education [Paper Presentation]. NASPA Annual Conference, Baltimore, MD (refereed).

West, N. M., & Bertrand Jones, T. (2018). Architects of change in the ivory tower: The role of professional counterspaces for Black women in higher education. In U. Thomas (Ed.), *Navigating micro-aggressions toward women in higher education* (pp. 23–52). IGI Global.

Womble, M. N. (1995). Transition from a teaching institution to a research institution: An African American female perspective. *Innovative Higher Education, 19*(4), 241–254.

14

NAVIGATING A WOMANIST CARING FRAMEWORK

Centering Womanist Geographies within Social Foundations for Black Academic Survival

Taryrn T.C. Brown and E. Nichole Murray

Black women educators have historically aided in assisting students in navigating their realities both inside and outside the classroom (Beauboeuf-Lafontant, 2009; Collins, 2000; Delpit, 1988; Dillard & Neal, 2020); with their roles not solely connected to teaching the formalized curriculum, but rather inheriting and embodying a communal responsibility to uplift Black communities and Black families (Beauboeuf-Lafontant, 2009; Dillard & Neal, 2020). The first Black woman professor in the USA, Sarah Jane Woodson Early, was an educator, and a political and social activist who urged Black educators to lead their race. Willa Beatrice Player, the former president of Bennett College for women and the first Black woman president of a four-year fully accredited liberal arts college, saw her role as an activist educator and actively encouraged students to fight racial oppression (Sanders, 2019). Black women educators embodied an ethic of care that prioritized holistic development for their students and their communities. Such care considered how social, economic, and moral structures affected children's experiences both within and outside of school (Beauboeuf-Lafontant, 1999; Goldstein, 1999; Sanders 2019). Black women's care reflected an interdisciplinary approach that often mirrored the field of social foundations.

Social Foundations as an academic field of study is a meeting ground of scholarship, research, and praxis from many differing orientations (Shujaa, 1995). Deeply rooted in the inter-and intra-personal development of students within teacher education programs, social foundations contribute to perspectives that align with ethical and communal responsibilities inside and outside of schools (Cozart & Gordon, 2006). As a discipline, it embodies an ethical and political framing of responsibility and guides a deeper understanding of human culture's interconnectedness, with the requisite responsibility to leave

DOI: 10.4324/9781003184867-17

the communities as viable and healthy environments for future generations (Shujaa, 1995). This notion, intertwined with the intersectional aspects of an educator's identity, creates pedagogical spaces that impact individual practice and experience (Beauboeuf-Lafontant, 2002; Cozart & Gordon, 2006; Ladson-Billings, 1996).

As two Black women scholars whose research and teaching have been grounded in the multidisciplinary areas of social foundations, this paper utilizes duo-ethnography (Sawyer & Norris, 2009) and sista circle methodology (Johnson, 2015) to explore the embodied *womanist caring framework* that guided our teaching in the classroom. We suggest there is learning, and professional growth found when *(re)membering* our experiences as Black women faculty; experiences critical in understanding the tensions and power dynamics of racial, ethnic, and gender inequities within the academy and the strength and resilience that rests in critical collaborative self-reflection of pedagogical practice.

Centuries-Long, Experiences of Black Women in Education

Black women educators' caring has been guided by historically gendered and racialized experiences that have long been decentered and underutilized as sites for educational theorizing and pedagogical praxis. With the onerous duty of uplifting a nation, Black women navigate cultural, social, political, historical, global, and maternal connections in the teaching and learning of their students (Beauboeuf-Lafontant, 2002; Collins, 2000; Houchen, 2015; Whitaker, 2013). Moreover, on a collegiate level, Black women educators historically have been positioned to be more than cognoscente in their teaching and learning for students to become moral and social change agents. However, historical narratives often centralized in dominant white-centric experiences within the K-12 landscape did not value the pedagogies of Black women (Acosta, 2019; Graham, 2007; Whitaker, 2013). The lack of acknowledgment for the role that race, gender, and culture play in the relational attributes of the ethics of care (Noddings, 1995, 2003) omits the intersectional lived experiences of Black women, who often within the academy navigate limited and often traumatic experiences with care ethics as praxis. This marginalization, however, continues to be disrupted through Black feminist epistemological frameworks.

Coined by social activist Alice Walker, *womanism* centers perspectives within the collective experiences of Black women (Walker, 1983). As a framework, womanism makes connections between pedagogy and positionality (Beauboeuf-Lafontant, 2005). A *womanist-centered* perspective seeks to center the impact of Black women who make significant contributions in equitable realities for all (Beauboeuf-Lafontant, 2002; Houchen, 2015; Ladson-Billings, 1996). Womanist-centered perspectives validate Black women's voices through storytelling, proverbs, affirmations, prayer, idioms, lyrics, technology, and social media (Littlefield & Roberson, 2005; Phillips, 2006). While Black women's stories are often silenced in schools, womanist epistemologies (Marr, 2015) respond to the absences of race and gender in dominant narratives while addressing the intersections of class, race, power, and culture (Beauboeuf-Lafontant, 2005; Walker, 1983). A womanist approach enhances inclusive epistemologies and uplifts the voices of the minoritized by promoting the equity of resources, honoring histories and traditions, and valuing lived experiences (Espino, 2012; Marr, 2015; Walker, 1983).

Amidst educational narratives inundated with racist and sexist ideologies, Black women educators at the intersection of their pedagogy and positionality navigate deeply rooted realities in the struggle for racial and gender equity. Beauboeuf-Lafontant (2002) accounts for this intersection of praxis as *womanist caring*. Beauboeuf-Lafontant (2002) describes the "*womanist caring framework*" as consisting of three characteristics: an embrace of the maternal, political clarity, and an ethic of risk. These characteristics bring awareness to the relationships that exist between schools and society; and the radical collectivism among people in authentic commitment for injustice (Beauboeuf-Lafontant, 2002).

In the social foundation's classroom as Black women who now had language through the *womanist-caring framework*, we found that we navigated internal and external tensions within the predominantly white spaces of academia. Through duo-ethnography and sista circle methodology, this space of critical self-reflection gave us language to grapple with who we were as we identified the source of our frustrations in our experiences with students, peers, and colleagues. It created space to realize the connections in our praxis as Black women educators. This chapter centers our collaborative inquiry as Black women faculty in (a) the responsibility of challenging limited world views; (b) the obligation in disrupting one-sided portrayals of the world to offer invaluable insights to students; (c) navigating the weight of sharing oneself to deepen a student's cultural understanding; and (d) carrying the weight of humanizing our personal cultural experiences for the benefit of student consciousness.

Framing Our Teaching in Context

What started out as two sista scholars exchanging stories about their experience teaching social justice courses in the academy evolved into a transformative, dialogical narrative that examined the realities of being Black, woman, and in academia. To construct our dual perspectives, we intertwined tenants of duoethnography (Norris et al., 2012; Sawyer & Norris, 2009) and sista circle methodology (Johnson, 2015). The two approaches provided a guide for us to center our truths around Beauboeuf-Lafontant's (2002) *womanist caring framework*.

Duoethnography is grounded in social justice and is defined as "two or more participants bringing different life experiences and ways of knowing, and perspectives to a shared phenomenon" (Monzó & SooHoo, 2014, p. 155). Collaboration, critical dialogue, and transformative methodology are the three main components. Collaboration occurs from understanding the other participant's experience (Norris et al., 2012). Articulating, exploring, and presenting counternarratives in contrast to dominant narratives is part of the critical dialogue (Norris et al., 2012). At the transformative stage, self-reflection and critical dialogue help to create meaning of the experience through self-discovery and another's perspective (Monzó & SooHoo, 2014). These three crucial components allowed us to work through our vulnerability and embrace our lived truths.

Parallel to duoethnography, sista circle methodology provided the counter space for social engagement. Sista circle methodology is a qualitative research method conducted in a supportive—"sister to sister" context (Johnson, 2015). Rooted within the Black church and Black women's club movements (Giddings, 1984, Neal-Barnett et al., 2011), Johnson's (2015) sista circle methodology has three distinguishing features. The first feature, communication dynamics, refers to the intra-cultural verbal and nonverbal communication between Black women. For us, it was sometimes the "*Girllll, let me tell you…*," or the quick side-eye reaction to our experiences. The second feature, centrality of empowerment, emphasizes the values in Black women's knowledge and operates to uplift and validate Black women's experiences. The third is the researcher as a participant, where the researcher actively engages and exchanges dialogical content with the group or other participants. Analyzing data through personal stories, social media posts, journals, and memos, duoethnography, and sista circle provided the collaborative space for us to (de)construct our experiences, authentically engage in intimate discourse, and validate our lived experiences.

Being the First: Introspection in the Social Foundations Classroom

"You're my first Black teacher" were words we heard every semester from at least one student. This declaration forced us to reflect on the weight the statement carries in a hyper-racialized climate. Probing deeper into our teaching experience, we began to conceptualize how the term "ethics of care" looked for two Black women teaching a social justice course at a PWI, and how our experiences deviated from the dominant narrative of care. To create meaning of our experiences, we reflected on the central question, "how do our racialized and gendered identities shape how students view our ethics of care in a social justice course?" We explored the topic by sharing our personal stories and discussing how our expertise differed from white professors who taught the same course.

This led to reflecting on our narratives via phone conversations, virtual meetings, and text messages. The personal exchanges were recorded digitally. In addition, we complemented our discourse with social media posts from the group Black Women PhDs on Instagram, Twitter, and Facebook as discussion points to situate our stories and even reinforce our experiences. Diving further into our introspection, we replayed the recordings (phone conversations and virtual meetings) three times. During the playback, we paused the recording as needed to jot down any questions we had for the other researcher, journaled our innermost thoughts, noted our emotions or feelings, and recorded reactions to the shared experiences. Knowing that sista circle (Johnson, 2015) and duoethnography (Bhullar & Grain, 2012; Breault, 2016) relied heavily on a substantial degree of trust and as friends and sista scholars for over eight years, we were able to expose our truths genuinely and freely. Reflexivity encouraged us to challenge each other to deconstruct experiences, become vulnerable as we processed our feelings, and confronted tension within ourselves. Then we exchanged notes via email to disrupt our dogmatic thinking (Breault, 2016). The intellectual transaction granted us insight into each other's interpretations and perspectives. Sharing our writing also helped to validate our stories while helping us name our experiences. Once we finished reading and taking notes on each other's reflections, we scheduled two virtual meetings to process, debrief, and discover where our stories intersected. Our synergy created a hybrid narrative about the realities present within teaching courses focused on systemic and structural inequities in education. The following sections outline our experiences in the classroom within a *womanist caring framework*.

Embracing the Maternal, Without Reciprocated Care

Embracing the maternal requires teachers to treat all children as their own and to meet children's particular needs by whatever means necessary, ultimately involving shared responsibility with families and communities (Beauboeuf-Lafontant, 2002). In the reflective process of our womanist caring pedagogy, tensions emerged at the intersections of how we came to navigate the classroom's physical and psychological space with our students. We both had recollections of tensions in the maternal caring exchange between teacher and student, knowing the care, emotionally, physically, and psychologically, was not prioritized for us in the same way.

One researcher recalls navigating her teaching about white privilege in her classroom and having the realizations of the emotional baggage it took to challenge her students on the validity of whiteness within inequitable educational systems and structures. She recalled a student's reflection paper, "*White privilege is not real. I have a family that grew up in a poor community. Why are we talking about this?*" This student quote is just one of many fielded by the researchers in which the maternal caring for student learning had to supersede the heavy personal realities of hearing the discredit and devaluing of minoritized narratives. It was also a strain on our identities as some students looked at us as Black women who had privilege and challenged the privilege narrative because of our professional status.

We were reminded every semester that we were a student's "*First Black Female Teacher*." Our intersections of identity constantly came into play in our negotiation with the classroom and with our students. Navigating points of discussion both in and outside these spaces often left us feeling as though our desire to care for the student, especially in their limited consciousness of systemic and structural histories, often resulted in constantly defending minoritized narratives and oppressive realities. We both discussed our attempts to disrupt students' unconsciousness with care while also protecting those considered to be the most vulnerable, from future generations of ill-informed and deeply rooted inequities. While we extended care to our students, we often wondered who would offer us reciprocity.

Political Clarity and Being Called into Question

Political clarity is the understanding that oppression is systemic rather than individually motivated (Beauboeuf-Lafontant, 2002). This aspect of womanist caring pushed us to reflect on when we were called into question about having a personal agenda, especially concerning the criticality that undergirded explorations of racial tensions and inequities in U.S. education. One researcher remembered notations on her course evaluation in which the student shared, "*I wish the professor wouldn't focus so much on race in this class, I mean it seems as if she is more interested in centering voices for her own benefit.*"

This sentiment was expressed on different occasions from students during class times and emails, with the underlying assumption that we were somehow attempting to perpetuate a personal agenda. Our identities as Black women educators were blurred with the idea that we personally sought to center the experiences of minoritized communities, as a distraction to the "*alleged*" real tensions that plagued issues of achievement, access, and equity for all. We faced our teaching being challenged based on our identities as Black and woman. Meanwhile, our white counterparts were rarely charged with promoting an "agenda." We were subjected to triaging student emails, commentary, and implicit insinuations that our teaching within social foundations contexts is an effort to promote a personal platform.

Deeply entrenched in the dominant US discourse is the notion of meritocracy—the ideology that if people work hard, they will be rewarded and overcome any obstacle. Most students who came from a white middle- or upper-class backgrounds, often relied on meritocracy to rebuttal inequities. As one student wrote in a critical reflection paper, "*Brown v. Board of Education has made it where all people can succeed in school, just look at my Black female professor.*" The student's insinuation—that one researcher's intersectional identities of Black, woman, and educator, somehow proved parity—demonstrated the politicization of our embodiment in the classroom. It is in these situations, where we had to make the troubling decision to sacrifice our lived experiences for a deepening of the privileged students' learning or use some impersonal data with less emotional resonance. As Black women, we were forced to navigate and challenge dominant ideologies by getting students to think critically about systemic oppression while also having to explain our positionalities.

Ethic of Risk and the Struggle for Black Academic Survival

An ethic of risk concerns understanding the obligation to change schools even when there is no guarantee of success. A critical component of an ethic of risk is a teacher's commitment to not only herself, but also to the community of the children with whom she works. The responsibility in the ethics of risk is the idea of a lifelong struggle. We both felt the metaphoric heaviness of what it meant to sustain *critical hope* (Duncan-Andrade, 2009) within an ethic of risk amidst a system built without us in mind. This heaviness presented its own emotional and psychological challenges as we sought to persist in academia. We experienced comments such as, "*We live in a post-racial society, just look, we had a Black U.S. President and a Black First Lady,*" "*I'm a feminist so I can't be racist,*" or "*I'm a liberal and progressive so I can't be (racist, sexist, homophobic, xenophobic, etc...).*" These sentiments invalidated our lived experiences. We felt the pain when we heard of Black women like Deborah Danner and Charleena Lyles who brutally lost their lives to institutional violence (Henery, 2017). It is a constant reminder that makes us hypervigilant of our bodies. But these same comments also remind us of our work and social justice calling and signals to us that we cannot let the dominant discourse distort our narratives and realities.

While most of the students we teach are white and our extension of care is given to white students, it is worthwhile to echo Lee and Johnson-Bailey's (2004) view of privilege and care. They asserted being cared for is a privilege because one benefits from it, while the carer is usually less privileged (Lee & Johnson-Bailey, 2004). As Black women educator-activists, we also wondered how to confront systemic injustices and care for students, without perpetuating oppression synonymous with centering whiteness. It is within this tension we felt the burden of humanizing our personal cultural experiences for the benefit of our student consciousness.

Strategies and Lessons Learned in Our Womanist Caring Framework

The African proverb, "she who learns must also teach," echoes the historical importance preceding Black women faculty's efforts to care and share their knowledge with those around them, regardless of the opposition, tension, or challenges they face. Living at the intersection of being Black women educators in predominantly white university classrooms reinforced this narrative in our reflective sharing. The following section offers interrelated strategies we worked through as we navigated our womanist caring framework. We hope in sharing our voices as Black women social foundation educators, our experiences are helpful in praxis to others as they reconcile realities of their identity intersections.

Self-Care: An Internal Process and an External Idea

Social Foundations is rooted in challenging the hegemony of oppressive systems. It is our duty as educators to critically encourage our students to think about ethical and communal responsibilities both inside and outside of schools. Engaging in such political and social works means we inevitably encounter some resistance to the material presented, especially due to some students' postulation that our intersectional identities fuel our teaching. As Black women who feel committed to exposing societal inequities, the work can be taxing. Our extended care, receptive attention, and empathy in the classroom are sometimes rejected by students (and administrators). Black women educator-activists have documented how incurring racial fatigue, Black women superwoman syndrome, and double consciousness, have created internal conflict, trauma, and health issues (Beauboeuf-Lafontant, 2009; Woods-Giscombé, 2010). Black women have always had to be the carer and are rarely cared for, but we learned it was necessary to tend to our well-being. For us, this meant tapping into our womanism and our spiritual agency. Meditation, finding peace in silence, and proclaiming positive affirmation, helped preserve our essence and led to liberation consciousness.

The Power of Sista Scholars

In our sista support network, we were able to develop an invaluable counter space for our praxis. With very little representation of Black women in academia, this space allowed us to unpack our navigation through our (still developing and growing) womanist caring frameworks. The sista counter space centered our voices to focus less on the tensions we navigated in our teaching, and instead, allowed us to focus on important components of our shared experience and teaching narratives. Our sista scholar network has extended into our continued professional lives and translates across our respective teaching and research practices. The care translated in our sista support network remained at the forefront of our experience and ultimately guided our praxis as educators.

Thriving through Voice in the Academy

As co-researchers, we realized one of our most powerful tools was our voices. We needed to collectively navigate tensions and positionalities to survive in these educational and community spaces. We often used our voices to disrupt dominant narratives that suggested the maintenance of problematically oriented student–teacher exchanges. Our collective voice brought us together in our shared experiences and efforts to truly make sense of the phenomena at the center of our teaching. We realized the strength in framing our teaching wherein we could center our interests as tools to engage our students more critically and intentionally; while refusing to be silenced when our voices created opportunities for more transformative learning for students.

Embracing the Strength of Your Positionality

Our position as Black women in academia placed us at several intersections. Our racialized and gendered identities were on display, while our occupational identity, as social foundation educators, was visualized once we began facilitating the class. For some students, our identities brought discomfort, for others, it was an anomaly to have someone like us teaching. In this othering space, we used our identities and positionalities to disrupt systems, resist dominant ideologies, and challenge status quos, while still exhibiting womanist caring. Our innate spiritual and ancestral connection has helped us overcome oppression, depression, and suppression. Seeking solace in our womanist identity helped us know we were not alone; we were liberated to authentically exist as Black woman educators. We encourage all Black women academics to embrace their positionality, rewrite the narratives, and know we are the branches of fierce justice warriors, such as Audre Lorde, Chikwenye Okonjo Ogunyemi, and Sarah Parker Redmond.

Conclusion

Our chapter sought to amplify the womanist geographies of social foundations educators through a duo-ethnographic and sista circle methodology. By sharing our stories, we illuminate Black women educators' pedagogical experiences in social foundations, and we expose how the locale mattered for us within teacher education. Our stories support the need to critically understand the racialized and gendered tensions and inequities within pedagogical praxis.

References

Acosta, M. M. (2019). The paradox of pedagogical excellence among exemplary black women educators. *Journal of Teacher Education, 70*(1), 26–38. https://doi.org/10.1177/0022487118808512

Beauboeuf-Lafontant, T. (1999). A movement against and beyond boundaries: "Politically relevant teaching" among African American teachers. *Teachers College Record, 100*, 702–723.

Beauboeuf-Lafontant, T. (2002). A womanist experience of caring: Understanding the pedagogy of exemplary Black women teachers. *The Urban Review, 34*(1), 71–86. https://doi.org/10.1023/A:1014497228517

Beauboeuf-Lafontant, T. (2005). Womanist lessons for reinventing teaching. *Journal of Teacher Education, 56*(5), 436–445. https://doi.org/10.1177/0022487105282576

Beauboeuf-Lafontant, T. (2009). *Behind the mask of the strong Black woman*. Temple University Press.

Bhullar, S. A., & Grain, K. (2012). Mirror imaging diversity experiences: A juxtaposition of identities in cross-cultural initiatives. In J. Norris, R. D. Sawyers, D. Lund, & L. M. Given (Eds.), *Duoethnography: Dialogic methods for social, health, and educational research* (pp. 199–222). Taylor & Francis Group.

Collins, P. H. (2000). *Black feminist thought: Knowledge, consciousness, and the politics ofempowerment*. Routledge.

Cozart, S., & Gordon, J. (2006). Using womanist caring as a framework to teach social foundations. *The High School Journal, 90*, 9–15.

Delpit, L. (1988). The silenced dialogue: Power and pedagogy in educating other people's children. *Harvard Educational Review, 58*(3), 280–298.

Dillard, C., & Neal, A. (2020) I am because we are: (Re)membering Ubuntu in the pedagogy of Black women teachers from Africa to America and back again, *Theory into Practice, 59*(4), 370–378. https://doi.org/10.1080/00405841.2020.1773183

Duncan-Andrade, J. (2009). Note to educators: Hope required with growing roses in concrete. *Harvard Educational Review, 79*(2), 181–195.

Espino, M. M. (2012). Seeking the truth in the stories we tell: The role of critical race epistemology in higher education research. *The Review of Higher Education, 36*(1), 31–67. https://doi.org/10.1353/rhe.2012.0048

Giddings, P. (1984). *When and where I enter: The impact of Black women on race and sex in America*. Quill William Morrow.

Goldstein, L. (1999). The relational zone: The role of caring relationships in the co-construction of mind. *American Education Research Journal, 36*(3), 647–673.

Graham, M. (2007). The ethics of care, Black women and the social professions, implications of a new analysis. *Ethics and Social Welfare, 1*(2), 194–206.

Henery, C. (2017). *Black women, police violence, and mental illness*. Black Perspectives. https://www.aaihs.org/black-women-police-violence-and-mental-illness/

Houchen, D. F. (2015). *The transcendent pedagogy of Lincoln high school, 1921–1955: The aims, pursuits, and professional development of African American educators during de jure segregation* [Unpublished doctoral dissertation]. University of Florida.

Johnson, L. S. (2015). *Using sista circles to examine the professional experience of contemporary Black women teachers in schools: A collective story about school culture and support* [Unpublished doctoral dissertation]. University of Georgia.

Ladson-Billings, G. (1996). Silences as weapons: Challenges of a Black professor teaching White students. *Theory Into Practice, 35*(2), 79–85.

Lee, M., & Johnson-Bailey, J. (2004). Challenges to the classroom authority of women of color. *New Directions for Adult and Continuing Education, 102*, 55–64.

Littlefield, M. B., & Roberson, K. C. (2005). Computer technology for the feminist classroom. *Affilia, 20*(2), 186–202. https://doi:org/10.1177/0886109905274676

Marr, V. L. (2015). Ditchin' the master's gardening tools for our own: Growing a womanist methodology from the grassroots. *Feminist Teacher, 24*(1–2), 99–109. https://doi.org/10.5406/femteacher.24.1–2.0099

Monzó, L. D., & SooHoo, S. (2014). Translating the academy: Learning the racialized languages of academia. *Journal of Diversity in Higher Education*, 7, 147–165. https://doi.org/10.1037/a0037400

Neal-Barnett, A. M., Stadulis, R., Payne, M. R., Crosby, L., Mitchell, M., Williams, L., & Williams-Costa, C. (2011). In the company of my sisters: Sister circles as an anxiety intervention for professional African American women. *Journal of Affective Disorders, 129*(1), 213–218.

Noddings, N. (1995). Teaching themes of caring. *Education Digest, 61*(3), 24–29.

Noddings, N. (2013). *Caring: A relational approach to ethics and moral education* (2nd ed.). University of California Press.

Norris, J., Sawyer, R., & Lund, D. E. (2012). *Duoethnography: Dialogic methods for social, health, and educational research.* Left Coast Press.

Phillips, L. (Ed.). (2006). *The womanist reader.* Routledge.

Sanders, C. R. (2019). Pursuing the "Unfinished business of democracy": Willa B. Player and liberal arts education at Bennett College in the civil rights era. *North Carolina Historical Review, 96*(1), 1–33.

Sawyer, R. D., & Norris, J. (2009). Duoethnography: Articulations/(re)creation of meaning in the making. In W. Gershon (Ed.), *Working together in qualitative research: A turn towards the collaborative* (pp.127–140). Sense.

Shujaa, M. (1995). Cultural self meets cultural other in the African American experience: Teachers' responses to a curriculum content reform. *Theory Into Practice, 34*(5), 194–201.

Walker, A. (1983). *In search of our mother's gardens: Womanist prose.* Harvest Books.

Whitaker, F. (2013). The color of teaching: Expectations of mammy in the classroom. *The Feminist Wire.* Retrieved from https://thefeministwire.com/2013/11/the-color-of-teaching-expectations-of-mammy-in-the-classroom/

Woods-Giscombé, C. L. (2010). Superwoman schema: African American women's views on stress, strength, and health. *Qualitative Health Research, 20*(5), 668–683.

15

BLACK FEMINIST THOUGHT FROM THEORY TO PRACTICE

"This is MY LIFE"

Tiffany L. Steele

Black Feminist Thought (BFT) has been my trusted companion throughout my life journey. As most Black girls and women, I engaged BFT long before I knew it had a name and long before I could recognize how it was influencing my thoughts and actions. When thinking about my journey specifically throughout education, BFT was the guiding frame on how I made decisions, cultivated relationships, viewed myself, and ultimately, developed into a scholar. It was not just the presence of BFT as a theoretical abstract work but more so as a way of life and knowing. Essentially, BFT was and continues to be my paradigm, the worldview that aids me in decoding my surroundings and those who inhabit them. In addition, expanding my understanding of BFT introduced the possibility of identifying tools, such as portraiture methodology, to evoke the essence of BFT in research. In this chapter, I will explore my development as a scholar through my engagement with BFT in practice through relationship, research, and responsibility.

Black Feminist Thought as a Personal Paradigm

According to Collins (1989), BFT specializes in formulating and rearticulating the distinctive self-defined points of view of Black women. In this regard, Black women are the experts on their own experiences of oppression and offer a different view of experiences within structures such as political, educational, or economical systems and how these experiences catalyze a unique development of consciousness. Black women's self-definition challenges the power of controlling negative images attached to them by validating the power of Black women as human subjects (Collins, 1986). This form of independent thinking threatens the internalization of societal norms which causes groups in the

DOI: 10.4324/9781003184867-18

position of dominance to find ways to suppress the utility of this thinking in the lives of Black women to maintain control and continue suppression.

When reflecting on my doctoral journey, the power of academic socialization under the guise of dominant white norms was suffocating (Gildersleeve et al., 2011). I can recall the feelings of misalignment between myself and the unspoken expectations and rules I gathered about "the academy." This intuition screamed loudly when I tried to fit myself into qualitative boxes provided by the ivory tower to describe just who I was, how I approached my work, and what I cared about. It was not until it was time for me to fully engage my dissertation research that I allowed myself to step into who Tiffany was as a scholar doing work not just *for* Black girls and women but *with* them every step of the way. I had to accept that my internal conviction to turn away from the doctrine of the academy was my own personal commitment. It was not guaranteed to be readily understood or accepted, it would not come with a step-by-step guide, and it would be invisible to many but necessary for the survival of my spirit. Unbeknownst to me, this journey with BFT and resistance influenced my pursuit of the professoriate to encourage future generations of Black girls and women to come home to themselves and find community to thrive, particularly in education.

Collins (1989) described BFT through the following contours that shape ways of knowing for Black women: (a) the use of knowledge and wisdom; (b) the use of dialogue; (c) the ethic of care; and (d) the ethic of personal responsibility. The use of knowledge and wisdom is unique for Black women as knowledge is not enough for their survival (Collins, 1989). Within Black communities, previous experiences develop one's wisdom in determining how to navigate the world, and wisdom is recognized as more valid than mere knowledge gained from absorbing text. However, to develop new knowledge, there is a necessary component of connectedness to validate the developing knowledge among Black women through dialogue (Collins, 1989). The ethic of care highlights how the validation of knowledge cannot be separated from "the value of an individual's expressiveness, the appropriateness of emotions, and the capacity for empathy" (Collins, 1989, p. 767). Most importantly, Black women have a personal responsibility for the knowledge they develop and possess as this knowledge is viewed as connection to their personal values, morals, and beliefs (Collins, 1989).

In the creation of my dissertation study, BFT, as a paradigm, allowed me to reimagine new possibilities for my research outside of foundational texts originally used to develop my understanding of qualitative research. I wanted to not only capture the contours of BFT but also embody them in action. What did it mean for me to be a Black woman conducting research with Black girls about their experiences in education? What was my responsibility to the field to share the knowledge I cultivated in the relationship with the Black girls in my study? Most importantly, what was my responsibility to these Black girls as a Black woman generally? I was presented with the idea of portraiture as a methodology to begin answering those questions to shape not only my study but also my identity as a scholar.

Portraiture Methodology as a Tool for BFT

Lawrence-Lightfoot (1997) captured the essence of portraiture in describing her personal experience of having a self-portrait created by a painter, "I was never treated or seen as object, but always as a person of strength and vulnerability, beauty and imperfection, mystery and openness" (p. 4). Described as a more radical approach to research, portraiture methodologists are expected to imagine more for their participants, research, and overall field of study to evoke liberation and change (Lawrence-Lightfoot, 1997). Through an asset-based lens, researchers focus on representing the overarching story in a way that arouses emotions from readers. Therefore, the focus of the study is not to maintain an "inner circle" conversation among those in your field but to produce practical research that can be readily and broadly understood to make the change (Lawrence-Lightfoot, 1997). Undertaking this responsibility should produce an outcome of social transformation for the researcher and participant(s) using dialogue and actively listening to and interpreting the story within the stories participants share (Lawrence-Lightfoot, 1997).

After absorbing literature on the use of portraiture, I found its alignment to BFT through the need for both researchers and participants to be seen as contributors to the development of knowledge based on the lived experiences they bring to a study (Dixson et al., 2005). Overall, the portraiture methodology called for me to not only discuss the contours of BFT but to also *live* them out through engagement. While conducting my research, I had to be intentional about the development of rapport with the Black girls of my study. It meant modeling vulnerability through sharing my own journey in hopes to cultivate a safe space for them to in turn share their vulnerable stories about the genuine hurt educational spaces afforded them. I had to utilize their words in their entirety instead of perpetuating the idea of making their stories palatable for much of the academy. I had to be creative with the qualitative tools I learned in creating authentic opportunities for them to engage with one another versus bending to the traditional qualitative methods of data collection. Ultimately, I chose to speak life into them as a fellow Black girl instead of only viewing myself as a researcher throughout the entire study. The product of engaging in this study *with* Black girls utilizing portraiture and BFT was a necessary reflection of my own experience.

BFT Contours in Action

Use of Knowledge and Wisdom

Conversations with participants evoked suppressed memories of my educational journey from elementary school to doctoral studies. The language provided by

BFT helped me paint my memories in relation to the influential forces that led me to my current landing. There was a clear *use of knowledge and wisdom* I garnered throughout this journey by being mentored by a countless number of Black women faculty and peers. Drs. Porter, Patton Davis, Bertrand-Jones, Croom, and Polite's of the world, just to name a few, were the models of BFT personified for me to begin visualizing my own path in academe. These Black women pulled from their journeys, vulnerabilities, lessons, and overall knowledge to paint new possibilities for what my experience could be. The *beauty and imperfection* of their collective experiences were the permission I needed to begin thinking of myself as a scholar and ultimately, a faculty member. I could fill this chapter's pages solely on the interactions and conversations with these Black women and many others, and it still would not capture the power Black women possess as beings in the articulation of BFT.

The *use of knowledge and wisdom* displayed by those I consider mentors was present in my interactions with participants. Outside of considering them as just study participants, I *viewed* them also as Black women and humans. They were more than just first-year students who successfully matriculated into higher education on a predominantly white campus. They were humans with real fears, doubts, and questions about how to navigate their new journey. However, they had also been conditioned to turn away from the relationship I was offering due to the mistrust they experienced with past educators. Therefore, I created intentional moments throughout our interviews to check-in with each student personally. I wanted to know about how they were acclimating to campus, if they knew of all the campus resources available to them, and if, in any way, I could be a source of knowledge and wisdom to them during their journey. It was a way to impart knowledge relevant to their needs as people instead of monopolizing or exploiting their stories for my personal gain.

Use of Dialogue

Dialogue was at the center of my dissertation and remains in my current research approach. It captures my innate leaning toward qualitative research to co-construct understanding through sharing experiences. The *use of dialogue* was present in rapport building with the Black girls of my study but also building community among themselves. I can recall the day my participants and I gathered to complete a focus group discussion and activity. Most were unfamiliar with each other and more so, unfamiliar that they shared a harmful experience in educational spaces. As hours flew by, each student heroically shared their intimate thoughts. The courage and comfort to do so grew as each girl discussed their journey in full *truth and transparency*. They began to see the connection I had already witnessed between their experiences and innately bonded over just how alone they felt in their educational journeys.

Before long, one student said aloud to the group, "this helped me see that our stories really do matter."

I left the focus group reflecting on the life-giving power of dialogue in my doctoral experience. For me, the *use of dialogue* was essential to my relationships with Black women mentors and peers. Our connections were more than casual conversations; they were curated spaces for authentic dialogue that ultimately led to my survival and ability to complete my dissertation. This was most felt during my experience at the *Sisters of the Academy Signature Research BootCamp.* The week spent with fellow Black women doctoral students and scholars the summer before completing my dissertation study was life changing, to say the least. The *use of dialogue* during my time in the boot camp became an avenue to face my fears. In dialogue with other students and mentors, I expressed the doubt I felt in my ability to finish, the anticipated weight of my dissertation topic and participant stories, the fear of rejection from the academy in relation to my ideas, and the overall fear of my future career in academia. Members and scholars of the boot camp met me where I was and matched my fears and doubts with empowerment through dialogue. Speaking life and continuous encouragement were found in conversations with Drs. Bertrand-Jones, Cobb-Roberts, Mensah, and Foster Pierre. These dialogues cushioned my feelings of fragility around my scholarly identity as most conversations began in tears of fear and ended with tears of joy. It was this experience that readily enhanced and validated the ethic of care in which my research is grounded.

Ethic of Care

The development of my dissertation study was influenced by BFT as not just a theoretical framework but also a mode of practice. When asking participants to share their raw emotions unguardedly, the space I created for them to share was important both physically and emotionally. The *ethic of care* within BFT goes beyond finding a space to ensure participant confidentiality. This contour encourages researchers to consider the space both you and participants occupy as *liberating* while proving you as the researcher can be *trusted* with participant's stories. To do this successfully, I heavily engaged in being reflective in the moment to evoke the *empathy* necessary to support participants as they unpacked their educational journeys. My ability to do so, however, was largely due to my own experience as a Black woman. I could recall my educational journey and the amount of mistreatment I experienced from K-12 teachers and spaces. I could recall stepping onto my predominantly white campus as an undergraduate and processing my first apparent experience of *othering.* It was these memories that guided how I showed up for participants in a responsible way that was not self-serving but validating to their experiences as I engaged in data collection and constructed their individual portraits.

Ethic of Personal Responsibility

As an assistant professor, I try to embody the concluding contour, *personal responsibility.* I am indebted to Black girls and women due to the knowledge and wisdom I have gained throughout my experiences, to the skills I possess, and for the sanctity of my research. I speak the names of mentors and peers to show the lineage of BFT as a paradigm and practice in higher education. With that lineage comes the responsibility to continue engaging in knowledge creation *with* Black girls and women to share with the world. This responsibility and collaboration easily defined my pursuit of the professoriate. I wanted to be in a position to always engage BFT through research, practice liberation and change making on university campuses, and directly mentor and support future generations of Black girls and women in education. Although I start with acknowledging these tasks as my *personal responsibility*, I also remember it as one of the greatest opportunities I have been given throughout this educational journey.

References

Collins, P. H. (1986). Learning from the outsider within: The sociological significance of Black feminist thought. *Social problems*, *33*(6), 14–32.

Collins, P. H. (1989). The social construction of black feminist thought. *Signs: Journal of Women in Culture and Society*, *14*(4), 745–773.

Dixson, A. D., Chapman, T. K., & Hill, D. A. (2005). Research as an aesthetic process: Extending the portraiture methodology. *Qualitative inquiry*, *11*(1), 16–26.

Gildersleeve, R. E., Croom, N. N., & Vasquez, P. L. (2011). "Am I going crazy?!": A critical race analysis of doctoral education. *Equity & Excellence in Education*, *44*(1), 93–114. https://doi.org/10.1080/10665684.2011.539472

Lawrence-Lightfoot, S. (1997). A view of the whole: Origins and purposes. In S. Lawrence- Lightfoot & J. H. Davis (Eds.), *The art and science of portraiture* (pp. 3–16). Jossey-Bass.

16

HOW POSITIONALITY AND INTERSECTIONALITY IMPACT BLACK WOMEN'S FACULTY TEACHING NARRATIVES

Grounded Histories

Rhonda C. Hylton

The term "grounded histories" might evoke different types of feelings for various groups of people: pride, dignity, honor, joy, confidence, or respect. For others, it might elicit languishing, yearning, or even a hungering for those outside of a group to understand the history of not only a people, but of a place. Johnson (2010) suggested, "a critical pedagogy of place recognizes the concrete experiences of communities grounded in shared histories, stories and challenges based within a politics of place" (Abstract, para. 1). The histories in which Black women ground our narratives impact how we navigate and negotiate our positionality and intersectionality within the academy and in the world. This chapter will advance an exploration of specific teaching experiences to help Black women faculty interpret our positionality within these spaces. Theories of positionality (Acevedo et al., 2015; Bourke, 2014; Hall, 1990; Merriam et al., 2001; St. Louis & Barton, 2002), intersectionality (Crenshaw, 1995), and critical race feminism (CRF; Wing, 1997; Zinn & Dill, 1996) frame the interdisciplinary voices and practices in teaching that influence systemic, institutional, and personal change for Black women.

The narratives of Black women are not only powerful; they are critical in helping us teach others about who we are, where we have been, and the struggles we face within higher education contexts. These components inform how we experience our personal and professional lives; they dictate how we advocate for ourselves and for each other; they influence the classes we teach; and they guide our pedagogical decisions in and out of the classroom. This chapter recognizes the stories of two Black women faculty and myself, and calls for readers to learn from us as they consider their own lived experiences within and beyond the academy, and how we can work together to "better reposition ourselves at the center of our own inquiry" (Hylton, 2020, p. 16).

DOI: 10.4324/9781003184867-19

I also consider my positionality as a Black woman and pre-tenured faculty member at a predominantly white institution. I add my voice to the broader conversation of the importance of grounded histories and the beliefs within which we root ourselves, despite how we are positioned by those in power. I acknowledge the ways Black women perceive ourselves and how we are perceived by others complicates our experiences yet empowers us to strive for excellence in teaching and learning.

Before I discuss Black women and positionality, it is helpful to understand how positionality is grounded in the literature. In their exploration of positionality, Acevedo et al. (2015) uncovered two ways to view the subject of position: the first, positionality theory, was developed from postmodern feminist theory (see Alcoff, 1988; Collins, 1986; Harding, 1991). Contributors of this theory "challenged the essentialist views of identity as fixed, ongoing, and rooted in dominant individual and group characteristics (Acevedo et al., 2015, p. 32)." In this view, individuals hold multiple identities that are shifting, contextually situated, and grounded in prevailing individual and group characteristics.

The second framework, positioning theory, is rooted in social psychology. Acevedo et al. (2015) noted the theory "suggests that we are not simply actors of predetermined scripts, but agents and authors in our social participation" (p. 32). Both positionality and positioning theories work together to critically reflect upon how subjectivity is constructed and how people participate in social activities. Positionality reveals insider/outsider dynamics when engaging in research within and across cultures (Merriam et al, 2001); this view will be helpful when considering the three narratives of Black women portrayed in this chapter. Hall (1990) contested we must position ourselves somewhere to say anything at all. Bourke (2014) suggested it is important for us to recognize who we are as individuals and as members of groups and how our moving around affects our various social positions. St. Louis and Barton (2002) observed the role of our life experiences and how they also impact our positionality.

Black Women, Positionality, and Intersectionality

I draw upon Patricia Hill Collins (1999) to situate Black women's positionality. She identified the complications of race, gender, and social class and how they are experienced differently by Black women. Within the field of higher education at predominantly white institutions, intersectionality has become a popular analytical lens through which to investigate the varied experiences and realities of Black women (Boss et al., 2019). Born from the writings of women of color (Crenshaw, 1995), intersectionality calls for scholars to think more critically about gender and the conception of feminism, and to consider unique challenges Black women face, such as "racism, classism, and other threats to their equal opportunities and social justice" (Samuels &

Ross-Sheriff, 2008, p. 5). The framework also notes the complexity of the multiple demographic categories we embody, pushing us to consider the insider/outsider status Black women experience and how each status affords certain advantages and disadvantages.

CRF demonstrates the interdisciplinary voices and practices Black women adopt to create systemic and institutional change (Berry, 2009). Distinctive from other race or gender-only theories, CRF emphasizes intersectional identity, "which asserts that race and gender (among other identities) cannot be disentangled from the identity of women of color because they meet and overlap at a metaphorical crossroads" (Sulé, 2011, p. 171). Wing (1997) added about Black women:

> As representatives of groups oppressed on the basis of both race and gender, they cannot afford to adopt the classic white male ivory tower approach to abstract theorizing, removed from the actual needs of their communities.
>
> *(p. 5)*

CRF emanated from mainstream feminist movements (see Anzaldúa, 1987; Collins, 1986; Crenshaw, 1991, 2016; Delgado Bernal, 1998), and the framework has been used by numerous Black women scholars in education (Berry, 2015; Collins, 1990, 1998; hooks, 1990; James, 1999). My use of Collins (1999) to situate Black women's positionality relates to intersectionality, in that both lenses probe women's multiple identities and the challenges faced in their day-to-day lives. Along with CRF, attention to Black women's positionality and intersectionality can lead us to better understand the relationship between praxis and theory, and how Black women faculty perceive their literacy pedagogy. Berry (2015) observed the interconnected relationship between praxis and theory and how the two must work together to be useful. It is within this exchange between praxis and theory I situate the narratives of the Black women faculty featured in this chapter. The next section provides brief context for the narratives.

Research Methodology

The first two counternarratives of Black women faculty in this chapter are drawn from a larger study on Black women faculty's lived teaching experiences, their positionality within the university, and their literacy pedagogy (Hylton, 2020). Qualitative methods were used to examine each participant's subjective experiences and the processes in which they engaged to make meaning of them. The participants in this chapter identify as Black or African American and women and are classified as assistant professors at their respective universities.

Data Collection and Analysis

Data were collected over a three-month period. I collected the following four sources of data: (1) a short qualitative survey that gathered basic demographic information about each participant; (2) two semi-structured, in-depth interviews, which allowed participants to share their teaching narratives with me in a conversational format; (3) personal reflections on two prompts—one on their collective teaching experiences, and one on the similarities between their positionality and their perceptions of their literacy pedagogy; and (4) course syllabi from the fall 2019 semester, which provided insight into the decisions they made regarding their literacy pedagogy and how they conveyed their teaching goals to their students. Two research questions guided the study:

1. What teaching experiences have helped Black women faculty understand their positionality within the university?
2. How does the positionality of Black women faculty influence their perceptions of their literacy pedagogy?

To analyze the data, I transcribed the participant's audio interviews and used values coding (Saldaña, 2014) to determine emerging themes. This type of coding identifies values, attitudes, and beliefs about our "interpretive perceptions of the social world" (Saldaña, 2009, p. 89). After transcribing and listening to the participants' audio interviews, I examined their syllabi and compared those codes to the interview and reflection codes generated to verify that they matched. Additionally, I wrote analytic memos about how I related to the participants; patterns, categories, themes, and concepts that emerged during the interviews; possible connections among those elements; personal dilemmas within the study; and future directions for the work. As I interpreted the data, I selected a series of teaching instances from the participants and looked for recurring patterns in the data to explore similarities between categories.

Black Women Faculty Narratives: Nyanganyi, Sisyphean Task, and Rhonda

Nyanganyi

Born in St. Lucia, Nyanganyi's various identities provide insight into her teaching narrative, particularly how her identities transformed when she moved to the United States from the Caribbean, and how the struggles she experienced in the academy helped her transition from distancing to acceptance. Nyanganyi holds a Ph.D. in Curriculum and Instruction with a specialization in Literacy Studies and a concentration in Multilingual Education. Her research focuses on "the cross-cultural and crosslinguistic challenges faced by Black immigrant adolescents and educators in literacy instruction, assessment, and multicultural teacher education" (Hylton, 2020, p. 91). Her literacy pedagogy and practices shed light on her teaching experiences; special attention is given to the histories in which her narrative is grounded.

Nyanganyi's early life seemed to be heavily influenced by her family and community members. Her mother advocated for Nyanganyi and her siblings to receive a good education; literacy was a key aspect of their home life. There was an abundance of books and even though she and her siblings were homeschooled, no one talked to her about the books they read. Religion was also a significant part of their lives. Her father discussed the Bible and used it to promote critical thinking around implicit messages contained within the pages; this furthered Nyanganyi's view of literacy from a religious standpoint.

When Nyangani considered who guided her on the path to become a teacher, she was adamant it was not the path she chose for herself. A self-proclaimed introvert, she insisted she did not want to be a teacher. She related, "But I was good at it because my dad would have only said to do it because he felt I was good at it and that I would be good at teaching and everybody loves it when I'm teaching" (Hylton, 2020, p. 92). Nyanganyi admittedly got lost in what her father and her community wanted her to be simply because she was good at it, and she exhibited the characteristics of a good teacher. Nyanganyi's father told her she was going to be a teacher; therefore, she invested a substantial amount of time into learning about the profession. Her decision to pursue teaching was largely based on her father's authority, and on cultural norms that superseded her own desires. As she excelled in her career, she recognized the importance of cultural and societal norms, and how her early experiences in St. Lucia transferred to her perception of teaching and learning in the United States.

Important to Nyanganyi's narrative is the consideration of social class. It seemed Nyanganyi came from a middle to upper-class family because they could afford to outsource books and literature. Her father was a school principal, and her mother had the time and financial resources to stay home and teach Nyanganyi and her siblings. This dynamic revealed a great deal about her family's position in St. Lucia, and what it meant for her father to work as a school administrator, while choosing for his own children to be homeschooled. Brannon et al. (2017) wrote,

> Survey and experimental research demonstrate that social class is tied to rank (e.g., status, hierarchy) and resources (e.g., material, social and cultural capital) [2–4]. Yet, at the intersection of race and social class the consequences of being working-class or middle-class are not so Black and White.
>
> *(p. 117)*

Thus, we see how from a broader perspective, race, social class, and even ethnicity intersect to benefit and burden those who experience the constructs in their daily lives. Furthermore, the lines between social classes are not always clearly visible. For Nyanganyi, her perceived social class in St. Lucia helped her achieve academically, and it also burdened her by thrusting her into a profession she would not have chosen on her own. Furthermore, although Nyanganyi self-identified as Black/African American, her ethnicity was the Caribbean. Ethnicity is used to classify people according to their cultural expression and identity, and Nyanganyi understood that she would always be Caribbean, but she had to learn to adjust that identity when she moved to the United States and embrace a different identity as a Black scholar.

Nyanganyi's positionality as a Black, Caribbean, immigrant woman living in the United States prompted her to critically reflect on how she needed to transform her identities as she adjusted to a new way of life. Her lived experiences up to that point propelled her to shift her various identities based upon her desire to be true to herself in the academy. From the beginning, Nyanganyi was keenly aware of how she was perceived in the academy. As an emerging scholar, she focused her energy less on race and more on culture. However, she was more critical than what her colleagues were comfortable with. When she attempted to engage them in conversations around sensitive topics, her efforts were rejected because people were not ready to address them.

The distancing Nyanganyi named and experienced from her colleagues—and that she offered in return by distancing herself from them—led her to use her work, specifically writing, as a path to acceptance of her strategies to thrive in the academy. In the process, she learned to write about issues that frustrated her instead of letting her feelings build up inside of her, a method that proved helpful.

> At least it's more at least a positive channel to get the conversation to people out there, and then there are like, some particular people who are kind of similar to the people I feel, who are just completely opposed to people of Color, who might be able to take up that conversation and then maybe share with their friends or something, you know, but anyways.
>
> *(Interview 2, November 22, 2019)*

Thus, distancing inspired Nyanganyi to create space for herself and allowed other scholars to initiate discussions around sensitive subjects, despite their comfort levels. Moreover, distancing can lead other scholars of color, particularly women, to reconceptualize what it means to thrive in the academy and the approaches we can use—particularly writing—to do so. We can also use our university and community involvement as vehicles to share critical messages that might otherwise go unheard.

In their general observations of intersectionality and social theorizing, Harris and Leonardo (2018) offered, "Prescriptively, 'intersectionality' serves as a powerful reminder to pay attention to the margins of all identity-based organizing and analysis" (pp. 4–5). Nyanganyi learned to develop a new perspective on an old problem by recognizing her identities as positioned at the margins of the academy and calling attention to them by using writing to prevent further invisibility. Furthermore, she understood how "intersectionality disrupts group-based formulations such as 'women,' 'people of color,' and 'sexual minorities'" (Harris & Leonardo, 2019, p. 5). Through her writing, Nyanganyi proved that through a lens of intersectionality, no label is complete; we must work to find new ways to solve established problems to sustain long-term change. Thus, through the lens of intersectionality, the ways Nyanganyi moved between her personal and professional lives to reach a point of acceptance were major themes of her narrative.

As Nyanganyi worked in different universities in the United States, she was intentional about her teaching practices and made sure they were useful to her students in the real world. Even in online courses, she created a strong sense of community for her students and used language to help them feel a sense of solidarity with one another. Once Nyanganyi discovered coping skills to combat challenges within the academy, she was able to negotiate her positionality as a Black, woman, Caribbean immigrant in the United States. Within the context of higher education and in the world, Nyanganyi reimagined these spaces and her position within them to serve her professional and personal needs.

Sisyphean Task

Sisyphean Task is the second narrative I explore. She holds a Ph.D. in English and concentrates her research on basic writing, composition, digital literacies, and andragogy. The concepts of knowing and being are targeted, as well as how they influence her intentional praxis and ethos of care. Sisyphean Task identified as a Black, woman, but not as African American. She noted her identities felt ambiguous because though she was born in the United States, her parents were born in Panama. She and her family readily embraced the African pieces of their heritage and culture, but not the Hispanic and Latina elements. Sisyphean Task knew she presented multiple identities to the outside world and often felt the need to explain them to others. To the world, she appeared to be a Black woman, yet her ethnicity, which could not be easily detected, was grounded in rich Hispanic and Latin American cultures.

The uncertainty Sisyphean Task felt points to why intersectionality is useful in framing and showcasing the diverse voices and experiences that influence Black women. She did not view herself as African American; she recognized her ethnicity as Panamanian. Yet her nationality could be considered American because she was born in the United States, a country dominated by white people. Sisyphean Task's multiple, overlapping identities illustrated systems of power that were influenced by social interactions, relationships, and organizations (Vardeman-Winter & Tindall, 2010).

Sisyphean Task's parents initially moved from Panama to the United States to obtain better opportunities for their family. Although her parents' native language was Spanish, Sisyphean Task and her sisters spoke little of the language because Americans did not speak it where they lived in Texas. However, the little bit of the Spanish she did hear at home influenced the way she learned to write and speak. Like Nyanganyi, Sisyphean Task engaged in early literacy experiences at home with her mother that eventually led her to become a teacher. As an undergraduate, she recalled taking a Chicano Studies course taught by a Chicana professor, which shaped how she came to view teaching and learning. Of a particular pedagogical move by the professor, Sisyphean Task shared,

> It felt like a hug. It was so inclusive and mind you, I had enough credits. I was a junior at this time. And it was all throughout that I never (emphasis added), ever had a professor, you know, be so inclusive of me, and of the entire class. Because even though my parents are from a Central American country, they do identify as um, Hispanic and their first language is Spanish . . . (I) stood out as a Black woman in that class . . . it's a Chicana literature class . . . and just for her to say that I was like damn! Ok!
>
> *(Interview 1, November 21, 2019)*

Her early life experiences, her ethnicity, her understanding of language and literacy, and her keen sense of awareness about her identities and how they impacted her position in the world, led Sisyphean Task to understand intersectionality as an analytical frame. She recognized her multiple identities and the complexity that comes with being a person of color and a sexual minority. Instead of evading her identities, she embraced them and used them to highlight her conceptions of knowing and being. She also realized that comfortability with and acceptance of herself were key to her embodiment of her multiple identities.

In these ways, Sisyphean Task felt seen, heard, and validated and used her professor's practice in her own work to demonstrate the recursive process of teaching and learning. However, the most critical experience that opened her eyes to the possibility of becoming a teacher was her work as a writing tutor at a community college. There, she had ideas of becoming a teacher but did not know how to prepare for reality. When she earned her Ph.D., she was intentional about how her multiple identities and positionality connected and explained her thinking processes to her students in this way: "And I show it, and talk about it, and explain it to students because so often I feel that we're asking people, specifically students to be one way" (Interview 2, November 25, 2019). Sisyphean Task recognized identities as diverse and constantly unfolding and believed students should feel comfortable to share every part of who they are—not only the parts professors desire to see. The notion of care and allowing students to be their authentic selves contributed to her conceptions of knowing and being. Again, knowing, being, and racially identifying as one way or another aligned to the idea that comfortability and acceptance were critical to epitomizing multiple identities.

Sisyphean Task fostered a non-traditional, safe classroom in which students were encouraged to share all parts of themselves with others. She critiqued traditional forms of power in education to help them identify new ways of knowing and being in the literacy classroom. For example, she would not directly answer students' questions to transfer the power she held as the professor to students as learners, and as agents of their own knowledge. Her focus on critical pedagogy and power was evidenced by her approach to teaching; she intentionally surrendered some of the power placed upon her and offered it to students. Thus, Sisyphean Task's praxis and ethos of care were influenced by her narrative which she willingly shared with others. Her conceptions of knowing and being were paramount to her advancement and comfortability within the academy.

Rhonda

Through my narrative, I acknowledge my positionality as a gendered minoritized person and early career faculty member at a predominantly white institution to contribute to the larger conversation around the importance of grounded histories and the beliefs in which we root ourselves. A teacher by nature and by trade, service is the essence of who I am and how I live my life; it is also the common thread that weaves my narrative together. The history I ground myself in signifies the pride, dignity, honor, joy, confidence, and respect alluded to in the introduction to this chapter.

I did not know what race implied the first few years of my life. I grew up in predominantly white spaces in Georgia. My family was working middle-class and though I felt comfortable knowing we had certain privileges other Black people did not have, as a child, I was unaware of the price that came with that contentment. I belonged to a Black family that was the first to live in a majority white subdivision in Milledgeville, a small city that once served as the capital of Georgia. My father and uncles sat on our front porch at night with shot guns, protecting our family from unveiled threats of racism. When we moved from Milledgeville to a suburb of Augusta, Georgia, I became keenly aware that I was the only Black girl in academic spaces. In the after-care program I attended, I was called a nigger, despite my attempts to fit in with my white peers. I sensed that the use of the word was wrong, but I could not articulate how it made me feel. This scene illustrates my positioning in the world by others and reveals how I was seen by my peers. I was not comparable to them; my race was perceived first, and because of it, I was assumed to be lesser than, not equal to the white children. That racialized piece of my identity was characterized as a negative element, despite me belonging to the same social class as my white counterparts.

When my parents and I moved to Metro-Atlanta, I grappled with what it meant to transition from being one of the only Black girls in my school to being a part of a racial majority. After completing high school, I enrolled in a historically Black university in Atlanta and was exposed to the diversity of the Black diaspora. I learned Black people came from varied backgrounds and positions, and we all carried with us life experiences that made us who we were. I wanted to pursue teaching as a career, and after I enrolled in a master's degree program, I quickly determined that white, male privilege still ran rampant and trumped my Blackness, despite the diversity and support the university offered. In my second master's degree program, I surrounded myself with other Black students in our cohort to establish a sense of togetherness based on shared commonalities. Our group was formed based on markers of our intersecting identities such as social class, race, ethnicity, and age.

As I moved into my teaching career, I experienced what I knew was racism. My first two years as a teacher were filled with excitement, worry, and eventually, a need to escape an environment that became toxic. Once again, my intersecting identities, particularly my race, age, and gender identification were attacked by white supervisors based on their perceptions of who and what they thought I was. In my everyday professional interactions, these markers of my identity were discredited by systems of power considered superior to my knowing and being.

When I began teaching in higher education, I realized my previous teaching experiences and my positionality—how I was perceived and positioned by others—were different from what was portrayed. My teaching experiences and positionality have greatly impacted how I understand the academy, my evolving literacy pedagogy, and my current role as a faculty member. At the institution where I work, I am one of three Black women in my school and the youngest person. These statistics are not unique to my narrative; I have been in professional situations like this before. However, I have an ongoing responsibility to myself to critically examine my position, particularly as a Black woman at the school level and at the university at large; this reflection is crucial, considering the volatile racial and political climate we live in. The university continues to grapple with ways to engage in tough conversations that center the experiences of the Black, Indigenous, and people of color, and the experiences of those with minoritized genders. I am learning to be more intentional about adding my voice to these conversations to support others in their understanding of the intricate nature of the societal issues that affect us.

Strategies

As a tenure-track faculty member and as a Black woman with intersecting multiple identities, my primary interests lie in discovering and sharing the narratives and stories of other Black women faculty to highlight our common interests and to celebrate the ways in which we uniquely approach teaching, learning, and the world around us. The three narratives I present here represent only a fragment of the stories and the grounded histories Black women faculty possess. Together, we should continue to share our stories to create sustainable change within and beyond the academy. Sisyphean Task offered a point that resonated with me, and I hope resonates with other Black women faculty,

> As a Black woman in higher education, I am often a physical representation of the fact that what is "dominant" i.e., white men in higher education or even white women, is not the only (even though I am, quite frankly, the only). What is often seen as the "only" is not in fact the "only;" that there is more and that what is "other" than dominant is not lesser.
>
> *(Reflection Two, December 27, 2019).*

Her idea of Black women and our positionality as the "only" or the "other," particularly at predominantly white institutions, reminds us that our intellectual efforts are not subordinate because we do not belong to a dominant group. Rather, in combination with the histories, we ground ourselves in, we should confidently wield our teaching experiences, positionality, and pedagogical skills to challenge the thinking and assumptions of those who do belong to dominant groups.

The ways Black women view ourselves and how we are perceived by others complicates our experiences, yet also empowers us to collectively strive for excellence in teaching and learning. How do we do this and engage in the work that lies ahead of us? I offer three strategies for consideration. First, Black women faculty should use our positionality and positioning by others to push back against established norms and cultures in the academy. We can do so by offering alternative ways of viewing and engaging in teaching, learning, and talking about our experiences. Hollis (2018) suggested working with departments of Academic Affairs to ensure social justice teaching is included in the curriculum across disciplines.

Second, Black women faculty should use our counternarratives to encourage students to critically examine their beliefs around what it means to teach literacy, particularly in minoritized communities. We must teach students to develop meaningful relationships with the children and families they serve to help them understand how interrogating their own decision-making practices can set them up to be more informed and empathetic educators.

Third, Black women faculty should make our health and wellness a priority by practicing radical self-care to remain rooted and grounded in our histories. Self-care is traditionally viewed as "a deliberate practice to prevent major illness for those with chronic conditions such as high blood pressure, diabetes, and heart disease" (Nicol & Yee, 2019, p. 134). However, we must explore and engage in radical self-care, which is defined as "practices that keep us physically and psychologically fit, making time to reflect on what matters to us, challenging ourselves to grow, and checking on ourselves to ensure that what we are doing aligns with what matters to us" (Nicol & Yee, 2019, p. 134). Participating in this practice can change how we think about time, money, and energy in all facets of our lives, leading us to transform our workplace practices.

Immersing ourselves in radical self-care also impacts our personal lives. Though we are not all athletes, Black women faculty take on a mental toughness to meet the demands of the academy. We can look at recent—though not new—stories of how the professional grit we display for the world affects us personally. These stories are seen in Black women like Simone Biles and Serena Williams, who, because of the unfair demands of their professions, have been honest about what it looks like to struggle with mental health as athletes, but also as Black women who are critically examined by others who position them in ways that highlight their professional accomplishments, but ignore their varied and multiple identities that intersect and represent who they are. Similarly, Black women faculty must tend to our own needs and transform ourselves personally as we aim to do the same professionally.

CRF offers a mechanism through which Black women can push back against and disrupt dominant systems not only as gendered people, but as women whose lives are deeply influenced by our locations in and embodiments of various spaces. CRF's utility can help Black women faculty and those interested in our lived and teaching experiences, move forward in practical ways. Black women faculty can offer thoughts and practices that intentionally aid in our teaching and learning about ourselves and urge those in dominant groups within and beyond the academy to do the same.

References

Acevedo, S. M., Aho, M., Cela, E., Chao, J-C, Garcia-Gonzales, I., MacLeod, A., ... Olague, C. (2015). Positionality as knowledge: From pedagogy to praxis. *Integral Review: A Transdisciplinary and Transcultural Journal for New Thought, Research and Praxis, 11*(1), 28–46.

Alcoff, L. (1988). Cultural feminism versus post-structuralism: The identity crisis in feminist theory. *Signs, 13*(3), 405–436.

Anzaldúa, G. (1987). *Borderlands/la frontera: The new mestiza.* Aunt Lute.

Berry, T. R. (2009). Women of color in a bilingual/dialectal dilemma: Critical race feminism against a curriculum of oppression in teacher education. *International Journal of Qualitative Studies in Education, 22*(6), 745–753.

Berry, T. R. (2015). Me and Bill: Connecting Black curriculum orientations to critical race feminism. *Educational Studies, 51*(5), 423–433.

Boss, G. J., Davis, T. J., Porter, C. J., & Moore, C. M. (2019). Second to none: Contingent women of color faculty in the classroom. In R. Jeffries (Ed.), *Diversity, equity, and inclusivity in contemporary higher* education (pp. 211–225). IGI Global.

Bourke, B. (2014). Positionality: Reflecting on the research process. *The Qualitative Report, 19*(33), 1–9.

Brannon, T. N., Higginbotham, G. D., & Henderson, K. (2017). Class advantages and disadvantages are not so Black and White: Intersectionality impacts rank and selves. *Current Opinion in Psychology, 18*, 117–122. http://dx.doi.org/10.1016/j.copsyc.2017.08.029

Collins, P. H. (1986). Learning from the outsider within: The sociological significance of Black Feminist Thought. *Social Problems, 33*(6), S14–S32.

Collins, P. H. (1990). *Black feminist thought: Knowledge, consciousness, and the politics of empowerment.* Unwin Hyman.

Collins, P. H. (1998). *Fighting words: Black women and the search for justice.* University of Minnesota Press.

Collins, P. H. (1999). Reflections on the outsider within. *Journal of Career Development, 26*(1), 85–88.

Crenshaw, K. (1991). Mapping the margins: Intersectionality, identity politics, and violence against women of color. *Stanford Law Review, 43*(6), 1241–1299.

Crenshaw, K. (1995). Mapping the margins: Intersectionality, identity politics, and violence against women of color. In K. Crenshaw, N. Gotanda, G. Peller, & K. Thomas (Eds.), *Critical race theory: The key writings that formed the movement* (pp. 357–383). New Press.

Crenshaw, K. (2016). *On intersectionality—A keynote.* WOW 2016. https://www.youtube.com/watch?v=-DW4HLgYPlA

Delgado Bernal, D. (1998). Using a Chicana feminist epistemology in educational research. *Harvard Educational Review, 68*, 555–583. doi:10.17763/haer.68.4.5wv1034973g22q48

Hall, S. (1990). Cultural identity and diaspora. In J. Rutherford (Ed.), *Identity: Community, culture, difference* (pp. 2–27). Lawrence & Wishart.

Harding, S. 1991. *Whose science? Whose knowledge?* Cornell University Press.

Harris, A., & Leonardo, Z. (2018). Intersectionality, race-gender subordination, and education. *Review of Research in Education, 42*(1), 1–27. https://doi.org/10.3102/0091732X18759071

Hollis, L. P. (2018). Bullied out of position: Black women's complex intersectionality, workplace bullying, and resulting career disruption. *Journal of Black Sexuality and Relationships, 4*(3), 74–89.

hooks, b. (1990). *Yearning: Race, gender, and cultural politics.* South End Press.

Hylton, R. C. (2020). *Who are we? My sisters and me: A multiple case study of Black women faculty and how their Teaching experiences and positionality influence their perceptions of their literacy pedagogy* [Doctoral dissertation, Kent State University]. OhioLINK.

James, J. (1999). *Shadowboxing: Representations of Black feminist politics.* St. Martin's Press.

Johnson, J. T. (2010). Place-based learning and knowing: critical pedagogies grounded in Indigeneity. *GeoJournal, 77*, 829–836. https://doi.org/10.1007/s10708-010-9379-1

Merriam, S. B., Johnson-Bailey, J., Lee, M.-Y., Kee, Y., Nteeane, G., & Muhamad, M. (2001). Power and positionality: Negotiating insider/outsider status within and across cultures. *International Journal of Lifelong Education, 20*(5), 405–416. https://doi.org/10.1080/02601370110059537

Nicol, D. J., & Yee, J. A. (2019). "Reclaiming our time": Women of color faculty and radical self-care in the academy. *Feminist Teacher, 27*(2–3), 133–156.

Saldaña, J. (2009). *The coding manual for qualitative researchers.* Sage Publications.

Saldaña, J. (2014). Coding and analysis strategies. In P. Leavy (Ed.), *The Oxford handbook of qualitative research* (pp. 581–605). Oxford University Press.

Samuels, G. M., & Ross-Sheriff, F. (2008). Identity, oppression, and power: Feminisms and intersectionality theory. *Affilia: Journal of Women and Social Work, 23*(1), 5–9.

St. Louis, K., & Barton, A. C. (2002). Tales from the science education crypt: A critical reflection of positionality, subjectivity, and reflexivity in research. *Forum: Qualitative Social Research Sozial Forschung, 3*(3).

Sulé, V. T. (2011). Restructuring the master's tools: Black female and Latina faculty navigating and contributing in classrooms through oppositional positions. *Equity and Excellence in Education, 44*(2), 169–187. https://doi.org/10.1080/10665684.2011.559415

Vardeman-Winter, J., & Tindall, N. T. J. (2010). Toward an intersectionality theory of public relations. In R. L. Heath (Ed.), *The SAGE handbook of public relations* (pp. 223–233). Sage Publications.

Wing, A. K. (1997). Brief reflections toward a multiplicative theory and praxis of being. In A. K. Wing (Ed.), *Critical race feminism: A reader* (pp. 27–34). New York University Press.

Zinn, M., & Dill, B. T. (1996). Theorizing difference from multiracial feminism. *Feminist Studies, 22*, 321–331. https://doi.org/10.2307/3178416

SECTION IV

Canary in the Coal Mine

Journeying from Associate to Academic Administrator and Full Professor

17

SUPPORTING BLACK WOMYN ASSOCIATE PROFESSORS TO THE FULL PROFESSORSHIP

Stacey D. Garrett and Natasha N. Croom

Persistent in the academy is the conversation around representational diversity. Despite the ever-increasing rate at which Black womyn earn terminal degrees, they continue to be underrepresented at every level of academia. For Black womyn on the tenure track, many conversations with mentors and peers focus on attaining tenure. However, this limited approach fails to prepare Black womyn for the complete career trajectory and pathway to promotion. The full professor rank is said to bestow prestige, influence, and status as faculty gain (inter)national content expertise (Finnegan & Hyle, 2009) and play a vital role in the governance of higher education institutions. What opportunities are missed for Black womyn faculty as well as the field of higher education when Black womyn are left out of the conversations happening at the highest levels of the institution? The purpose of this chapter is to center tenured Black womyn associate professors' perspectives on advancing to the full professorship and the roles of mentors, academic administrators, and institutional initiatives in their advancement opportunities.

Background

The professoriate emerged as a highly coveted space in the late 1970s as college enrollment slowed (Youn & Price, 2009). Standards for faculty rewards increased and tenure became increasingly difficult to obtain. The job security tenure provided was even more important with a decline in available positions. Colleges and universities seeking to maintain enrollment numbers fought to distinguish themselves by hiring top-tier faculty to conduct cutting-edge research and provide the best educational experience (Youn & Price, 2009). This historical lens demonstrates the ways in which institutions continue to use

DOI: 10.4324/9781003184867-21

faculty to drive/maintain enrollment. In the espoused pursuit of a more diverse student body today, historically white institutions (HWIs) seek a diverse faculty body. Unfortunately, the questions of who can be educated, who can teach, and who can lead, still plague today's colleges and universities (Smith, 2015).

A significant amount of literature documents the experiences of faculty seeking tenure and promotion to the rank of associate professor. Achieving this level of security is a hurdle many Black womyn strive to overcome. Less, however, is known about the experiences of Black womyn mid-career faculty and their experiences seeking promotion to Full Professor. Black womyn represent ~2% of faculty at the Associate and Full Professor ranks across institution type in the USA (National Center for Education Statistics, 2019). The nebulous path to full is riddled with inconsistent or undefined promotion guidelines leaving Black womyn—commonly left without the mentoring and institutional supports to navigate this uncharted territory—to advocate for themselves in ways that may be read as unwelcome at best and aggressive at worst. Croom (2017) found that when faculty of color (FOC) aspired for promotion to the full professorship, their white full professor colleagues viewed them as interlopers and arrogant for seeking assistance and insights into advancing. Despite multiple frameworks for making the change in higher education settings (Dowd & Bensimon, 2015; Smith, 2015), institutions continue to avoid the necessary work for creating environments in which Black womyn can thrive and advance. HWIs must name the history of oppression that has limited access and inclusion, and then create the policies to reshape practices for a more equitable experience (Down & Bensimon, 2015). Therefore, this chapter contributes to the literature of mid-career faculty by giving insights into how Black womyn's intersecting marginalities and society's systems of oppression manifest in the professoriate.

Theoretical Framework

Aligning with the goals of this text, we frame the research guiding this chapter with critical race feminism (CRF). This theory provides us the space to identify and interrogate the systems of privilege and oppression that help and hinder the advancement of Black womyn in the academy. We utilize the tenets of CRF as structured in Croom (2017) to design the study, analyze the data, and contextualize the findings. The five tenets of CRF include (1) intersectionality and anti-essentialism; (2) racism, sexism, and classism are endemic; (3) valuing experiential knowledge and challenging ahistoricism; (4) challenging liberal ideologies; and (5) praxis.

Intersectionality and anti-essentialism represent the convergence of social identities and the subsequent systems of oppression. For Black womyn, our marginalized race and gender identities, coupled with other salient and latent identities, are perceived in particular ways as we navigate various social institutions. This tenet provides space to highlight and name historical and present-day perceptions of Black womyn and their experiences. This tenet also informs the purpose of our study and interview protocols. *Racism, sexism, and classism are endemic* asserts the embeddedness of interlocking systems of privilege and oppression in social institutions (e.g., academia) and practices (e.g., tenure and promotion; Croom, 2017). We use this tenet in subsequent rounds of data analysis. *Valuing experiential knowledge and challenging ahistoricism* necessitates counterstorytelling and individual/group narratives in the understanding of the effects of racism, sexism, and other forms of oppression, particularly for womyn of color. We can center the voices of our participants in our data collection with the use of this tenet. Including this tenet in our framing creates space to speak to the historical and continued exclusion of Black womyn in the academy at individual and institutional levels in intentional and systematic ways. *Challenging liberal ideologies* concerns debunking the myths of meritocracy, objectivity, race- and gender-neutrality, and other "bootstrap" mentalities that plague social institutions and practices. We use this tenet in our analysis process to name the barriers our participants' encounter while advancing in a racialized and gendered environment. Informed by Hughes and Giles (2010), Croom (2017) noted, "*Praxis* requires the bringing together of theory and practice to act toward the empowerment of womyn of color and the elimination of racism, sexism, and classism" (p. 567). We assert the use of CRF as a liberatory epistemology and theoretical framing to effect change in the policy and practice of academic institutions.

Research Design

The data informing this chapter were collected as part of a larger study exploring the aspirations of men and womyn of color faculty across the country. The call for participants was shared through social networks, direct contact with various campus-based organizations supporting FOC, and snowball sampling. Using CRF and purposive sampling, this critical qualitative inquiry centers the experiences of three Black womyn to "problematize the cycle of socialization, incorporate marginalized voices within the research processes, and make visible alternative paradigms" (Pasque et al., 2012, p. 27) toward creating more equitable policies and practices. Our specific research questions were: (1) what influences Black womyn's aspirations to full professor, and (2) what role do mentors, academic administrators, and institutional initiatives play in supporting or thwarting the advancement opportunities of Black womyn?

Sampling and Participants

To center the experiences of Black womyn faculty, we utilized purposive sampling to select participants who: (1) self-identified as Black or African American; (2) self-identified as a womxn; (3) had earned tenure; (4) held the rank

TABLE 17.1 Participant Demographics

Institution Control		*Institution Type*		*Years at Associate*	
Private, not for profit	1	R1/Highest Research	2	0–2 years	1
Public	2	R2/Higher Research	1	3 or more years	2

of Associate Professor; and (5) was serving as a faculty member at the time of participation. We use the terms *womxn (singular)* and *womyn (plural)* to decenter "men" as a discursive practice and assert womyn as separate, albeit not unconnected, in analyses of the sociopolitical world that constructs normative gender roles. We identified three participants who met the desired criteria. Additional demographic information is given in Table 17.1. Each participant served within a different discipline at a different HWI, which was not included to provide anonymity. We intentionally chose to focus on the Black womyn faculty participants to highlight the specific aspirations, motivations, and implications of this underrepresented group seeking promotion to full professorship. Each participant was able to select a pseudonym for use throughout the study and publication phases. Only one participant offered a name for this purpose, and pseudonyms were assigned to the other womyn. Additional safeguards were in place to protect the identities of our participants (e.g., removing names of individuals and institutions mentioned in interviews).

Data Collection

We collected data through semi-structured interviews with each participant. Our interview protocol was designed utilizing the CRF tenets of intersectionality and anti-essentialism and valuing experiential knowledge and challenging ahistoricism. Our questions were divided into four sections to explore the following: (1) establishment of aspirations to full; (2) levels of support and the role of mentoring; (3) influence of identity on aspirations; and (4) knowledge of the professorship. We created space for participants to share their stories of previous tenure and promotion experiences and ways in which their race, gender, and other salient identities influenced their aspirations. Other sections of the interview focused on the role of various institutional agents and initiatives, teasing out the written and unwritten rules of advancing on the tenure track. We held interviews via phone which were recorded and professionally transcribed.

Data Analysis

Uplifting the voices of our participants was central in our analysis. Thus, we engaged in multiple rounds of analysis. The first round of analysis consisted of analytic memoing (Saldaña, 2016), which allowed for us to note interpretations of the data based on our insider positionality and the literature around Black womyn faculty experiences. The memoing process also allowed for us to maintain a level of separation between our experiences and thoughts from what was in the data specifically. The second round of analysis focused on open coding, or emergent coding, and provided space for us to create codes from participant responses that we could apply to each transcript. This series of codes, such as *seeking information about the process* or *having a mentor in an administrative leadership position*, were then arranged into like categories, or themes.

Trustworthiness

We employed multiple strategies to ensure credibility and trustworthiness in our data and analysis. First, our research design was structured in a way that aligned our framework with our methods. Privileging the voices of our participants, the critical qualitative inquiry, and our use of semi-structured interviews, opened the door for rich data collection. Second, our emergent coding process maintained much of the original sentiments expressed from our participants without ignoring important details that did not fit into a particular mold of an *a priori* approach. Finally, we utilized self-reflection to separate ourselves from the data during our analysis. This allowed us to acknowledge our own experiences (lived and researched) as Black womyn in tenure-track faculty positions and monitor our interpretations of participant experiences.

Positionality

With our racial, gender, and professional identities aligned with our participants, we, as Black womyn faculty members, accepted the opportunity to collect, interpret, and present these experiences as real and valuable. The tenets of CRF push against essentialism, discouraging a singular Black womyn's reality. The findings we present in this chapter describe a commonality of experiences and understanding among our participants without the goal or purpose of generalization. As authors, we chose to show up in this chapter through a first person, plural, active voice that foregrounds ourselves, Black womyn, as knowledge producers.

Findings

We present our findings as direct responses to our research questions. Each theme was informed by the experiences of each participant.

The Influence of Identity in Black Womyn's Aspirations

When questioned about the influence of their identity on their aspirations, each participant had a perspective based upon their unique (and shared) intersections of identity. Regarding their shared racial identity, two participants discussed *access* as a primary concern: access for themselves and access for others. Khadijah spoke to wanting to guard against "getting stuck" at associate. It was important for her to obtain "her full rights and privileges" by claiming a seat at table of institutional governance, a space she noted was only accessible with the rank of Full Professor. Olivia mentioned wanting to open doors for Black undergraduates. She asserted,

> The [B]lack undergraduates that I've worked with who are some of the most talented young people of this generation never even get a chance to think about graduate school because there's not one other black faculty member in [this discipline].

Her goal is to change the demographics of her field and that starts with the classroom experience for undergraduates. Regine acknowledged the influence of her racial identity in connection with her "racial uplift background, missionary Baptist church background," saying, "that's kind of part of what we do that just makes me who I am."

Khadijah and Olivia discussed what it means to be a womxn seeking the full professorship, while Regine was not feeling motivation from her gender identity independently. Each participant had a different meaning associated with their gender identity which could be a result of our questioning as we asked participants to separate their identities and consider the influence. Olivia spoke to the support she has had from womyn over time and part of her inspiration was to pay that forward. She stated,

> Nobody gets tenured [here] in my mind without that handful of senior women pitching that for you, like senior full...Part of being full for me is just standing in the shoes of these senior women and carrying the banner forward.

Similarly, Khadijah mentioned taking pride in inspiring other womyn to accomplish their goals.

We opened the door for participants to also discuss identities beyond race and gender that served as an influence on their aspirations. Two participants discussed how class (specifically, low socioeconomic status) interacted with their race and gender identities. One participant acknowledged her sexuality (described as queer), and another brought up her caregiver status as a mother and age (or perceptions of age) as factors in their aspirations and experiences working toward promotion. This led to participants considering the totality of their identities as an influence on their aspirations. For example, Khadijah said, "I've always kind of feel like I'm the exception to most rules anyways just because I'm a black female [in STEM]. So, it's like, 'Well, then I'll be the exception to that rule too. Let's do this [get to Full].'" Olivia acknowledged the way various identity-based networks became sources of support for her scholarship. Regine described what happens at the intersection of her identities and the way ageism operates. Regine felt herself discredited and disrespected because the physical signs of aging looked different for her as a Black womxn. She extended this to discuss how choices around motherhood could have impacted her had she listened to the advice or concerns of previous deans, encouraging her to push back her tenure clock despite having met the criteria for tenure and promotion to associate.

Supports and Barriers to the Advancement of Black Womyn

When seeking to answer this question, we structured our interview protocol to specifically ask for experiences with various individuals or initiatives. While each participant had a story to share, we named similarities in their stories as self-advocacy. Within the other themes that speak directly to the second research question, our participants illustrated the ways Black womyn faculty look out for themselves in the face of institutions not built for their participation or success.

Black Womyn's Self-Advocacy

Each of our participants successfully navigated their tenure and initial promotion experiences. A renewed, or continued, need for self-advocacy was a clear part of their path and promotion to full. Participants discussed the various meetings they requested to speak with administrators, mentors, or full professors in their units or institutions. They were under no illusion that the opportunity for advancement would be handed to them, given the lack of information in institutional and department policy. They had to take the steps to learn about the process, express their aspiration to full, and gather feedback on their work. The notion of self-advocacy connotes the requirement for Black womyn to take a much more active role in their process than some of their white and/or men colleagues.

Khadijah noted her department had no shortage of womyn; however, many were concentrated at the assistant and associate levels. She emphasized the importance of not "getting stuck" at the associate and engaged her department chair in specific conversations regarding next steps. Regine discussed repeat conversations with an Associate Dean in her college. She shared, "In my initial [conversation] with her, her response was, 'I didn't even know you were interested in going up for full.'" The Associate Dean assumed Regine would be content with staying at the Associate Professor rank. If Regine had not expressed interest and asked about the requirements for promotion, her Associate Dean would not have volunteered that information. Regine went on to describe subsequent meetings, one in which she received confirmation from that Associate Dean to prepare her promotion materials for submission the following year. In this way, our participants demonstrated the dangers of a passive approach to advancement. Without the internalized push to advance and express their aspirations, Black womyn may be overlooked and unconsidered. We continue to note evidence of self-advocacy in mentoring experiences, the power of academic administrators, and the role of ineffective institutional initiatives.

The Necessity of Cross-Cultural Mentoring

Our participants readily presented stories and experiences that demonstrated the role of mentoring in their advancement decisions and preparations. For Khadijah and Regine, having someone as a mentor with experience in administrative roles contributed to their aspirations. Regine acknowledged a mentor who served as a dean and discussed what it took to make the change on campus and operate as a full professor. Similarly, Olivia looked externally to find examples of the responsibilities of a full professor, specifically in her discipline. Notably, sponsorship came up for each participant as something that aided their advancement or influenced their aspiration. In academia, where Black womyn are so underrepresented, cross-cultural sponsors are necessary. Khadijah mentioned the ways white men colleagues operated in tandem, one as a mentor, one as a sponsor, to help her advance. Regine and Olivia provided examples of how sponsorship can be integral in one's experiences and something they can do once promoted to bring others through the ranks with them.

Each participant identified white men, and some white womyn, who served as mentors or supporters. With the abundance of white men holding the rank of Full Professor, it only makes sense that these individuals would be the group to mentor and sponsor all aspiring associate professors. Unfortunately, given the ways racism and sexism continue to plague our institutions, men continue to operate as gatekeepers, limiting access to the information, resources, and support needed to advance (Croom, 2017).

The Power of Academic Administrators

Participants discussed conversations with various administrators from department chairs to college deans as a part of their preparations for promotion. The consistent theme we saw here again centered around Black womyn seeking out information to navigate the nebulous system. The responses varied demonstrating the problematic and random nature of a process built on the will of individuals. Khadijah found support in her department chair, as an extension of her decision to switch institutions after tenure and promotion at another institution. She acknowledged the arbitrary response of her former chair when inquiring about promotion to full as a contributing factor in her departure. At her current institution, the conversation around promotion began as part of her negotiations and, luckily, her chair was consistent after she transitioned.

Regine's story illustrated the variation in responses that can complicate a process. Seeking support from multiple sources, she experienced a possible delay in her advancement. Her chair and the associate dean were not actively supportive nor actively unsupportive. They withheld endorsement, which did little to build confidence in her readiness to apply. Regine presented accounts of multiple conversations with a senior mentor and other full professors in her department. She even met with the newly appointed dean of her college to get a sense of their expectations. Her familiarity with the vagueness of institutional policy caused her to continue these types of meetings to, in a sense, shore up the votes for a successful bid.

Olivia, with less time at rank, spoke mainly about her observations of her department and informal conversations with senior members of her department. She described a specific conversation with her college-level dean, but their expectations seemed to counter her department expectations and what she had observed for others on campus. This variation in expectations could prove to be detrimental without further confirmation given the college-level standard was lower than the observations and messaging she received from her department colleagues. She also perceived different expectations for Black faculty in her department, with Black faculty having to exceed the limited espoused guidelines for promotion.

Ineffectual Institutional Initiatives

Participants reported a lack of notable supports and resources from the institutional level. They mentioned only having general guidelines for promotion to full professor which provided little clarity. The vagueness of the process and expectations influenced the heightened need for our participants' self-advocacy. Through the seeking of information, participants found few answers at the department, college, or institutional level. They mentioned attending workshops held by their institutions, but found the general nature to be unhelpful, particularly when not applicable to their specific discipline. More often, workshops were designed for junior faculty seeking tenure rather than tenured faculty seeking promotion.

Loose guidelines for promotion do allow for more holistic reviews and would, reasonably, create more opportunities for advancement. The lack of detail forced our participants to create their own road maps and engage in additional labor to understand what was expected of them. Each participant noted looking to other colleagues or most recently promoted faculty to see what their promotion dossiers included. They engaged in conversations with those who would ultimately evaluate their materials to get a sense of how their work would be received. This level of subjectivity, however, could lead to delays in the promotion. Regine painted a picture of "readiness" in her story—she was waiting for indicators from colleagues and administrators at each level to tell her she was ready to apply. With too many opinions and too little criteria, Black womyn could, and are, left waiting for an invitation that may never come.

Overall, we found mentorship to be a consistently helpful part of advancement for these Black womyn faculty members. Having the ability to choose a mentor also worked in their favor. Academic administrators can have a positive or negative impact on progress. The amount of chance or luck in a process with so much at stake leaves Black womyn vulnerable to the whims of the academy, a place that routinely disserves, devalues, and dehumanizes Black womyn. With virtually ineffective institutional initiatives, there are little to no protections for Black womyn faculty in current structures. The implications for praxis given our findings can shift the academy to create an environment supportive of Black womyn's advancement.

Discussion

Throughout the findings, we see how intersectionality and anti-essentialism manifested in the experiences of our participants. They acknowledged their identities as an influence on their professional aspirations—an expression of who they are, but also a response to the ways in which they are perceived. This point was evident in Regine's discussion of herself as a Black mother with a youthful appearance. She provided examples of multiple administrators' and senior colleagues' dismissal of her as an ambitious faculty member. Until she made her aspirations known, many did not consider her interest in promotion. There was an element of false neutrality in which she stated folks were "not *not* supportive" of her goal. By not actively supporting or blocking her promotion, they were in effect delaying her advancement.

The embeddedness of systems of privilege and oppression is evident in our participants' stories. The multiple marginalization Black womyn face in the academy shows up when the rules for promotion change, with bias in teaching evaluations, and other forms of gatekeeping enacted by those with the most power in the system (i.e., white men; Croom, 2017). Olivia discussed her observations of Black faculty in her department facing different research expectations. Khadijah mentioned the directive to increase her scores on teaching evaluations before applying for promotion, despite exceeding expectations in research and service and meeting the department average for teaching. The differential treatment of Black womyn inhibits advancement. With subjective policies and an unstructured system for promotion, myths of meritocracy, and objectivity operate as designed. The power in our participants' counter-stories is the ability to illuminate the intentional and systematic ways Black womyn are excluded from the highest levels of the institution (Croom, 2017).

Our participants' self-advocacy embodies each of the tenets of CRF. Their particular social location motivated them to fight against controlling images and inaccurate perceptions of who they are, to what they can aspire, and what they can achieve. These Black womyn faculty were motivated beyond simply being in the academic space. They envisioned themselves in a role with a greater impact on the university. Predictably though, when systems of oppression and privilege are challenged, there is a counterattack to suppress the challenge(r) (Croom, 2017).

Even the initiatives designed to support all faculty across an institution continued to exclude Black womyn. One experience our participants shared was their attendance of workshops held at the institutional or college level. Not only were these workshops unhelpful, but they were not led by anyone who could speak to the ways Black womyn may experience faculty life. We found no evidence these workshops were led by FOC. Similarly, when discussing interactions with administrators, once again, FOC were not holding these chair or dean positions. White womyn were present in these spaces; however, they were not described as supportive for all participants. Collectively, we found more barriers than bolsters for Black womyn seeking to advance in the academy.

Implications

Black womyn routinely carve out a place for themselves in unwelcoming and, occasionally, hostile environments. Increasing the number of Black womyn full professors provides the opportunity for change at the highest levels. Sponsorship is a key element of being a full professor from an access perspective. Youn and Price (2009) and Croom (2017) found institutional agents can invite associate professors whom they choose as worthy or meritorious to submit their dossiers for promotion. Black womyn institutional agents could create the opportunity for more FOC to be invited into these spaces. There is value to cross-cultural mentoring, however, it remains an exception and not a rule in most institutions. Thus, more Black womyn in a position to mentor and sponsor from a higher level, could increase the pipeline of faculty and shift the demographics across ranks.

Further, Black womyn full professors can access the highest levels of governance in an institution. This provides new ontological and epistemological perspectives in curriculum conversations and policy decisions. The classroom experience contributes to the retention of students of color (SOC) and can change how they aspire to higher levels of education. The faculty pipeline has significant leaks in postsecondary environments. What is being taught and who is teaching can impact the aspirations of SOC and lead them into further studies. Policies around admission, funding, and matriculation have direct impacts on students. When decision-makers share a single educational experience, it is impossible to fully understand the real limitations facing a diverse student population. Leaders adopting a critical race feminist approach can acknowledge and respond to the limitations of a white supremacist, heteronormative, patriarchal, and capitalist institution.

Full professors can be changemakers in the academy. Opening doors through policy and practice is one of their key responsibilities should they choose to accept it. As prolific self-advocates, Black womyn are primed to serve in these roles. We understand the current landscape better than most and utilize liberatory frameworks to set ourselves, and others, free. Supporting the advancement of Black womyn to the highest levels of governance would be a benefit to institutions at every level.

Conclusion

In this critical qualitative inquiry, we explored how intersecting social identities and interlocking systems of oppression, influenced Black womyn's aspirations to full professor and the role of institutional agents and initiatives. Our participants demonstrated how their identities influenced their aspirations for promotion and the ways cross-cultural mentoring supported their advancement. We found evidence of inconsistent support with institutional agents and ineffective institutional initiatives. We contend that having Black womyn as full professors can shift the current landscape of HWIs with new perspectives at the highest levels of governance.

References

Croom, N. N. (2017). Promotion beyond tenure: Unpacking racism and sexism in the experiences of Black womyn professors. *The Review of Higher Education, 40*(4), 557–583. https://doi.org/10.1353/rhe.2017.0022

Dowd, A. C., & Bensimon, E. M. (2015). *Engaging the "race question": Accountability and equity in U.S. higher education*. Teachers College Press.

Finnegan, D. E., & Hyle, A. E. (2009). Assistant to "full": Rank and the development of expertise. *Teachers College Record, 111*, 443–479.

Hughes, R., & Giles, M. (2010). CRiT walking in higher education: Activating critical race theory in the academy. *Race Ethnicity Education, 13*(1), 41–57.

National Center for Education Statistics. (2019). *Full-time faculty in degree-granting postsecondary institutions, by race/ethnicity, sex, and academic rank: Fall 2015, fall 2017, and fall 2018*. Digest of Education Statistics. https://nces.ed.gov/programs/digest/d19/tables/dt19_315.20.asp

Pasque, P. A., Carducci, R., Kuntz, A. M., & Gildersleeve, R. E. (2012). *Qualitative inquiry for equity in higher education: Methodological innovations, implications, and interventions*. Wiley.

Saldaña, J. (2016). *The coding manual for qualitative researchers* (3rd ed.). Sage Publications.

Smith, D. G. (2015). *Diversity's promise for higher education: Making it work* (2nd ed.). Johns Hopkins University Press.

Youn, T. I. K., & Price, T. M. (2009). Learning from the experience ofo others: The evolution of faculty tenure and promotion rules in comprehensive institutions. *The Journal of Higher Education, 80*(2), 204–237.

18

BLACK WOMEN IN ACADEMIC LEADERSHIP

Reflections of One Department Chair's Journey in Engineering

Meseret F. Hailu and Monica F. Cox

Historically, Black women have been mostly absent from upper-level university administration. Despite increased racial and gender diversity at the student and faculty level, Black women remain an aberration in higher education leadership (Kelly, 2011; Langan, 2019; O'Meara et al., 2018; Ospina & Foldy, 2009). National data show that Black women make up only 2% of full professors, while women of color make up only 5% of university presidents (American Council on Education [ACE], 2017; National Center for Education Statistics [NCES], 2021).

Black women rarely ascend to senior-level administration positions in higher education (Miles, 2002). In fact, Johnson and Fournillier (2021) explained how Black women who do advance in administration usually stay in a mid-management role. Research also shows there are 59 Black women presidents in the United States (Jackson & Harris, 2005). This lack of representation in leadership is unsurprising, considering previous literature has supported the prevalence of racism and sexism in higher education institutions. Racism and sexism permeate faculty hiring practices (Sensoy & DiAngelo, 2017), tenure and promotion cases (Croom, 2017; Durodoye et al., 2020), access to mentorship and sponsorship (Boveda & McCray, 2020), and informal networks that help individuals advance in their academic careers (Espino & Zambrana, 2019). Meanwhile, scholarship about department chairs suggested they often encounter much resistance when trying to initiate organizational change (Gaubatz & Ensminger, 2017).

As pathways to top leadership have remained largely uncharted for women of color, some have abandoned the pursuit (Cox, 2021; Flaherty, 2020). We gather that women of color, and Black women specifically, likely experience structural challenges when pursuing leadership positions in higher

DOI: 10.4324/9781003184867-22

education. Recognizing these issues, many universities and affiliated organizations have created initiatives to promote successful trajectories for women within the professoriate. For example, the Higher Education Resource Services (HERS) is a program for women in collegiate leadership (HERS Network, 2021). Housed at the University of Denver, the HERS program offers training, career planning, and a professional network for women seeking to climb the ladder of academic leadership.

Within science, technology, engineering, and mathematics (STEM) higher education, institutional diversity efforts have focused more on diversifying the professoriate (McGee et al., 2021) and less on upper-level administration. For example, 19 universities across the nation have recently joined the third cohort of Aspire: The National Alliance for Inclusive & Diverse STEM Faculty. Funded by the National Science Foundation, this program works to increase STEM faculty diversity (Padilla, 2020). Meanwhile, the organization 500 Women Scientists seeks to make public engagement and leadership in science more inclusive by "...fighting racism, patriarchy, and oppressive societal norms" (500 Women Scientists, n.d.). While these efforts are promising, they do not squarely address the barriers faced by mid-level managers in STEM, such as Black women administrators in engineering.

This chapter is timely because it presents a deeper insight about a population scarcely represented in the literature. Moreover, we offer a distinct contribution to the literature by shining a light on a specific discipline (engineering education) and how one Black woman leader's narrative illuminates some of the challenges and possible opportunities for reforming pathways in academic leadership.

Purpose and Guiding Questions

In this qualitative inquiry, we highlight one Black woman's trajectory within the engineering professoriate, specifically in academic leadership. The purpose of this study was to examine and contextualize the legacy of a Black woman institutional leader in a department of engineering education. We focused on engineering because of the underrepresentation of Black women academics in this field. As of fall 2018, Black faculty of all genders made up 2.4% of all engineering faculty, across all levels (assistant, associate, and full). Women of all races made up 17.4% of all engineering faculty (Roy, 2019). In empirical and public scholarship about upper-level administration, the emphasis is often on how the department chair can support faculty research (Aziz et al., 2005; Mickey et al., 2020). The relationship between administrative authority and race, in the context of engineering education leadership, has been relatively understudied. We contend women of color administrators occupy a liminal space: simultaneously in a position of power (by virtue of their administrative position) and in a position of marginalization (by virtue of their embodied identity). Thus, our chapter was guided by two questions: What are the important moments/pertinent aspects of one Black woman's trajectory through the academy? and how does reflection on these formative events shape our understanding of the existing challenges and possible opportunities for reform?

Conceptual Orientation: Intersectionality

Intersectionality theory, per scholars such as Collins (2000), Crenshaw (1991), and Ladson-Billings (1998), helps us understand how systems such as racism, genderism, and classism function synergistically to oppress Black women in US society. As a heuristic for education research, intersectionality is valuable because it captures how deeply entrenched structures shape the educational opportunities available to a person. Often used by women of color engaging in critical work, intersectionality provides an evergreen critique of social justice ethos that only prioritizes a single form of oppression above all others. To this end, Crenshaw (1991) stated,

> The failure of feminism to interrogate race means that the resistance strategies of feminism will often replicate and reinforce the subordination of people of color, and the failure of antiracism to interrogate patriarchy means that antiracism will frequently reproduce the subordination of women.
>
> *(p. 1252)*

We use intersectionality to help us understand how racism and sexism rendered one Black woman leader vulnerable in her organization, despite her position of administrative authority.

Intersectionality has both theoretical and methodological utility. In a qualitative investigation of four Black women in educational leadership, Johnson (2021) articulated how the race-gender dyad shaped these individuals' socialization and ability to do their jobs well. Specifically, the study revealed:

> … (1) the importance of an established identity, (2) the complexity of equity as more than a singular construct, (3) navigating through the educational leadership sphere (i.e., context), and (4) balancing race, gender, and responsibility, all coalesced (i.e., intersected) within the realm of educational leadership.
>
> *(Johnson, 2021, p. 8)*

Considering the utility of intersectionality as a conceptual tool for complex social phenomena, we follow the tradition of Crenshaw (1991) and Johnson (2021) and use it to frame the reflections presented in this chapter.

Methodological Approach: Collaborative Counter-Narrative Essay

We use the collaborative counter-narrative essay as our primary methodological approach. A counter-narrative is a form of storytelling that foregrounds the experiences of people of color. Conceptualized by Solórzano and Yosso (2002) as a component of critical race methodology, a counter-narrative can take the shape of personal narratives, life histories of other people, or composite narratives. A panoply of scholars has used this approach to generate empirical research that underscores the impact of intersecting oppression with the educational trajectories of people of color (Anthym & Tuitt, 2019; Espino, 2008; Gonzales & Terosky, 2020). We employed a counter-narrative structure because it centers the narrative of a Black woman as legitimate. We posit this type of storytelling is necessary since Black women are less likely to feel valued, respected, and fairly treated in the workplace (Lloyd, 2021).

The subject and first author of this analysis is Dr. Monica Cox, a full professor and former department chair in a College of Engineering. The second author is Dr. Meseret Hailu, an assistant professor of higher and postsecondary education. Moreover, Dr. Cox was the principal investigator during Dr. Hailu's postdoctoral appointment. Since then, we have continued to work together on academic research projects. This collaboration is an example of the many ways researchers cultivate emotional connections that occur in both geographical and virtual contexts, which are central for professional success and personal value (Metcalfe & Blanco, 2021). We posit this type of relationship makes this type of research more accessible, full of rapport, and enjoyable.

Reflections

In the following sections, Dr. Cox narrates in the first person her reflections on four aspects of her time in administration: (1) a performance review test, (2) her approach to ethical decision-making, (3) the challenges of not being able to select members of her administrative team, and (4) her reflections on code-switching. We decided on these four aspects of her experience after engaging in reflective journaling and open-ended interview questions from Dr. Hailu. These selections are part of a larger narrative of Dr. Cox's four-year appointment as an academic leader. We collectively agreed on which portions to present here because these four reflections act as "historical moments" (Denzin & Lincoln, 2008, p. 1) and reflect the emotional, social, and political realities of being a Black woman department chair.

Performance Review Test

For me, performance reviews were formal and informal. They were like faculty annual reviews in that I produced documents and had something of a structure in which to talk to my supervisor. These reviews differed in that there was this newfound freedom that came along with being a leader. However, once they started, I found there were limited opportunities for me to provide additional details about some of the situations that were going well and some of the situations that were not going well. I could speak about visioning strategies for my department and could discuss ways the college might work with me to execute my vision and achieve the goals that were expected of me.

In my role as department chair, in every meeting I had with my supervisor, I identified the unique perspective I brought as a woman of Color in the organization. I felt it was worth mentioning I was a woman of Color, particularly a Black woman, because people in the department told me how different my leadership was from the previous older white man's leadership who came before me. In the previous leadership structure, many people were used to doing what they wanted to do. There were no constraints on the budget. There were limited expectations for them to align with goals within the department (which was a center at the time), and they operated in their silos. With my view of inclusivity, there was an expectation that people would work together to achieve an organizational goal.

I also took leadership literally, and I knew it was my responsibility to answer for the organization. I would make the final decisions and take responsibility when things went wrong. For some reason, however, there was resistance from many of the people who were considered senior when it came to my role in the organization. In my department chair performance reviews, I spoke with my supervisor about what could be done to ensure I was not the final woman of Color to ever obtain a leadership position in the department. As such, I often said the organization was not ready for women of Color department chairs, particularly because the organizational structure did not seem to support the dynamics at play between myself and others.

Every annual performance review was difficult because the same problems existed each year. Even with an open-door policy, calling people out, and trying to identify new ways to engage with the naysayers, I could not connect with some faculty and staff. By the end of my four-year term as department chair, I knew things had to change. I told my supervisor that I could not continue in this position if they refused to transform the organization at its core. Without organizational interventions to address the oppression I felt, I could see myself going through four more years of stress, isolation, and trouble. That was not beneficial to me, the department, or to my family.

Looking back, I wish the performance reviews could have been sessions where we had actionable items that addressed the concerns I had. There should have been follow through and discussions of progress. When I observe the recent increased focus of higher education organizations on diversity statements, they often feel like empty promises with more reactive than proactive strategies. I wish people would have listened when I asked them to listen. With the benefit of hindsight, I realize the major problem is higher education institutions espouse inclusivity ideals but are quite resistant when leaders, particularly women of Color leaders, try to enact inclusive changes. Overall, these performance reviews were a missed opportunity to strategize around situations rooted in systemic oppression.

Ethical Decision-Making Practices as a Leader

One of the most difficult choices I had to make as a department chair was to decide between being a leader of integrity regardless of what came my way or to focus on disciplinary status and my future. I had to choose between doing my job as chair and reprimanding people who had never been reprimanded before. The culture in my organization was conflict-averse so I had to tread carefully to achieve the goals as I lead people. I realized people could use their privilege to undermine me in the future. Many of those people also were more senior than I was and could retaliate if I did not give them what they wanted. I had to choose between engaging in conflict or letting people have their way to avoid conflict. I chose to call issues out. This resulted in HR complaints and division in the department. A lot of people hated me at the time. I knew I could be removed for not doing my job as chair, and I knew I could be persecuted if I did my job as chair. It was a win/win and lose/lose situation at the same time. I chose to do my job and be equitable, despite the resistance to my stance by many people in the department.

One example that stands out in my memory had to do with membership in a professional society. In my position as department chair, I led individuals who were members of a professional society to which I aspired to be a member. I had to be voted on to become a member. Some members of the society in my department were used to getting what they wanted. When I came in as a unit leader, I was determined to be a chair for all people, not just a few people with the loudest voices or the most senior titles. As a result, there were many fights and nasty conversations and experiences.

I recall sitting with one of my mentors as I discussed having to decide between giving people what they wanted, knowing I may never become a member of this professional society or standing firm on my leadership principles such that these individuals may never endorse me or respect me. In the end, I did what was best for my organization. I chose to be the leader for all people, not just a few and not just for people who could do something for me.

It was scary to speak up. It was scary to correct people who were disrespectful to me all the time. It wore me out. It was frustrating and humiliating. At the time, it was difficult to determine what the long-term impact of my decisions would be, but in February 2020, I finally became a member of that professional society. In July 2021, I gave a Distinguished Lecture in that society. What I know now is I would have been judged regardless of the leadership decisions I made. If I had chosen to appease a few at the expense of others in the organization, I could have been labeled an unproductive or poor leader. By choosing to stand up for what I believed was right for everyone, however, I held fast to my values. I hope I proved I was a moral leader—who was inclusive and who thought of the greater good more than I did for myself.

This leads to a conversation about martyrdom. I was all in this position. I now know I sacrificed my health—my mental health, my physical health, and my emotional health—for the organization. It is often said that a woman of Color or a person of Color must be two to three times better than anyone else in an organization. I believed and I embraced that idea. I worked extremely long hours for the organization.

Although I was successful in many ways, I am unsure what the long-term implications of my efforts will be. Yes, I am a member of my professional society, but there have been assaults on my character and conflicts I never could have predicted. These are unlike any conflicts I have ever heard of in higher education. The sacrifices were real and are still felt months after leaving this position and not being around those individuals. Through this experience, I chose to be an ethical decision-maker, regardless of the implications that it would have on my professional trajectory and personal comfort.

Not Picking My Own Team

One of the biggest regrets I have as a department chair is not being able to pick my own team before or after I arrived. When I entered the organization, I was one of the few external hires in the organization since there was a tradition of identifying department chairs from within the college. As a result, I was an outsider, and it was obvious that I was an outsider.

My department chair experience was also difficult because I was an inaugural chair in a department that required many changes. The department had previously been a unit where many people did not hold tenured and tenure-track positions. This meant several of the people attended the university where we worked, earned advanced degrees from this university, and worked there for several years. It was their primary higher education experience. Several people had never lived outside of the state. They were accustomed to what they were accustomed to in this environment.

Additionally, there was the complexity of the lack of racial diversity in the college and the department. I was the only tenured Black woman faculty in the college. I was the first Black full professor in the university in its almost 150-year history; and I remained so for five years after being hired. Coming into the organization was a transition on top of a transition. In addition to being Black, I was a woman. I was young. I was from another university. I was from the

South. I also have an outgoing personality, which is not typical in engineering. So, if you could put so many different layers of complexity on top of this, I brought that to a conservative organization set in its ways.

When you think of any team, you usually think of people who align with you. You have someone near you, whether it is an administrative assistant or someone close, who gets you, someone who understands you, your background, and your perspective. The problem was I did not have that. I was expected to run an organization at a high level, and I was expected to run a department in a field that was new in this college. At the same time, I had to work with people whose perspectives differed from my own. I had to balance the old and the new. I was hired to be a change agent, but I eventually realized that several people in the organization did not want change. There was so much resistance.

One thing I recommend to anyone is you at least have some people around you who embrace your expectations for productivity and your expectations for communication, diversity, equity, and inclusion. If you are an open communicator, find someone who is that as well. Find someone who wants success for you as much as you want success for yourself. Find people who are loyal to you not because they must be but because they want to be. Find people whose values align with yours and whose morals align with yours. Find someone who cares about people being their best and fulfilling their purpose. Get some of those people in your organization as well. Hire and appoint some of those people on your team, because that is going to make or break your success in that organization.

Code-switching

There is controversy among various people about what code-switching means. I see a lot of people who have been successful in corporate America and academia, who in their training, teach people how to behave and how to work so they get their feet in the door and gain access to opportunities. Many people of Color are taught how to be safe and how to make members of the majoritarian community feel they are not a threat.

I thought I understood that concept and tried to play that game until I was in a position where I was repeatedly disrespected and misunderstood. It was as if a light bulb went off in my brain, and I realized even if I was the best minoritized employee, I would not be exempt from discrimination, harassment, misunderstandings, and miscommunication.

Code-switching does not exempt me from being left out, being marginalized, and being perceived as a token. It does not exempt me from the pain and suffering that comes from being the only or the first in my environment. It does not exempt me from being omitted from crucial conversations about my future and the futures of others. I must move beyond assimilation and code-switching because what I want people to remember is my authenticity, my ability to be transparent, and my willingness to say what I mean and mean what I say and to own that. I operated from these positions prior to becoming a department chair but coming into this leadership position made me question this approach. After serving as a leader, I now see the importance of this type of sincerity.

Discussion and Implications

In the above counter-narrative, Dr. Cox described the particulars of her time as a department chair. What unifies her journey is a constant friction: she was tasked with balancing her administrative responsibilities with interpersonal conflicts and (micro)aggressions shaped by racism and misogyny. The challenges Dr. Cox faced are not new, and it is unlikely she will be the last Black woman to have these experiences in institutional leadership. However, her narrative, in addition to the narratives of many others, is an important component of the pushback against the norms which have been created in contemporary higher education.

While it is not possible to extrapolate these stories to all women, they help us consider changes to the intersecting systems of oppression (Crenshaw, 1991) individuals are expected to navigate. For example, Dr. Cox's recounting of performance reviews suggests Black women's leadership is not seen as legitimate, even when the Black woman in question is well-credentialed and professionally experienced. Arguably, the role of the department chair involves the management of many different types of personalities and priorities. While the dominant narrative about this position would suggest this leadership position is uniformly challenging for all leaders—regardless of race and gender, the identity of the leader does indeed matter (Croom & Kortegast, 2018). Specifically, Dr. Cox's narrative suggests raced *and* gendered identities matter because Black women's merits (i.e., leadership in this case) are often dismissed; her narrative reminds us that no role in the social world is difference neutral.

In response to this, individual faculty members should critically reflect on how they respond to the presence of a minoritized leader in general, but specifically of a Black woman leader. Meanwhile, her experience with making principled decisions reflects her commitment to equity, which she is attuned to as a minoritized person who experiences inequitable environments daily. We conclude Dr. Cox's curtailed efforts to select members of her own administrative team show that Black women may be put in leadership positions as a symbolic gesture, rather than as evidence of trust in their ability to engage meaningfully in academic governance. Finally, her reflections on code-switching emphasize Black women leaders are often expected to compartmentalize themselves and are not provided with the same cognitive and social safety to be their full selves in the workplaces. This reflection should be a reminder to institutions to create workplace norms, traditions, and values so minoritized people—especially leaders who balance both power and marginalization—can express their full identity. Combined such institutional changes might mitigate the intertwined impacts of racism and sexism and make leadership a less arduous pursuit for other Black women in the future.

References

American Council on Education [ACE]. (2017). *American College President Study*. https://www.aceacps.org/minority-presidents/

Anthym, M., & Tuitt, F. (2019). When the levees break: the cost of vicarious trauma, microaggressions and emotional labor for Black administrators and faculty engaging in race work at traditionally White institutions. *International Journal of Qualitative Studies in Education, 32*(9), 1072–1093.

Aziz, S., Mullins, M. E., Balzer, W. K., Grauer, E., Burnfield, J. L., Lodato, M. A., & Cohen-Powless, M. A. (2005). Understanding the training needs of department chairs. *Studies in Higher Education, 30*(5), 571–593.

Boveda, M., & McCray, E. D. (2020). Writing (for) our lives: Black feminisms, interconnected guidance, and qualitative research in special education. *International Journal of Qualitative Studies in Education*, 1–19.

Collins, P. H. (2000). *Black feminist thought: Knowledge, consciousness, and the politics of empowerment* (2nd ed.). Routledge.

Cox, M. F. (2021, February 19). *The exit interview I never had*. Medium. https://drmonicacox.medium.com/

Crenshaw, K. (1991). Mapping the margins: Intersectionality, identity politics, and violence against women of color. *Stanford Law Review, 43*, 1241–1299.

Croom, N. N. (2017). Promotion beyond tenure: Unpacking racism and sexism in the experiences of Black womyn professors. *The Review of Higher Education, 40*(4), 557–583.

Croom, N. N., & Kortegast, C. A. (2018). When ignoring difference fails: Using critical professional praxis. *About Campus, 23*(1), 27–31.

Denzin, N. K., & Lincoln, Y. S. (2008). Introduction: The discipline and practice of qualitative research. In N. K. Denzin & Y. S. Lincoln (Eds.), *Strategies of qualitative inquiry* (pp. 1–43). Sage.

Durodoye, R., Gumpertz, M., Wilson, A., Griffith, E., & Ahmad, S. (2020). Tenure and promotion outcomes at four large land grant universities: Examining the role of gender, race, and academic discipline. *Research in Higher Education, 61*(5), 628–651.

Espino, M. M. (2008). *Master narratives and counter-narratives: An analysis of Mexican American life stories of oppression and resistance along the journeys to the doctorate* [Doctoral dissertation, University of Arizona]. https://repository.arizona.edu/handle/10150/195733

Espino, M. M., & Zambrana, R. E. (2019). "How do you advance here? How do you survive?" An exploration of under-represented minority faculty perceptions of mentoring modalities. *The Review of Higher Education, 42*(2), 457–484.

Flaherty, C. (2020, October 13). *A Profound Act of self-preservation*. Inside Higher Ed. https://www.insidehighered.com/news/2020/10/13/spitzer-architecture-dean-quits-profound-act-self-preservation

Gaubatz, J. A., & Ensminger, D. C. (2017). Department chairs as change agents: Leading change in resistant environments. *Educational Management Administration & Leadership, 45*(1), 141–163.

Gonzales, L. D., & Terosky, A. L. (2020). On their own terms: Women's pathways into and through academe. *Journal of Diversity in Higher Education, 13*(3), 274–287.
HERS Network. (2021). *Contact us*. Retrieved January 1, 2021, from https://www.hersnetwork.org/contact/
Jackson, S., & Harris, S. (2005). African American female college and university presidents: Career path to the presidency. *Journal of Women in Educational Leadership, 3*(4), 1541–6224.
Johnson, N. N. (2021). Balancing race, gender, and responsibility: Conversations with four black women in educational leadership in the United States of America. *Educational Management Administration & Leadership*. https://doi.org/10.1177/1741143221991839
Johnson, N. N., & Fournillier, J. B. (2021). Intersectionality and leadership in context: Examining the intricate paths of four black women in educational leadership in the United States. *International Journal of Leadership in Education*, 1–22.
Kelly, M. L. (2011). *Next in line: Women chief academic officers, their experiences and career aspirations* (Order No. 3455418) [Unpublished doctoral dissertation]. University of Pennsylvania.
Ladson-Billings, G. (1998). Just what is critical race theory and what's it doing in a nice field like education? *International Journal of Qualitative Studies in Education, 11*(1), 7–24.
Langan, A. (2019). Female managers and gender disparities: The case of academic department chairs. https://scholar.princeton.edu/sites/default/files/alangan/files/langan_jmp_current.pdf
Lloyd, C. (2021). *Black women in the workplace*. https://www.gallup.com/workplace/333194/black-women-workplace.aspx
McGee, E. O., Main, J. B., Miles, M. L., & Cox, M. F. (2021). An intersectional approach to investigating persistence among women of color tenure-track engineering faculty. *Journal of Women and Minorities in Science and Engineering, 27*(1), 57–84.
Metcalfe, A. S., & Blanco, G. L. (2021). "Love is calling": Academic friendship and international research collaboration amid a global pandemic. *Emotion, Space and Society, 38*, 100763.
Mickey, E. L., Kanelee, E. S., & Misra, J. (2020, June 5). *10 small steps for department chairs to foster inclusion*. Inside Higher Ed. https://www.insidehighered.com/advice/2020/06/05/advice-department-chairs-how-foster-inclusion-among-faculty-opinion
Miles, S. (2012). *Left behind: The status of Black women in higher education administration* [Doctoral dissertation]. Retrieved from Florida State University database.
National Center for Education Statistics. (2021). *Race/ethnicity of college faculty*. https://nces.ed.gov/fastfacts/display.asp?id=61
O'Meara, K., Templeton, L., & Nyunt, G. (2018). Earning professional legitimacy: Challenges faced by women, underrepresented minority, and non-tenure-track faculty. *Teachers College Record, 120*, 1–38.
Ospina, S., & Foldy, E. (2009). A critical review of race and ethnicity in the leadership literature: Surfacing context, power and the collective dimensions of leadership. *The Leadership Quarterly, 20*(6), 876–896.
Padilla, D. (2020, October 30). *19 universities join the national alliance for inclusive & diverse stem faculty*. Diverse Issues in Higher Education. https://diverseeducation.com/article/195137/
Roy, J. (2019, July 15). *Engineering by the numbers*. American Society for Engineering Education. https://ira.asee.org/wp-content/uploads/2019/07/2018-Engineering-by-Numbers-Engineering-Statistics-UPDATED-15-July-2019.pdf

Sensoy, Ö., & DiAngelo, R. (2017). "We are all for diversity, but...": How faculty hiring committees reproduce whiteness and practical suggestions for how they can change. *Harvard Educational Review, 87*(4), 557–580.

Solórzano, D. G., & Yosso, T. J. (2002). Critical race methodology: Counter-storytelling as an analytical framework for education research. *Qualitative Inquiry, 8*(1), 23–44.

500 Women Scientists. (n.d.). *About us.* Retrieved January 1, 2021, from https://500womenscientists.org/

19

IN CONVERSATION

Engaging (with) the Narratives of Two Black Women Full Professor Leaders

Christa J. Porter, V. Thandi Sulé, and Natasha N. Croom

In reviewing chapters for this edited book, and specifically reflecting on this section (Canary in the Coal Mine), we (co-editors) desired an intergenerational dialogue. We invited two Black women full professors who also served as department chairs to engage in a joint conversation in the form of a semi-structured interview. Our goal, however, was not simply to pose questions and record their responses; we desired to provide an opportunity for them to share their reflections of Black feminist epistemologies in dialogue with us as co-editors. We highlight our reflections of the conversation while presenting their narratives; the space we created while reviewing their narratives was reflective, (re)affirming, and revealing. Within this chapter, we briefly discuss the metaphorical social positioning of Black women full professors as canaries via three themes: (1) competence as overachievement: Black women as intruders/interlopers; (2) intentionally disrupting and abolishing structural oppression; and (3) taking up space: connected ways of being, knowing, and leading.

Black Women Full Professors as Canaries in the Coal Mine

"Molly. You in danger, girl!" This line, made famous by Whoopi Goldberg's character in the movie *Ghost*, captures the overarching sentiment that higher education (i.e., Molly) is indeed in danger if Black women's experiences in and throughout are any indicators. Lani Guinier and Gerald Torres (2002) introduced the metaphor of the miner's canary as a way for postsecondary leaders to think about the relationship between racially minoritized communities and college and university environments. Namely, they argued that just like the canary, communities of color were signaling warnings to the larger

DOI: 10.4324/9781003184867-23

community about the dangers of the environment – dangers that affect everyone. While Black women still make up less than 3% of the full professorship, we take up this metaphor of the miner's canary to move beyond narratives of underrepresentation, which are certainly a problem, into narratives of epistemology, experience, connectedness, and praxis.

Despite the limited literature based on Black women as full professors and as academic leaders, what is there helps us to discern some of the ways Black women's existences in the coal mines of academia surface larger systemic, that is ideological, cultural, and structural, issues abound throughout higher education (Croom & Patton, 2011). Some of these issues include:

- being viewed as interlopers or folks who do not belong in certain spaces of the academy, such as the full professorship or academic leadership (Croom, 2017);
- having merit assessed in ways that undervalue their contributions to their departments, institutions, and fields (Croom, 2017), see for example:
  - Relegating scholarship by Black women about Black women to spaces often viewed as less than (i.e., edited volumes, book chapters, and lower-tiered journals) in advancement and promotion processes (Patitu & Hinton, 2003; Stanley, 2007);
  - Constant questioning about the merits of centering Black women in scholarship or foci on diversity, equity, and inclusion (DEI) (Benjamin, 1997; Croom, 2017);
- being pigeonholed in spaces only meant to support minoritized communities or issues of DEI (as to suggest that this work does not permeate the institution) (Turner, 2002; Turner et al., 1999);
- experiencing racial and gendered microaggressions meant to invalidate, assault, and insult Black women (Croom, 2017; Myers, 2002), see for example:
  - The disdain shown through how students use teaching evaluations to spew misogynoir – often making the feedback about identity rather than substantive evaluations of pedagogical moves and learning (Fries & McNinch, 2003; King, 1995; Pittman, 2010).

Rather than taking a position that these issues point toward group pathology, centering Black women's experiences about advancement and leadership point to systemic issues with ideas and practices related to meritocracy, advancement, belonging, community, epistemic violence/agency, and institutional transformation. Black women who survive and make it to the full professorship and academic leadership, while few and far between, have myriad stories to tell about the mines of academia – and we'd all be better off to listen.

Importance of Dialogue in Black Feminist Epistemologies

Collins (2000) emphasized Black feminism as a dialogic relationship. Through dialogue, Black women name, define, and change the world. As such, dialogue functions as an essential feature for information exchange and serves as the basis of Black women's feminist epistemology. Collins (2000) noted Black women's knowledge is rarely developed in isolation as "connectedness rather than separation is an essential part of the knowledge validation process" (p. 260). This reliance on dialogical connectedness is akin to many African communication traditions in which discourse is expected to be collective and purposeful. In other words, one does not speak in isolation, and what is spoken should be meaningful to the listener (Asante, 1987). Because Black women have a "unique angle of vision," in dialoguing with other Black women about a particular experience for the benefit of Black women, they are engaging purposeful discourse. The discourse is purposeful because Black women, theorizing from those experiences, can engage in praxis to facilitate Black women's empowerment. Through the participants' narratives and our dialogue with their narratives, we hope to encourage others to build upon our knowledge creation process as they seek a better understanding of the positionality of Black women as full professors in the academy.

Methodology

In alignment with dialogue as central to Black women's epistemologies, we engaged in a joint interview with both participants and the three of us as co-editors. We prepared questions that would allow them the opportunity to share specific examples and experiences. Questions included: (1) Share with us any parts of your individual journey into and through the academy; (2) How has raced gendered discrimination (or anti-Black woman oppression) shown up for you; (3) What does embodying a Black feminist epistemology or praxis mean to you; and (4) What advice would you give to those coming after you about embodying a Black feminist/womanist epistemology or praxis in the academy?

Participant Selection

We selected both participants because of their career trajectories, scholarly and embodied engagement with Black feminisms, and critical analysis of anti-Black woman oppression. In other words, because of our individual and collective socialization into and through the academy, we sought out Black women who not only achieved full professorships and who were leaders within their institutions and disciplines, but also those whose onto-epistemologies and praxis were congruent in ways that could add knowledge about the intersection of embodied Black feminisms and leadership practice.

Nia and Ivy

Both participants were in their third year as department chairs at Big Ten institutions. Nia has been at the same institution for 17 years, while Ivy was new to her institution. Nia had been in administration at her institution for five years before taking on the role as chair. Additionally, she was the second Black woman to obtain a promotion to full professor in her department. Prior to her role as chair, Ivy was a faculty member at several institutions and although she did not pursue administrative positions, "it kept calling."

Analysis

After the joint interview, we outsourced professional transcription and author two cross-checked the recording with the transcript (i.e., raw data) for accuracy. We individually read through the clean transcript and focused on coded small chunks of data (Charmaz, 2014). Example codes included: Black women's competence as overachievement, Black women as intruders/not belonging, Black women are undervalued, leadership challenged, association with Black men, white women's tears, violence, agency/taking up space, and spirituality. The three of us met to discuss our thoughts while analyzing (coding), share additional reflections, and brainstorm the collective meaning of our interpretations. We then reflected on our desire to converse among ourselves in relation to their dialogue (via the interview). We thought, "What would it mean for us to center their narratives while sharing our collective meaning in response to their experiences?" Author one compiled the composites based on our analysis; Authors two and three agreed with the (re)presentation of narratives. We collectively wrote up our discussions of each theme/composite.

Findings

We present findings as composite narratives (Patton & Catching, 2009; Porter & Byrd, 2021; Willis, 2019) wherein we compile combinations of full-length quotes and excerpts from both Nia and Ivy to (re)present their collective narratives in conversation with one another based upon our interpreted themes. Following each composite, we highlight our shared understanding of each respective theme. Our interpreted themes include the following: (1) competence as overachievement: Black women as intruders/interlopers; (2) intentionally disrupting and abolishing structural oppression; and (3) taking up space: connected ways of being, knowing, and leading.

Competence as Overachievement: Black Women as Intruders/Interlopers

Competence as overachievement represents the belief that Black women must exceed the standard of excellence to merely be perceived as competent. It is reminiscent of the Black American adage, "Black people must work twice as hard to get half as much" (or to be perceived as equal). Furthermore, in their overachievement, Black women are not perceived as welcomed or proper occupants of spaces originally imagined for white men, rather as uninvited guests. The following passages exemplify how Nia and Ivy described how their peers (de)valued them,

> … part of that competence has been because of what I've done to get through the academy and white people haven't had to do it. And so, I look qualified, because I've had to do things you didn't have to do. And so, it's the reward for doing; excellent work is more work. It's me trying to navigate it and do work, but you don't pay me and give me all the things. I've dealt with the micro and macro aggressions throughout, so I know what it looks like. There are so many white men who have such a tight grasp on power. It was interesting, my first year, just people trying to get over on me or me not feeling respected; people come because they're trying to prove something, not because they value me, but because they want a resource or want me to support something.
>
> I feel that all the time … some things people are saying to me, because I'm a woman, sometimes they're saying them to me or behaving in a particular way because I'm a Black woman… As a department chair, I don't know how many times my authority has been questioned. I think it is definitely raced, it's raced and gendered, because I'm a Black woman. The other department chairs have been white women, their authority wasn't questioned like that … I just want [white woman colleague] to know, you're not gonna jab me like this in a public meeting and expect me not to poke back. But I'm going to do it with a little bit of shade, where you probably don't really know what it means. But you need to know, I see you. What it has taught me was when we as Black women are assaulted, and other folks of color, whether at similar rank or below us see that, it's an assault on them, too. So, our assault and invalidations as scholars, as leaders, have ripple effects for other people of color. Throughout my career, I've had to maneuver and navigate in particular ways for people to understand that one, I'm here and two, it's a blessing for you that I'm here.

Poke Back

This passage reminds us of outsider-within, the marginal positioning of Black women in white spaces (Collins, 1986). Typically, Black women are allowed to exist in these spaces because they perform a service-albeit undervalued. Because their service is undervalued, they are "othered" and their marginality renders them both expendable and hyper-visible. It is no wonder they commented "what I've done to get through the academy." As perceived interlopers, their journey to full professor required more wit, patience, and productivity to be perceived as just competent. Most compelling from this narrative is the awareness that their experience does not exist in isolation; it has a rippling effect. Their pain is felt beyond the boundaries of their skin; it travels and is felt by other Black women. How they are treated, then, has implications for how other Black women will be able to move through academe. Their outsider-within positioning afforded them acute perceptiveness. They have no qualms about letting haters know they have been detected and are being watched. One thing is for sure, they will "poke back."

Intentionally Disrupting and Abolishing Structural Oppression

Intentionally disrupting and abolishing represents how Nia and Ivy's raced and gendered experiences informed their leadership style and purpose. Despite negotiating and navigating microaggressions and other affronts, they remained steadfast in their commitment to stay on purpose to eradicate policies and practices that do/did not elevate their work and the work of others, particularly as it relates to equity and inclusion:

> It [situation with a more senior (in rank) white woman gatekeeper] was very traumatic for me in the sense of, you know, you trust folks, and then you find out the enemy is warring behind your back. But I confronted her. I am telling you, this was a grown woman, the department chair - she came to my office and began to cry. At that moment, I sat there just as stoned face. I ain't have no sympathy, because here we go with the white women's tears and you in the position of authority. You know you were wrong. You know what I did? Because she ain't come with no Kleenex I reached right over to my desk, gave her that box and I kept on looking. You see what I'm saying? I can't trust anybody. And that for me was about invalidation. I don't know if that was raced, gendered, all that. But it was a microinvalidation. So, I was much more careful as I traversed for tenure, I lost the ability to really trust folks.
>
> I think that's what has given me, in part, the liberty to just say what I say, right? Because I'm like, if I step down tomorrow, they'll find another chair .... I didn't always have that confidence. But the notion of taking up space as an academic leader, as a Black woman ... how am I going to choose to take up space in this role? My business is about disrupting and abolishing structural inequities. Because I've seen a lot of them in my years as chair, and I'm like, "No, we're not going to do that anymore." So, I'm a disrupter. I'm going to disrupt and abolish, and I'm going to be unapologetic about it. Because can't none of y'all sit me down, only the dean can. You may not like every decision I make, but it's rooted in principle, inclusivity, the mission, and the vision ....it might not be aligned

with the cultural practices that y'all systematically have been enacting for years. As Black women leaders, we have to show up with an intention to disrupt and abolish.

The Assignment

In knowing the academy is wrought with injustice, Nia and Ivy are about the business of discarding and transforming (Sulé, 2014). Entwined in their narratives is the spirit of formidable Black women – Ida B. Wells, Bessie Smith, and Fannie Lou Hamer – who assessed the situation, rid themselves of boondoggle antithetical to their purpose, and took the uncharted path. Armed with their embodied knowledge, Nia and Ivy understood the assignment. They were unmoved by ploys, "white women's tears," to undermine their agendas to lead with the intention of obliterating structural inequities and establishing inclusive spaces. We understood this to mean that they moved through the academy with discernment because they recognized they posed a threat. We surmised Black women in positions of leadership must work against the tide by leading with the Black feminist epistemologies that called out the "white supremacist capitalist patriarchal values" (hooks, 2006, p. 6) in the first place. Otherwise, Black women full professors and academic leaders will not be honoring the very communities that anchored their journey.

Taking up Space: Connected Ways of Being, Knowing, and Leading

Taking up space captures how Nia and Ivy conceptualized their leadership. It represents a particular navigational style inspired by Black women role models intertwined with a strong spiritual framework. In other words, they are guided by familial and spiritual wisdom:

> I pull a lot of how I think about myself, how I show up, and take space are rooted in my mother and my aunt, my family. My mom was my first Black woman leader example; so much of her is in me. I realized the more I lead … it's all wrapped up in there. But she was my first example and I really appreciate the values and principles she taught. I do draw from Audre Lorde, bell hooks, Patricia Hill Collins in how I theorize my leadership style, pedagogy, and practice. hooks talks about taking up space, and liminal positionality; I don't want to be liminal. How you center, your marginality so that you aren't marginal anymore, you become center.
>
> … this wasn't always my scholarship; I didn't always theorize my leadership. I'm so glad I'm in this part of my journey, because I wasn't looking to ascend in higher education, it keeps calling me. But they're [my style, pedagogy, and practice] very much rooted in spiritual purpose. So, I be like, "God, wherever you want me to be I'll try to say yes." I try to have

a yes spirit. I don't know who would want to be a department chair. But I feel like God placed me here on purpose. So, I'm like, "okay, God, I'll do this work." So, it's feminist, it's womanist, it's spiritual; it's informed by my ancestors, my mother, my aunties, and other Black woman scholars.

Home

In 1892, Dr. Anna Julia Cooper proclaimed, "Only the Black woman can say when and where I enter" (1892/1988, p. 31) and in doing so she signified Black women's capacity for spaciousness. By spaciousness we mean the amplification of our authentic selves to the point our authenticity becomes the space. In becoming space, Black women's marginality is no longer marginal. Nia and Ivy embodied and embraced spaciousness. Their leadership is not about fitting a mold, it is about being immense by standing in their truth. What was compelling and comforting for us is how they linked their authenticity to their mamas and aunties – their homespaces. It reminded us of how we authentically show up as scholars and leaders and are influenced by our forebears. Hence, the homespun ordinariness of our girlhoods is fuel for how we take up space in academe. In our spaciousness, then, we are not forsaken. We are at home.

Implications/Concluding Thoughts

Just as Guinier and Torres (2002) suggested, we see systemic dangers in the academy through the lived experiences of Black women, and particularly the stories of Nia and Ivy. This final section is meant to surface such dangers and present a clear articulation of what is missed when we do not learn from the miner's canaries.

First, as outsiders-within, there are ongoing narratives about who belongs in upper-level academic ranks and administrative roles. By the time Black women reach the full professorship and academic administrative roles, their competence is likely to stand out. That is to say their very existence, and path to get there, often stands in direct opposition to others – particularly white men in the academy, who often fail up into academic administrative roles. Black women, however – no matter how long they have been at their institution or in an administrative role – are still viewed as interlopers and guests and thus often not considered to have the best interest of the community in mind in their decision-making and leadership. Higher education is in danger when folks would rather cut off their nose to spite their face. In other words, institutional agents would rather instigate controlling images and invalidate seasoned Black women's achievements, efforts, and directions than understand Black women's leadership and knowledge as viable and valuable. This forecloses many opportunities for institutional and organizational transformation as their experiences provide a particular view of the institution.

Second, senior Black women who operate from Black feminist epistemologies and critical framings of the world understand their role as that of disrupting and abolishing systemic inequity. Their experiences across their careers suggest misogynoir and gendered racism do not end as one climbs the academic ranks or transcends into academic administrative arenas. In fact, it might become heightened given that it was space they were never intended to take up. These ongoing inequities create a legacy of vicarious traumatizations whereby each generation of Black women scholars observe the experiences of the preceding generation and make conscious decisions about if and how they want to persist in the academy. Despite this legacy, those who do persist, recognize there is no disrupting and abolishing systemic oppression without the work of those who have come before. There is no disrupting and abolishing without understanding how true allies and co-conspirators show up. Each generation builds upon the progress of their predecessors. Higher education remains in danger, as they continue to try and keep and push out those who might be working toward not just a betterment of the institution but a betterment of a society. Higher education cannot afford to continue to be disconnected from the global majority, or those who are continually marginalized based on race, gender, and class.

Third, given their journey and long roads, Black women full professors and academic leaders possibly have come to a place of connectedness. Connectedness is a place wherein they can make sense of and bring together multiple worlds – including home, family, (in)formal schooling, and various iterations of spirituality. Higher education is in danger as it becomes a place where more and more people believe they can (and should) leave parts of who they are out of their learning, teaching, scholarship, and leading. It is in danger as a place that regularly asks people to assimilate and acculturate. Black women who have traversed this landscape and come to exist in a wholeness that pushes back against these narratives are seen as the enemy. Given the epistemic violence that higher education institutions have been instrumental in enacting, the epistemic agency shown by these women is a testament to the/our possibilities of existence in the academy.

References

Asante, M. K. (1987). *The Afrocentric Idea.* Temple University Press.

Benjamin, L. (Ed). (1997). *Black women in the academy: Promises and perils.* University Press of Florida.

Charmaz, K. (2014). *Constructing grounded theory* (2nd ed.). Sage.

Collins, P. H. (1986). Learning from the outsider within: The sociological significance of Black feminist thought. *Social Problems, 33*(6), S14–S32.

Collins, P. H. (2000). *Black feminist thought: Knowledge, consciousness, and the politics of empowerment* (2nd ed.). Routledge.

Cooper, A. J. (1892/1988). *A voice from the south.* Oxford University Press (Original work published in 1892).

Croom, N. N. (2017). Promotion beyond tenure: Unpacking racism and sexism in the experiences of black womyn professors. *The Review of Higher Education, 40*(4), 557–583. https://doi.org/10.1353/rhe.2017.0022

Croom, N., & Patton, L. (2011). The miner's canary: A critical race perspective on the representation of Black women full professors. *Negro Educational Review, 62–63*(1–4), 13–39.

Fries, C. J., & McNinch, R. J. (2003). Signed versus unsigned student evaluations of teaching: A comparison. *Teaching Sociology, 31*(3), 333–344.

Guinier, L., & Torres, G. (2002). *The miner's canary: Enlisting race, resisting power, transforming democracy.* Harvard University Press.

hooks, b. (2006). *Outlaw Culture.* Routledge.

King, T. C. (1995). "Witness us in our battles:" Four student projections of Black female academics. *Journal of Organizational Change Management, 8*, 16–25.

Myers, L. W. (2002). *A broken silence: Voices of African American women in the academy.* Greenwood.

Patitu, C. L., & Hinton, K. G. (2003). The experiences of African American women faculty and administrators in higher education: Has anything changed? *New Directions for Student Services, 104*, 79–93.

Patton, L. D., & Catching, C. (2009). 'Teaching while Black': Narratives of African American student affairs faculty. *International Journal of Qualitative Studies in Education, 22*(6), 713–728.

Pittman, C. T. (2010). Race and gender oppression in the classroom: The experiences of women faculty of color with white male students. *Teaching Sociology, 38*(3), 183–196.

Porter, C. J., & Byrd, J. A. (2021). Juxtaposing #BlackGirlMagic as "empowering and problematic:" Composite narratives of Black women in college. *Journal of Diversity in Higher Education.* Advance online publication. https://doi.org/10.1037/dhe0000338

Stanley, C. A. (2007, January/February). When counter narratives meet master narratives in the journal editorial review process. *Educational Researcher, 36*(1), 14–24.

Sulé, V. T. (2014). Enact, discard and transform: A critical race feminist perspective on professional socialization among tenured Black female faculty. *International Journal of Qualitative Studies in Education*, 27(4), 432–453. https://doi.org/10.1080/09518398.2013.780315

Turner, C. S. V. (2002). Women of color in academe: living with multiple marginality. *The Journal of Higher Education, 73*(1), 74–93.

Turner, C. S. V., Myers, Jr., S. L., & Creswell, J. W. (1999). Exploring underrepresentation: The case of faculty of color in the Midwest. *The Journal of Higher Education, 70*(1), 27–59.

Willis, R. (2019). The use of composite narratives to present interview findings. *Qualitative Research, 19*(4), 471–480. https://doi.org/10.1177/1468794118787711

ENACT, DISCARD, AND TRANSFORM

Black Women's Agentic Epistemology

V. Thandi Sulé

The literary conversation about Black women's ways of knowing and being in the academy is not new, arguably dating back to the 1990s (see Benjamin, 1997; Gregory, 1999). When compared to these earlier works, the narratives in this book overwhelmingly demonstrate one thing: anti-Black women oppression is pervasive and virtually unwavering. Black women, in response, created identity discourses that challenge frameworks failing to capture the contours of their intersecting gendered and raced experiences. To be a Black woman meant something distinct. In articulating their differences, Black women in academe challenged the erasure of their lineage, the disregard of their lived experience, and the questioning of their commonsense (Benjamin, 1997; Hull et al., 1982). In doing so, they let it be known that they understood their bodies represented a "disruptive incursion" (McKay, 1997, p. 19) into the academy—a space that was never meant for Black women to exist, much less to thrive.

As noted, the qualitative condition of Black women in the academy has changed very little. Rather than being eradicated, anti-Black woman oppression simply evolved (McKay, 1993). Similarly, the language we employ to illustrate our experiences is simultaneously nuanced and particular. For instance, misogynoir references particular ways Black women are pathologized in public spaces and in popular culture to the extent that the pathology is reinscribed within interpersonal and institutional spaces (Bailey & Trudy, 2018). Aligned with the articulation of how Black women are uniquely targeted, I want to revisit my model detailing how Black women faculty uniquely negotiate the academy (Sulé, 2014). The model, enact, discard, and transform (EDT), captures the subtleties of how Black women engaged faculty socialization processes and positioned themselves within historically white institutions. Pushing against the normative conversation about professional socialization, EDT represents how

DOI: 10.4324/9781003184867-24

Black women enact norms aligned with their standpoint, discard norms that conflict with their standpoint, and transform norms to correspond with their standpoint (Sulé, 2014).

Faculty socialization encompasses adaptation to institutional and professional norms (Sulé, 2014). However, for Black women faculty, adaptation is complicated by having to maneuver through processes emanating from norms that view Black women as the antithesis of intellectual (Croom, 2017; Evans, 2007). Black women, then, must contort themselves to fit into notions of academic leadership that are not inclusive of, and often in opposition to, the sanctity of their personhood. What is often undertheorized though is Black women's agentic performativity. As an agentic model, EDT, represents how Black women work to manifest self-affirming and equity-driven institutional norms. Even within the depths of anti-Black woman spaces, Black women academics were *theorizing Black feminisms* both in the recounting of their lived experiences and in the intentionality of their work (see also James & Busia, 1993). Black women upheld critical epistemology in that they brought their culture and positionality to their work, they tested their claims via self-reflexivity and community engagement, and they placed a premium on subjective knowledge to address the simultaneity of the oppressions they encountered (Evans, 2007; Sulé, 2009).

To be clear, Black women's standpoint is rooted in the similarities of their lived experiences without negating their intragroup diversity. The differences among Black women do not discount how oppressive stereotypes, policies, and practices factor in the lives of all Black women. As such, Black women operate from an ethos drawn from their historical, cultural, and political realities—realities both harsh and sublime that remind them they are a problem. The catalog of Black women's intelligentsia, including the narratives in this book, shows Black women as agential. Despite the oppressiveness of higher education, they have shown up and shown out. Essentially, they "have crafted a social contract that exposes a contested relationship between individuals and public institutions, where black women have engaged in defining and determining their roles...." (Evans, 2007, p. 5). It is within this context that I revisit EDT, a model centering Black women's agency, to position the narratives within this book.

Enact

As originally described, Enact encompasses beliefs and behaviors aligned with the tenor and protocols of higher education practice. At the very least, it captures elements of congruity between Black women's values and the norms of the institution. Although not as obvious as the other two components of EDT, enact reflects self-defining agency in that in their enactments, Black women are claiming their right to create and curate knowledge. This is indicative of the *Sisters of the Academy*, an organization that asserts Black women's rightful place in academe through mentoring and other supportive services (Sisters of the Academy, 2021). In Chapter 17, Garrett and Croom discussed how their participants found it necessary to self-advocate in their journey to full professor. Enact represents Black women's stance in defiance of what the world has carved out for them. As such, they affirm their identities as academics, and they demonstrate their commitment to scholarly endeavors.

Enact extends beyond asserting one's positionality as a viable member of academic spaces. Sometimes Enact can simply mean one is exercising their right to pick and choose their battles. Given their miniscule representation, Black women academics recognize their singularity makes them hyper-visible and vulnerable to surveillance. Bureaucratic surveillance acts as a form of disciplinary control of Black women (Collins, 2000). Poignantly, Collins (2000) posed, "if you can no longer keep Black women outside, then how can they best be regulated once they are inside?" (p. 280). Though all US institutions are invested in anti-Black racism, sexism, and classism, higher education can be particularly acidic for Black women because it is deeply yoked in undermining Black humanity under the guise of scientific objectivity and the public good (Dancy et al., 2018; Patton, 2016; Stanfield, 1985). Thus, when confronted with uncomfortable or questionable protocols, Black women choosing to acquiesce could be an act of survival—a way to conserve energy for the inevitable battles to come. Similarly, Hine (1994) called this pretense of compliance among Black women, the culture of dissemblance, a self-protective stance characterized by the appearance of openness while masking one's true feelings when working in white spaces. Black women, then, can devote their energy reserves to activities most aligned with their personal and professional goals.

Discard

At the dawn of Nina Simone's successful career, she decided to pivot. The 1964 Alabama church bombings inspired, *Mississippi Goddam*, a song that boldly articulated her frustration and anger with US-sponsored terrorism against Black people (Garbus, 2015). In writing and performing the song and several other pro-Black anthems, she made a choice to relinquish the promise of mainstream stardom. In her journey to be her most authentic self, she chose to discard components of what it meant to be a Black woman musician in the 1960s. Simone's trajectory is reminiscent of Harris-Perry's (2011) crooked room analogy,

> When they confront race and gender stereotypes, black women are standing in a crooked room, and they have to figure out which way is up. Bombarded with warped images of their humanity, some black women tilt and bend themselves to fit the distortion.
>
> *(p. 29)*

Black women like Nina Simone challenge the reality of the crooked room, rather than adjusting, they work to make the room aligned with who they are. In doing so, they reject what is presented to them as real because it simply does not serve them. In *Mississippi Goddam*, Simone's response to the United States' promise of human rights for Black people was "I don't trust you anymore" (Simone, 1964). Similarly, Discard, as a component of EDT, rejects aspects of the academy that are misaligned with a Black woman's standpoint and undermines a Black woman's authenticity. Most of the authors in this book discussed rejecting stereotypical assumptions about Black women both within and outside of the academy. In Chapter 12, Fields and Overby created a found poem with a theme of discarding the notion of inclusive, collegial academic spaces. Discarding conventional and often oppressive knowledge structures is the mainstay of Black women's epistemology which challenges the expunction of their lived experiences (Nelson, 1997) and tends to be accompanied by consequences (Sheth & Croom, 2021).

Although not a part of the original EDT model, a component of Discard is radical self-care. Black women experience the United States as a hostile space where there have always been factions vying for control of their labor and reproductive capabilities (Hine, 1994), thus radical self-care is endemic to Black women's culture (Chambers & Sulé, 2022; Lorde, 2017). Radical self-care is an embodied practice where Black women engage in body-mind regeneration. In a world that positions Black women as impossibly strong, radical self-care acknowledges their wounds and their vulnerabilities. As targets of *muling* or the expectation that Black women happily serve as a dumping ground for everyone's metaphorical shit (George, 2020; Hurston, 1978), radical self-care asserts Black women are entitled to proclaim their bodies as their own. Lorde (2017) emphasized, "caring for myself is not self-indulgence, it is self-preservation, and that is an act of political warfare" (p. 130). In Chapter 3, Gregory expressed the importance of habitual self-care after experiencing physical, mental, and spiritual decline resulting from the pressures of academe. In a world where Black women are reduced to an afterthought, radical self-care asserts that Black women are worthy.

For Black women who understand their positionality within higher education, to remain in academe requires work. The work needed is beyond what is required for promotion and tenure. Psychic labor is necessary to be mentally and physically well. Discarding aspects of the academy that are misaligned with Black women's ways of being and doing is a component of radical self-care.

Transform

The epistemology of Black women in academe extends beyond not subscribing to objectionable practices and beliefs. It extends to creating. Black women in academe engineer institutional transformation by insisting on *doing and being* in ways reflective of Black women's culture. In the original EDT article, transform was described as behaviors that "challenge cultural norms in non-trivial ways" (Sulé, 2014, p. 6). What inspires the drive to transform is the intersection of anger and pleasure. Audre Lorde's essays on the uses of anger and uses of the erotic further contextualize the nature of Transform. Anti-Black women oppression is reason enough to be angry. Lorde (1984) encouraged Black women to embrace anger, especially anger in service to themselves. She advised,

> Focused with precision, it [anger] can become a powerful source of energy serving progress and change...I do not mean a simple switch of positions or a temporary lessening of tensions...I am speaking of a basic and radical alteration in those assumptions underlining our lives.
>
> *(p. 127)*

The narratives in this book are manifestations of Black women's rage that are focused with precision to alter higher education spaces in *non-trivial and radical* ways. Hull, Scott, and Smith's, *But Some of Us Are Brave*, published in 1982, is an example of Black women making non-trivial change within higher education. In pushing against Women's Studies and Black Studies, Black Women Studies were positioned as a distinct and needed intellectual tradition. Similarly, in Chapter 8, Haynes et al. discussed how the establishment of the Black Women Scholars Writing Collective engages in *Write Us* research intended to impede narratives that undermine Black women's self-affirming praxis.

Transform is what happens after you discard what does not serve you. It is filling the open spaces with things that are self-affirming. In her explanation of the usefulness of rage, Cooper (2018) advised, "What you build is infinitely more important than what you tear down" (p. 275). Transform is about creating institutions that are optimally inclusive and just. Radical creation requires imagination and the belief that if people do better, the world will be better. According to Lorde (1984), to truly believe in the betterment of the world, one must experience intrinsic satisfaction or pleasure. By experiencing it, one can affirm the feeling as achievable, and one can work toward recreating that feeling in all aspects of their lives. Lorde (1984) stated,

> But when we begin to live from within outward, in touch with the power of the erotic within ourselves, and allowing that power to inform and illuminate our actions upon the world around us, then we begin to be responsible to ourselves in the deepest sense. For as we begin to recognize our deepest feelings, we begin to give up...being satisfied with suffering and self-negation.... Our acts against oppression become integral with self, motivated and empowered from within.
>
> *(p. 58)*

Satisfaction or pleasure is an extension of radical self-care because it means Black women are prioritizing their wellness. Through wellness they experience pleasure, and they are reminded of its attainability and of their worthiness. In Chapter 9, Collins and Hunter discussed dance as a liberatory praxis. They employed breathing and conditioning exercises to transform (heal) bodies battered by embodied oppression. Ultimately, actions to generate institutional transformation derive from the self-reflective and self-love work Black women have been doing on themselves. Transformative work, then, begins with Black women seeing the divinity and worthiness within themselves.

One Mo Again

The purpose of this elaboration of EDT is not to negate the responsibility of higher education to operate as *Black women inclusive spaces.* The point is to honor how Black women's ontology, epistemology, and praxis alter and enrich higher education. The goal is to push back against popular depictions of Black women as supernaturally strong and invulnerable—Black women feel pain and deserve healing and protection. The goal is to acknowledge Black women are worthy and their *flyness* derives from their perseverance, their creativity, their labor, and their agency.

References

Bailey, M., & Trudy. (2018). On misogynoir: Citation, erasure, and plagiarism. *Feminist Media Studies, 18*(4), 762–768. https://doi.org/10.1080/14680777.2018.1447395

Benjamin, L. (Ed.). (1997). *Black women in the academy: Promises and perils.* University Press of Florida.

Chambers, C. R., & Sulé, T. (2022). For colored girls who have considered suicide when the tenure track got too rough. In B. T. Kelly & S. Fries-Britt (Eds.), *Building mentorship networks to support Black women: A guide to succeeding in the academy* (pp. 121–135). Routledge.

Collins, P. H. (2000). *Black feminist thought: Knowledge, consciousness, and the politics of empowerment.* Routledge.

Cooper, B. (2018). *Eloquent rage.* ST. Martin's Press.

Croom, N. N. (2017). Promotion beyond tenure: Unpacking racism and sexism in the experiences of black womyn professors. *Review of higher education, 40*(4), 557–583.

Dancy, T. E., Edwards, K. T., & Davis, J. E. (2018). Historically White universities and plantation politics: Anti-blackness and higher education in the Black Lives Matter Era. *Urban Education, 53*(2), 176–195.

Evans, S. Y. (2007). *Black women in the ivory tower, 1850–1954.* University Press of Florida.

Garbus, L. (2015). *What happened, Miss Simone?* Netflix.

George, R. C. (2020). Holding it down? The silencing of Black female students in the educational discourses of the greater Toronto area. *Canadian Journal of Education, 43*(1), 32–56.

Gregory, S. T. (1999). *Black women in the academy: The secrets to success and achievement* [010 Books; 143 Reports--Research]. University Press of America.

Harris-Perry, M. V. (2011). *Sister citizen: Shame, stereotypes, and Black women in America.* Yale University Press.

Hine, D. C. (1994). *Hine sight: Black women and the reconstruction of American history.* Indiana University Press.

Hull, G. T., Scott, P. B., & Smith, B. (Eds.). (1982). *But some of us are brave.* The Feminist Press.

Hurston, Z. N. (1978). *Their eyes were watching God.* University of Illinois Press.

James, S. M., & Busia, A. (Eds.). (1993). *Theorizing Black feminisms.* Routledge.

Lorde, A. (1984). *Sister outsider: Essays and speeches.* The Crossing Press.

Lorde, A. (2017). *A burst of light and other essays.* Dover Publications.

McKay, N. (1997). A troubled peace: Black women in the halls of the White Academy. In L. Benjamin (Ed.), *Black women in the academy: Promises and perils* (pp. 11–22). University Press of Florida.

McKay, N. Y. (1993). Acknowledging differences: Can women find unity through diversity? In S. M. James & A. P. A. Busia (Eds.), *Theorizing Black feminisms* (pp. 267–282). Routledge.

Nelson, L. W. (1997). Begging the questions and switching codes: Insider and outsider discourse of African American women. In L. Benjamin (Ed.), *Black women in the academy: Promises and perils.* University Press of Florida.

Patton, L. (2016). Disrupting postsecondary prose: Toward a critical race of higher education. *Urban Education, 51*(3), 315–342.

Sheth, M. J., & Croom, N. N. (2021). Chronicles exploring hegemonic civility and the evisceration of academic freedom for critical womyn of color. In R. Dutt-Ballerstadt & K. Bhattacharya (Eds.), *Civility, free speech, and academic freedom in higher education: Faculty on the margins.* Routledge.

Simone, N. (1964). Mississippi Goddam. On *Nina Simone in Concert.*

Sisters of the Academy. (2021). *About.* https://sistersoftheacademy.org/

Stanfield, J. H. (1985). The ethnocentric basis of social science knowledge production. *Review of Research in Education, 12*, 387–415.

Sulé, V. T. (2009). Black female faculty: Role definition, critical enactments, and contributions to predominately White research institutions. *NASPA Journal about Women in Higher Education, 2*(1), 93–121.

Sulé, V. T. (2014). Enact, discard, and transform: A critical race feminist perspective on professional socialization among tenured Black female faculty. *International Journal of Qualitative Studies in Education, 27*(4), 432–453. https://doi.org/10.1080/09518398.2013.780315

AFTERWORD

Christa J. Porter, V. Thandi Sulé, and Natasha N. Croom

As a collection of pieces, our book illuminates the various ways Black women enact, discard, and transform in the academy, despite the manifestation of anti-Black woman oppression (Sulé, 2014). Black women's ways of knowing and being, our truths, and lived realities have been situated within institutional spaces that are crooked; spaces that perpetually relegate us to its margins (Harris-Perry, 2011; Porter et al., 2020). Black feminist epistemologies as a collective of philosophical traditions have provided (and continue to provide) the language within which we name and extend previous works, and honor Black women who paved a way for us. Our positionalities at the intersections of our identities and corresponding oppressions are grounded within Black/African feminist/womanist ontological and epistemological perspectives. Through the ways we learn, navigate, teach, lead, and advise as faculty and doctoral students, we embody an ethic or praxis centering who we are and how we make sense of the world (and the academy).

No matter one's (in)ability to traverse institutional spaces, Black women's narratives in and through the academy reveal the criticality of institutional responsibility. Black women deserve institutional support that intentionally honors our narratives, experiences, and knowledge, and radically alters the academic infrastructure. Yet and even still, when our institutions and those within it, collude in or perpetuate anti-Black women's oppression (or gendered racism) through an inability to center our voices, we will continue to speak our names, show up for, and on behalf of each other. We will continue to intentionally abolish and take up space, not because we necessarily want to, but because we have to. Our embodiment, personified through our Black/African feminist and womanist epistemologies, disrupts White- and patriarchy-centered philosophical traditions (pushing against and uprooting normalized ways of being and knowing in the academy). Our knowledge and histories provide insight into the ways Black women navigate and negotiate our respective institutional spaces, and (re)imagine our standpoint as faculty, academic administrators, and doctoral students.

References

Harris-Perry, M. V. (2011). *Sister citizen: Shame, stereotype, and Black women in America.* Yale University Press.

Porter, C. J., Moore, C. M., Boss, G. J., Davis, T. J., & Louis, D. A. (2020). To be Black women and contingent faculty: Four scholarly personal narratives. *The Journal of Higher Education, 91*(5), 674–697. https://doi.org/10.1080/00221546.2019.1700478

Sulé, V. T. (2014). Enact, discard, and transform: A critical race feminist perspective on professional socialization among tenured Black female faculty. *International Journal of Qualitative Studies in Education, 27*(4), 432–453. https://doi.org/10.1080/09518398.2013.780315

ABOUT THE EDITORS

Natasha N. Croom (she/her), Ph.D., is an Associate Professor of Higher Education and Student Affairs at Clemson University. As a critical race feminist scholar-practitioner, Dr. Croom is committed to identifying and disrupting interlocking systems of oppression that manifest within and are reinforced by institutions of higher education through centering the experiences of womyn of color faculty and students. Her work has been shared in *The Review of Higher Education*, *Negro Educational Review*, *Equity & Excellence in Education*, *About Campus*, and the *Journal for Student Affairs Research and Practice*. She is co-editor of *Envisioning Critical Race Praxis in Higher Education through Counter-Storytelling*, *Envisioning Critical Race Praxis in K-12 Education through Counter-Storytelling*, *Critical Perspectives on Black Women in College*, and the first special issue of the NASPA Journal About Women in Higher Education entitled *Centering the Diverse Experiences of Black Women Undergraduates*.

Christa J. Porter (she/her), Ph.D., is an Associate Professor of Higher Education Administration and Student Affairs at Kent State University. She critically examines policies and practices that influence the development and trajectory of Black women in higher education at diverse institutional types; college student development; and research and praxis in higher education and student affairs. Dr. Porter's work is grounded in a critical Black feminist and intersectional praxis and appears in various journals including *Review of Educational Research*, *Journal of Higher Education*, *Journal of College Student Development*, *Journal of Diversity in Higher Education*, and *Journal of Student Affairs Research and Practice*. Dr. Porter is co-editor of *Case Studies for Student Development Theory: Advancing Social Justice and Inclusion in Higher Education* (2020, Routledge).

V. Thandi Sulé (she/her), Ph.D., is an Associate Professor of Higher Education and the Coordinator of the Masters in Higher Education Leadership Program at Oakland University. As a critical race feminist hip-hop scholar, her work focuses on educational equity with an emphasis on Black women. Broadly, Dr. Sulé examines how marginalized students and faculty are socialized within, contribute to, and alter college communities. Her work is published in several journals including *Equity and Excellence in Education*, *Journal of College Student Development*, *The Journal of Higher Education*, *Feminist Teacher*, *Educational Policy*, *Teachers College Record*, and *the International Journal of Qualitative Studies in Education*.

ABOUT THE CONTRIBUTORS

Ebony J. Aya is a doctoral student at the University of Minnesota in Curriculum and Instruction, with minors in Culture and Teaching and African American and African Studies. Ebony works for the City of Minneapolis as the Resiliency in Community After Stress and Trauma Program Manager. In this role, Ebony has implemented community-based models to increase the understanding of trauma, healing, and resiliency. She also is the author of the Gospel According to a Black Woman and Incomplete Stories: On Love, Loss, and Hope, and the founder of the Aya Collective which focuses on cultivating and promoting Black women's stories.

Taryrn T.C. Brown, Ph.D., is a Clinical Assistant Professor of Social Foundations and Program Coordinator for the Schools, Society, and Policy Specialization at the University of Florida. Her teaching and research broadly examine interpretive, normative, and critical perspectives of education, with emphasis on the experiences of minoritized individuals and communities. Her interdisciplinary work promotes critical questions that challenge the standard assumptions about the purposes of schools in society and the role that race, class, and gender play in aspects of teaching and learning. As a scholar-practitioner, her scholarship focuses on Black girlhood studies, Black feminism, and critical race theory.

Shani Collins is core faculty of Africana Studies and an Associate Professor of Dance at Connecticut College where she has been on faculty since 2009. Shani's artistry focuses on fostering women's healing em(power)ment through performance, community ritual, and cultural engagement. Her work has been presented throughout the United States and abroad, including performance residencies in Seoul, Korea and Ghana, West Africa. She has presented choreographic work in such festivals as Performática Dance Festival in Cholula, Mexico and Kaay Fecc Dance Festival in Dakar, Senegal. In addition to her choreographic work, most recently she is leading international exchange programs to West Africa that are rooted in performance at the intersection of West African Dance, integrative embodied praxis, and identity exploration.

Monica F. Cox, Ph.D., is a Professor of Engineering Education at The Ohio State University. Prior to this appointment, she was an Associate Professor in the School of Engineering Education at Purdue University, the Inaugural Director of the College of Engineering's Leadership Minor, and the Director of the International Institute of Engineering Education Assessment (i2e2a). Her research is focused on the use of mixed methodologies to explore significant research questions in undergraduate, graduate, and professional engineering education and to develop reliable and valid assessment tools. She has most recently engaged in research exploring the persistence of women of color faculty in engineering.

Tiffany J. Davis, Ph.D., is a Clinical Assistant Professor of Higher Education and Program Director for the MEd and Ph.D. programs in Higher Education at the University of Houston. Her scholarship addresses two major strands: (1) issues related to diversity, equity, and inclusion within postsecondary contexts and (2) socialization and professional pathways for the higher education profession. Through these strands, she has been able to explore a range of topics including intercollegiate athletics, supervision, workplace experiences, and career development within the academy, particularly among minoritized faculty.

Venus E. Evans-Winters, LCSW, CCTP-I/CCTP-II, Ph.D., is a research and policy scholar interested in Black girls' and women's onto-epistemologies and critical race feminist methodologies. She is the author of *Black Feminism in Qualitative Inquiry: A Mosaic for Writing Our Daughter's Body* and *Teaching Black Girls: Resiliency in Urban Classrooms*, and co-author of *Introduction to Intersectional Qualitative Research*. She is co-editor of the books, *Black Feminism in Education: Black Women Speak Up, Back, & Out* and *Celebrating Twenty Years of Black Girlhood: The Lauryn Hill Reader*. Dr. Evans-Winters is also a clinical psychotherapist in private practice and founder of Planet Venus Institute.

Christina Wright Fields, Ph.D., is an Assistant Professor of Education at Marist College. Prior to Marist College, she was the founding Director of the award-winning Balfour Scholars Program at Indiana University-Bloomington. Her scholarship focuses on pre-college preparation, racial injustice, minoritized students' experiences in education, Black womxn, and the influence of teacher and student cultural identities. She has published work exploring fictive kinship, critical race theory in public administration, Black feminism, African-centered education and leadership, and inclusive classroom pedagogy and practice.

Stacey D. Garrett (she/her), Ph.D., is an Assistant Professor of Higher Education at Appalachian State University currently researching the experiences of students, faculty, and staff of color at predominantly white institutions. Her faculty-driven research explores the strategies for the success of Womyn of Color on the tenure track. She is particularly concerned with the role race and gender play in one's tenure pursuit, and the institutional structures that help and/or hinder Womyn of Color faculty advancement.

Sheila T. Gregory, MPA, Ph.D., is a Professor of Educational and Higher Education Leadership at Clark Atlanta University. Serving on seven faculties and publishing seven books, including *Daring to Educate: The Legacy of the Early Spelman College Presidents,* nominated for an NAACP Image Award. She is the author of over 60 scholarly publications and 6 International Visiting Research/Scholar Appointments. The proud wife and mother of four adults she's an SREB mentor to doctoral scholars of color, her major research interests include faculty/student recruitment/retention, professional/educational/social justice leadership, development/empowerment of women/girls, and student academic achievement with a special emphasis on race, ethnicity, class, and gender.

Meseret F. Hailu, Ph.D., is an Assistant Professor of Higher and Postsecondary Education in the Mary Lou Fulton Teachers College at Arizona State University (ASU). Her work focuses on the retention of minoritized women in STEM pathways and professions. Prior to coming to ASU, Dr. Hailu was a Postdoctoral Research Associate at The Ohio State University, where she studied the experiences of women of Color faculty in engineering departments. Her research has been funded by FHI 360, the Fulbright Program, and the National Science Foundation.

Debra A. Harley is a Professor in the Department of Early Childhood, Special Education, and Counselor Education at the University of Kentucky. She has published five books and more than 150 articles and chapters in the areas of diversity, intersectionality and marginalization, LGBTQ, mental health, disability, substance use disorder, and ethics. Dr. Harley is a licensed professional counselor and a certified rehabilitation counselor. She is nationally recognized in the field of rehabilitation counseling and disability studies.

Chayla Haynes is an Assistant Professor of Higher Education at Texas A&M University, where she teaches and conducts research on White racial consciousness and faculty behaviors in the classroom, Black women in higher education, and critical race theory and intersectionality.

Truth Hunter, M.A., is a doctoral student in the Department of Educational Leadership at the University of Connecticut with 14 years of experience as an educational advocate for underrepresented students in higher education. Her research focuses on post-colonial autoethnography, equitable classroom practices for faculty, racialized notions of intelligence, and embodied learning through dance.

Rhonda C. Hylton, Ph.D., is an Assistant Professor in the School of Teaching, Learning and Curriculum Studies in the College of Education, Health and Human Services at Kent State University. Her trajectories within and into the professoriate include Black women faculty, intersectionality, and academia, particularly the literacy pedagogical practices of Black women; and cultural and social issues embedded within schools, and in preservice teacher education. Dr. Hylton has shared her ideas in publications and through national and state conference presentations. A teacher and learner at heart, Dr. Hylton remains curious about the world and models her learning for students.

Nicole M. Joseph is an Associate Professor of Mathematics Education in the Department of Teaching and Learning at Vanderbilt University, where she researches Black women and girls, their identity development, and their experiences in mathematics and how gendered anti-blackness, whiteness, and white supremacy shape their representation, development, and retention in mathematics.

Reitumetse Obakeng Mabokela, Ph.D., is the Vice-Provost for International Affairs & Global Strategies and Professor of Higher Education at the University of Illinois at Urbana-Champaign. She was previously the Assistant Dean for International Studies and Professor of Higher Education at Michigan State University. Her research seeks to understand the experiences of marginalized populations in higher education to inform and influence institutional policies affecting these groups. Her research examines three interrelated themes: (1) organizational change and culture in higher education; (2) gender in higher education; and (3) higher education in transitional societies.

Yeukai Angela Mlambo, Ph.D., is Director of Mastercard Foundation Digital Initiatives and Assistant Research Professor at Arizona State University. Her research centers on *re*dressing the recruitment, retention, persistence, and career trajectories of women and Black women as underrepresented populations in STEM fields. Geographically, her research focuses on higher education institutions and faculty development in Sub-Saharan Africa and the developing world. Leveraging critical feminist and post-colonial perspectives and methodologies, she centers experiences of minoritized groups and attends to history when interrogating phenomena. Yeukai holds a Ph.D. in Higher, Adult, and Lifelong Education from Michigan State University.

Evette L. Allen Moore, Ph.D., is an Assistant Vice Chancellor of Diversity and Director of Multicultural Affairs at Arkansas State University. In this role, she works with the Multicultural Center, Access and Accommodation Services, and Beck Center for Veterans. Her leadership and research agenda focus on the experiences of students of color in higher education and social justice education.

E. Nichole Murray, Ph.D., received her undergraduate degree from Tuskegee University and her master's in Educational Psychology and Ph.D. in Social Foundations of Education from the University of Georgia. Throughout her career, she has taught in traditional and nontraditional education settings, including a youth correctional facility, a research one university, and a non-profit organization. Currently, she works to connect youth who are experiencing homelessness to education resources and opportunities. Her current research and scholarship focus on educational outcomes and students from underserved communities, homelessness and education, youth in the justice system and recidivism, womanism, and cultural inclusivity and humility.

Olivia T. Ngadjui, (she/her/hers) Ph.D., LPC, NCC is an Assistant Professor of Counselor Education at Western Michigan University. Dr. Ngadjui's clinical experience surrounds working with younger children to older adults in areas of trauma, grief/loss, anxiety, depression, suicidality, and homicidality. Her research interests include cultural inclusion efforts in education for K-12 and counselor education. She also has a background in education, teaching K-12 in various subjects and supervising education initiatives. Her advocacy efforts include varied public speaking engagements and presenting on subjects related to inclusion considerations for collective populations and cross-cultural connectedness.

Nadrea R. Njoku, Ph.D., is a senior research associate at the Frederick D. Patterson Research Institute (FDPRI) of UNCF (United Negro College Fund). Njoku conducts empirical research related to guided pathways and student success, as well as supports the evaluation of projects within the Institute for Capacity Building. She brings a critical race and feminist framework that is devoted to disrupting issues of race and gender within the post-secondary education context to FDPRI's research agenda. She has worked across multiple functions of higher education—housing, student affairs, fraternity and sorority affairs, alumni relations, and evaluation. She is a graduate of Xavier University of Louisiana and holds a master's and doctorate from Indiana University.

Katrina M. Overby, Ph.D., is an Assistant Professor in the School of Communication at Rochester Institute of Technology. Katrina is an activist scholar and Black feminist who broadly studies media, race, sexuality, and gender. Her current research focuses on African Americans and social media usage, Black Twitter, Black women in media representation and identity in higher education, race and gender in sports media, Black cinema representation, and activist/inclusive pedagogy. She is a graduate of an HBCU, Rust College and holds a master's degree from Oklahoma State University and a doctorate from Indiana University.

Shawna Patterson-Stephens, Ph.D., is the Vice President and Chief Diversity Officer at Central Michigan University. Her research interests include Black and Latinx issues in higher education, media influences in the postsecondary sector, and critical theory in higher educational contexts. She experiments with various modes of knowledge dissemination to ensure scholarship remains accessible, evidenced through projects like the podcast, "Scholar Tea." She is currently co-PI in a national project examining the experiences of Black doctoral women in higher education. She is also co-editor of the forthcoming volume, "Advancing Inclusive Excellence in Higher Education" (Information Age Publishing).

Lori D. Patton, Ph.D., is a Professor of Higher Education and Student Affairs at The Ohio State University, where she serves as Department Chair and maintains a research agenda on racial injustice in higher education, minoritized students' experiences on campus, and Black women and girls in education.

April L. Peters, Ph.D., is an Associate Department Chair and Associate Professor of K-12 Educational Leadership at the University of Houston. She is the principal investigator of the SistUH Scholars: Mentoring for African American Women Doctoral Students in Education grant. Dr. Peters' research interests include: (a) mentoring and support for early career administrators; (b) women in school leadership; (c) leadership and urban small school reform; and (d) leadership and career development for Women of Color.

Tiffany L. Steele, Ph.D., is an Assistant Professor of Education at University of Rochester in the Department of Educational Leadership. Her research interest centers a critical examination of the lived experiences of Black girls and women in education including students, faculty, and staff. Dr. Steele's dissertation research, "Disciplinary Disruption: Exploring the Connection between

High School Sanctioning and Black Collegiate Women's Experiences," examines how Black women's experiences with disciplinary action during their K-12 educational journeys influence their collegiate realities. Dr. Steele's intent for future research is to continue challenging current methodological choices in the study of Black girls and women in education.

Saran Stewart is an Associate Professor of Higher Education and Student Affairs and Director of Global Education in the Neag School of Education at the University of Connecticut. Dr. Stewart is an international and comparative educator who critically examines issues in anti-Blackness racism, Black women, intersectionality, decolonizing methodologies, postcolonial theories, critical/inclusive pedagogy, and access and equity issues in higher education.

Emerald Templeton, EdD, is a community college administrator and adjunct instructor with a background in higher education, student affairs, and counseling student development. Her research interests are emerging in two areas of work: the logic of valuing diversity and Black women in higher education.

Nicole M. West, Ph.D., is an Assistant Professor in Student Affairs in Higher Education at Missouri State University. As a Black feminist scholar-pracademic, Dr. West's research focuses on enhancing the experiences of Black women enrolled and employed in higher education; she has published a number of articles in top-tier, refereed student affairs and education journals. Her most recent scholarship focuses on her development of the concept of professional counterspaces, the application of Black feminist thought to her practice as a faculty member in student affairs, and her work on the conceptualization of the Hip Hop Feminism Model of Multiple Identities.

INDEX

Note: **Bold** page numbers refer to tables and *italic* page numbers refer to figures.

Lightning Source UK Ltd.
Milton Keynes UK
UKHW020053210123
415723UK00028B/511